DAVID MORGAN

1833 - 1919

THE LIFE AND TIMES OF
A MASTER DRAPER IN
SOUTH WALES

FIRST EDITION 1977

© THE STARLING PRESS LTD.

ISBN 0 903434 31 8

Printed in the United Kingdom by
THE STARLING PRESS LTD
RISCA   NEWPORT   GWENT
SOUTH WALES

The Author: portrait by Margaret Lindsay Williams.

DAVID MORGAN
1833 - 1919

THE LIFE AND TIMES OF
A MASTER DRAPER IN
SOUTH WALES

AUBREY NIEL MORGAN CMG

THE STARLING PRESS LTD.
PRINTERS & PUBLISHERS
RISCA NEWPORT GWENT
GREAT BRITAIN
1977

Foreword

Family history is the most ephemeral of all history. Unless diaries are kept and letters preserved, what is common knowledge to one generation becomes a jigsaw puzzle of unconnected stories, confused by the uncertainty of memory, in the next. After three generations little is left save such things as heirlooms, buildings, the occasional photograph, the stories which form the legends of family history.

The real continuity of a family lies in the genes handed down, producing the likenesses and characteristics which establish the mould that forms the visible family. It is impossible to assess the role the forebears have played in forming the family without some study of their lives.

C. V. Wedgwood in her biography of William the Silent writes: "History is lived forwards but is written in retrospect. We know the end before we consider the beginning and we can never recapture what it was to know the beginning only ".

It is not possible in this age of affluence to recapture the apparently inescapable poverty of the beginnings from which David Morgan emerged, those generations of hill farmers who spent their lives in a peasant existence devoid of any escape. For them life offered no prospect but an inevitable repetition of the unremitting lot of previous generations. They were, of course, totally unaware of the changes and opportunities to be brought about when the Industrial Revolution came to full force at the top of the valleys of South Wales.

From the Eighteenth Century hopelessness and despair of the impoverished Breconshire hill farms, David Morgan escaped into the Nineteenth Century industrial growth and progress of South Wales. Yet the experiences of his childhood and the memory of his background were to have a lifelong effect on him.

For these reasons this book attempts to recapture the beginnings and achievements of David Morgan.

Acknowledgements

For much of the information about David Morgan collected when I was preparing to write this story of his life I am deeply indebted to the children of William Morgan of Llanbrynean—Kate, Willie, Nellie and May—with whom I had the good fortune, due to their remarkable longevity, of talking about David Morgan and recalling their memories of their Uncle David. In particular I am most grateful to May (Mrs. Brummitt), with whom I greatly enjoyed celebrating her ninetieth birthday in Adelaide, Australia, when I spent twelve most rewarding days with her. Both Kate and May were very responsive correspondents to my letters of enquiry.

For help with the early part of the story I am grateful to Mrs. Gweneth Jenkins, the niece of John Arnott Lewis.

Amongst the very limited number of people who remember David Morgan, I have also been helped by Morgan Price, son of John Price, who was a first cousin of David Morgan, served his apprenticeship under him at Pontlottyn and ultimately became the owner of the Pont-lottyn shop, which is still in the hands of the Price family. Morgan Price's memories not only of David Morgan, but also his recollections of his father, have proved most helpful.

I am much indebted to my brothers, Trevil and Gerald, who before their deaths read the text thoroughly, making a number of suggestions and corrections. Gerald and his wife, Angela, discovered the position of Edgecumbe House, and emphasised the important coincidence that David Morgan sold Edgecumbe House when he bought Bryn Taff, drawing from that the possible conclusion that he never lived over the shop, but remained at Edgecumbe House until he moved to Bryn Taff. My sister, Margaret, has helped me by drawing my attention to various heirlooms, some of which she now possesses, which once belonged to our grandmother, after whom she was named; also by recalling stories she had been told about our grandmother.

The gap between the lifetime of David Morgan and the time of writing, together with a distance of approximately 6,000 miles between Plas Newydd in Washington State, USA, and South Wales would have made research a difficult problem if it had not been for the most willing co-operation of my second cousin, Kenneth Hughes, who with the greatest persistence has followed up successfully numerous enquiries and other trails. I am also grateful to him for his tracing of matters relating to our joint great-grandfather, John Llewellyn of Pontlottyn, and for his generous services as guide when we explored the family shrines. His cousin, Miss Margaret Llewellyn Lewis, OBE, one of the out-standing headmistresses in the history of Howell's School, has kindly spared the time to read some of the chapters and make most useful suggestions and corrections.

To this list of people who have been so kind and helpful, I must add the name of Mrs. Ruth Beckham, who has carried the secretarial burden of this book and has by her perceptive suggestions given much more help than just the tedious and arduous mechanical labour of producing the text. For the final stenographic work I add my gratitude to Mrs. Mary Richards and Mrs. Mary Mautz.

For the history of the shop on The Hayes and the life of the staff and the way they carried out their duties, I owe much to Miss Harnaman and Miss Glasson, who during their many years at The Hayes became pillars of the business and friends of the Morgan family. Leonard Horwood, son of my grandfather's right-hand man, Richard Horwood, most kindly wrote to me an admirable account of the impressions my grandfather made on him when he was a small boy. David Llewellyn Morgan, the great-grandson of the man about whom this story is told, has made a number of clear-headed editorial suggestions which have been incorporated in the text. I must also express my appreciation of the critical opinions of my friend the late D'Arcy Edmondson, who read the drafts of this book and made numerous suggestions concerning the presentation of this story. In the same way, the late Sir John Wheeler-Bennett, responding to the claims of friendship, gave me guidance stemming from his vast knowledge and experience of the art of writing.

The Archivist's Office of the Glamorgan County Council proved most helpful in obtaining the records of the various gas companies which had been deposited with the Archivist by the Gas Board of Wales, whose staff gave me a detailed report on what papers had been deposited.

The story of Rhymney and Pontlottyn could not have been attempted without reading first those most evocative memories of Rhymney and Pontlottyn entitled *Rhymney Memories* written by Tom Jones, C.H., a boyhood contemporary of my father. He was the son of D. B. Jones, the Manager of the Company Shop of the Rhymney Ironworks. Tom Jones became Deputy Secretary to the Cabinet under the Premierships of Lloyd George, Bonar Law, Stanley Baldwin and Ramsay MacDonald. After reading them it was possible to envisage what the life of David Morgan was like between his start in business and his marriage, and his departure to Cardiff.

I am equally indebted to Mr. E. E. Edwards for his most informative *Echoes of Rhymney*, published by The Starling Press Ltd. of Risca. He gives in full detail the facts of the growth of Rhymney from the coming of industry and its development as a town and the growth of its population. I am particularly grateful to Mr. Edwards for not only his encouragement and interest, but also his kindness in reading and editing in detail this text in its last stages.

The completion of this book is largely due to the encouragement and constant interest of Norman Hall and his wife, Heather. Fortunately, Heather Hall some years ago made a series of notes recording tales of the Hall family told to her by her father-in-law, David Hall. She generously informed me of these notes and her memories connected with them. Norman Hall frequently helped me from his memories acquired as a result of his legal connection with the Morgan family as a partner in his great uncle's firm of solicitors, James Morgan & Co.

There will be found in the text and footnotes acknowledgements of specific examples where help has been given in the collection of information.

After the typescript had been completed copies of letters written by David Morgan from Pontlottyn to relatives in Australia (children of the second marriage of John Morgan II of Bwlch Farm) were sent to me from Australia by Mrs. Gwen Kerr, who is the great-great-granddaughter of John Morgan II. These proved a great addition.

Professor Brinley Thomas kindly reviewed the industrial history.

The final text for publication was prepared by David Llewellyn Morgan, who not only redrafted the chapter on *The Will* but scrutinized carefully the whole text.

The many final detailed decisions necessary before the production of this book were spared me as a result of the close co-operation between Richard Morgan and Mr. F. E. A. Yates of The Starling Press, both of whom have earned my whole-hearted gratitude.

Contents

Publisher's Note

Reproduction of some of these photographs has been impaired due to age. They are included however since it is important to have them as historical records. The reader is requested to make allowances when bearing this in mind, since the Printers have attempted to overcome this difficulty. Blurred images and variations in tone are due to faulty photographs and are not the product of printing inadequacies.

1. The Beginnings

For the descendants of David Morgan "the land of our fathers" lies among the hill farms along the border of Breconshire and Radnorshire, near the town of Builth.

Throughout its history central Wales has been remarkable for the sparsity of its population, the emptiness of its great seas of mountain moorland and its persistent poverty. The only thing in abundance is the splendour of the scenery. When in 1655, in the time of the Commonwealth, Cromwell sent commissioners to levy fines on the estates of Royalists in Radnorshire, the paucity of the results of their efforts inspired a piece of doggerel:

> Radnorsheer poor Radnorsheer
> Never a park and never a deer
> Never a squire of five hundred a year
> But Richard Fowler of Abbey Cwm Hir[1].

What applied to Radnorshire applied equally to the bordering parts of Breconshire.

Generations of Morgans must have eked out a meagre existence in this remote and impoverished hill country. Little change would have occurred in their way of life from the time of the Cromwellian visitation to the end of "the Hungry Forties" of the Nineteenth Century. They would have been small farmers, or farm servants and labourers, or people who by their craft could supply the essential needs of the country people, such as the smith, the weaver, the saddler, the miller, or in some cases the innkeeper.

According to A. H. John in *The Industrial Development of South Wales*: "the standard of living of the Welsh labourer and small farmer . . . was very low. Potatoes were grown by the labourers but milk, flummery—sucan—barley bread, cheese made partly from ewes' milk and occasionally bacon or hung beef comprised their main diet". From the flock of sheep came the increases and replacements and the sales of fleece, mutton and lamb, which produced that scarcest of all their commodities, cash; an essential if they were to obtain those necessities which they could not produce for themselves, such as flour, sugar, salt, cloth by the yard, boots and other leather goods. For these things they went to the market at Builth.

Except in the more fertile land immediately around the town of Builth, the task of extracting a living from the soil was a harsh and desperate business. The adverse farming conditions which the Morgan forebears had to face were described in detail in a report written in 1794 by John Clark, Land Surveyor of Builth, for the consideration of the Board of Agriculture and Internal Improvement of His Majesty's Government entitled *General View of the Agriculture of the County of*

11

Brecknock with Observations on the Means of Its Improvement. The report divides the county into two divisions, the second of which " includes the hundred[2] of Builth including the other mountainous districts of the county ". Of this second division in which the Morgan ancestors lived, Clark observes that " the holdings are small, the soil ungrateful and the tenants poor ".

The unrewarding nature of the soil is explained by the formation of the rock in the hills which consists almost wholly of a brittle blue stone, so soft that " it does not strike fire with steel. . . Its lamina is so thin and its power of cohesion so feeble that on being exposed to the air it cracks, falls into small pieces and when mixed with water turns into clay. Its clayey nature makes it part with water with reluctance. This encourages the growth of rushes which the cattle will not eat. These wet lands are annually mowed for the small pittance of coarse hay for winter feed, for in the summer the cattle will not eat it ". The wetness is caused by the innumerable springs which ooze from the surrounding hills and mountains.

Unmoved by the heavy odds against the hill farmers who attempted to make a living in these extremely difficult and hostile conditions, John Clark was exceedingly critical of the hill farmers who existed on the profits of their stock and stated that " he depastures on the common land " and as a result of this " his farm is totally neglected ". Confirmation of this depressing picture can be found in the *History of Breconshire* written by Theophilus Jones, who spent some of his boyhood at the home of his grandfather at Llangamerch in the Irfon Valley. He refers to the wretched state of husbandry hitherto prevailing in the greatest part of the county.

It was in this setting that generations of Morgan forefathers struggled, survived and finally emerged. Theirs was a stern struggle, with no cushion of comfort in their lives. Their poverty was extreme. The Reverend Griffith Jones, founder of the Circulating Schools, referred to " the formidable poverty " of the ordinary folk of his time (circa 1750) " and their lack of bodily necessaries ".

The first three generations to appear in the Morgan family records were all born and married near Builth.

1 Quoted by A. G. Bradley in *The Romance of Wales.*

2 A hundred is an ancient subdivision of a county. [" In the Middle Ages the Hundred was chiefly important for its court of justice ". (*The Encyclopedia Britannica*).]

2. The Family Tree

Standing at the top of the family tree is the name of John Morgan of Abercneiddon, who was born about 1735. The Morgan family records do not reveal how John Morgan I came to live at Abercneiddon, a good farm with a handsome house two miles west of Builth, where the Cneiddon Brook reaches the Irfon River.

Fortunate indeed was the founding father of the Morgan family, John Morgan I, to have lived at Abercneiddon. According to the family records he appears to have lived previously at Pentre on the Radnorshire side of the River Wye near Builth.

All that is known of John Morgan I of Abercneiddon is that he had three children: a son, John Morgan II, who was baptized in 1760 in Llanfaredd Parish Church and was given his father's name, which has been carried in the Morgan family for eight consecutive generations; a daughter, Elizabeth, who married Rees Price of Llwyn-y-brain; and another daughter, Mary, who married William Pritchard of the Bell Inn, Builth. John Morgan II, the only son of John Morgan I, succeeded his father at Pentre. Pentre is a small and ancient farmhouse in a fold up in the Radnorshire hills above the River Wye about three miles east of Builth.

John Arnott Lewis wrote a letter in 1904 to James Morgan, the solicitor and the youngest brother of David Morgan the Draper, in reply to some enquiries the solicitor had made concerning his ancestors. John Arnott Lewis said: " The last time I saw D. P. Morgan (of Twyn Carno), I had some conversation with him about the two John Morgans, your grandfather (John Morgan II of Pentre and later Cwmrhibin) and great-grandfather (John Morgan I of Abercneiddon); the former of Cwmrhibin was a very bold and daring character who would put his bare hands in a foxhole and pull out the fox ".

John Morgan II married on 17 June, 1786, Jane Jones of Cwmrhibin. It would appear that John Morgan II, like many a bold man, was also an ardent and persuasive wooer, for their first child, John Morgan III, was born on 9 October, 1786, not quite four months after the wedding.

Of the eight children born to John Morgan II and his wife Jane, three were born at Lower Goytre: William in 1788, Jane in 1791 and Elizabeth in 1793. Jane married Thomas Samuel in 1820. A grandson of this marriage, Tom Samuel, was an apprentice of David Morgan at Pontlottyn.

Elizabeth, the youngest child of Lower Goytre, married Philip Jones, who first farmed at Poityn Farm, then moved to the Swan Inn and later to the Greyhound at Builth. Philip and Elizabeth Jones had nine children. The ultimate destinations of this family are an example of the widespread emigration that took place at that time. Emigration was for many people the only door to opportunity. Of Philip and Elizabeth's nine children, two sons (John and William) went to Australia and two daughters went to Salt Lake City, where one of them married a Mormon. The eighth child married Morgan Lewis, a saddler who lived on Bridewell Street, Bristol. John Arnott Lewis, the eldest son of this marriage, was apprenticed to David Morgan at Pontlottyn and was an early member of the staff in the shop on The Hayes, Cardiff.

By 1795, John Morgan II and his family had moved to Cwmrhibin, the old home of Jane, on the hillside of Mynydd Eppynt overlooking the Irfon Valley.

The three farms of John Morgan II—Pentre, Lower Goytre and Cwmrhibin—were all typical hill farms, and by strange coincidence all had the 700′ contour line running through their farmyards. As is nearly always the case with hill farms, these three small farms were remote and distant from the road and were adjoining or had easy access to common land[1] on the moors at the top of the hills.

Pentre, Lower Goytre and Cwmrhibin fit so closely the description of hill farms given by John Clark in his report of 1794 that it is possible to draw from this report a picture of the likely methods of farming of John Morgan II. It is not an impressive picture. Most probably poverty, rather than a love of sheep, deterred John Morgan II from seeking a valley farm like Abercneiddon in the good land near Builth, and forced him into accepting instead the Spartan ruggedness of those hill farms. Perhaps he also observed that the better soil of the good lands immediately around Builth was too demanding and therefore preferred the less laborious "catch-as-catch-can" methods of hill farming. A. H. John in *Industrial Development of South Wales* described the type of agriculture of the small Welsh hill farm as "one that minimized losses from lack of attention".

According to John Clark there were a number of small holdings which bordered on the common land and were let for five to ten pounds a year. He leaves little doubt about his opinion of the men who lived on these farms when he describes their grievous lack of good husbandry:

These extensive commons which as an appendage to his farm the farmer enjoys gratis, furnish so wide a range for his flocks that he can subsist without the drudgery of that hard labour which the cultivation of his farm would subject him. . . He will scarcely take the trouble to keep up the fence between his farm and the common. He will however, plough up in the spring a few spots in the dry part of the field, the wet he leaves in the same state in which it has lain for a thousand years. The same part of the field is ploughed up over and over again because when the land has once been broken up it is more easy ploughed than fresh land and they are from habits of idleness very averse to labour. Their cattle are also small and in the spring after a whole winter's starvation they are very weak, for they never think of ploughing in the winter. Two little ponies and two cows often in calf are the team. This horrible practice however is most prevalent on the verge of the extensive commons. (Which is precisely where Pentre, Lower Goytre and Cwmrhibin are located.)

14

Opened the Shop at 5 P.m. Friday Oct 31 1879
first sale on Tuesday the 28th 2/7
& sold goods Every day up to & on
including this Evening making the   } 7   3   9¾
total receipts ——————————

David Morgan

First Shop on The Hayes.

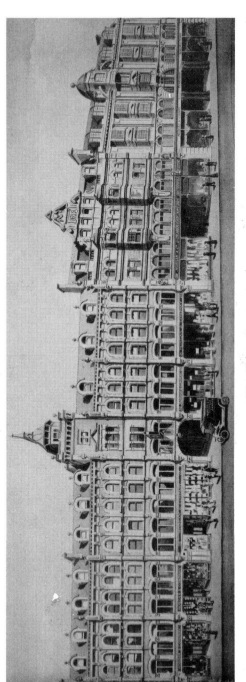

The Hayes Front.

David Morgan, 1868.

Margaret Llewellyn, Mrs. David Morgan, 1868.

The Guv'nor.

This indictment, written in 1792, is almost certain to be an accurate description of the primitive, destructive methods of farming practised by John Morgan II of Cwmrhibin and taught to his sons.

Contemptuous of the stubborn ignorance of the hill farmers in the hundred of Builth, Mr. Clark made only one comment which could in any way be interpreted favourably to these men, and that was in the form of a back-handed compliment: " It must at first view, excite some degree of astonishment that a class of men endowed by nature with a keenness of penetration and a solidity of judgement which may be equalled but which has not been surpassed by any of their fellow subjects in this island should from father to son persevere in a practice so destructive to themselves." The destructive practice was the planting of oats over and over again in the same places, thereby ultimately destroying the fragile fertility of the ploughed land.

This picture of hill farming drawn by John Clark in the year that John Morgan II and his wife Jane moved to Cwmrhibin reveals the methods of John Morgan II. By his boldness, his shrewdness, " his keenness of penetration and solidity of judgement " he would survive, marry twice and bring up thirteen children.

It was from this stock that David Morgan the Draper sprang, for John Morgan II was his grandfather.

John Morgan III left Cwmrhibin when he was twenty-two years of age to marry Anne Price of Llwyn-y-brain in Llanlleonfel Church on 5 January, 1808, a highly unfashionable time for a wedding, which doubtless took place in a cold and wintry setting. After their marriage John Morgan III and Anne went to live nearby at Corrin, a farm similar in many respects to that of his father at Cwmrhibin. Once again the seven-hundred-foot contour line passes through the farmyard of Corrin; there is easy access to the common lands on the Eppynt. The parallel may have discouraged John III and Anne from repeating another Cwmrhibin in very hard times. They left Corrin, and John Morgan III became landlord of the Garth Inn, originally known as Maesygenfford. A description of this lonely inn appears in Theophilus Jones' *History of Breconshire 1809*.

> On the turnpike road leading from Builth to Llandovery and near the falls of the Dules into the Irvon is a public house called Maesygenfford where the magistrates hold their meetings, and here though there is but one house there are seven fairs annually.

This solitary inn was a meeting place for drovers coming from West Wales and gathering at this inn before taking their cattle up onto the Eppynt, which was the start of their journey to London.

The magistrates used to sit on Sundays to settle disputes and legal matters arising from these fairs and the meetings of drovers. Unfortunately for the magistrates, the landlord, John Morgan III, was, like many of his family, a Welsh Calvinistic Methodist and a strict adherent to the stern rules of this sect; as a result he refused to serve the magistrates anything of an alcoholic nature on the Lord's Day. Feeling the

15

needs of their comfort, the magistrates were understandably inconvenienced and irritated. Having failed to persuade the landlord to overcome his religious principles, they removed his licence. This remarkable reversal of the customary relationship between licensee and magistrate must surely be some sort of record. Of the many landlords of public houses in Wales who have lost their licences there must be very few, if any, who could challenge the claim that John Morgan III was the one and only landlord to lose his licence for NOT serving a drink on a Sunday.

At least three generations of Morgans were brought up in the strict rules of the Welsh Calvinistic Methodists, an earnest body who were ardent teetotallers, anti-smoking, and held the strictest views on the observance of the Lord's Day.

Rees, the eldest son of John Morgan III, the strict innkeeper at Garth, followed in the footsteps and principles of his father and became landlord of the Britannia Arms, Caerleon. Here he objected strongly, and effectively, to Lord Tennyson writing poetry in the inn's garden on a Sunday. Calvinistic Methodists did not, however, prevent John Morgan III or Rees from earning their livings as publicans.

After John Morgan III lost his licence at the Garth Inn, he moved to the inn at Erwood on the River Wye. Like the Garth Inn, this was a stopping place used by drovers. Having crossed the Eppynt, the cattle were brought down to the River Wye at Erwood, where the drovers would either ford or ferry the cattle across the river, according to its state. The cattle were then driven on to Painscastle, where they were shod for the hard roads they would travel for most of their journey to London. This was a route used by David Price of Maesllech, maternal grandfather of David Morgan the Draper, when he drove cattle to London.[2]

The second son of John Morgan III was named David Price Morgan, after his mother Anne Price of Llwyn-y-brain. He later opened a shop called Albion House at Twyn Carno, the village at the top of Rhymney.

Alfred Phillips Morgan, a son of David Price Morgan, was born over the shop at Albion House. He was a gifted musician and composed a number of hymns which appear in various hymnals, especially the Presbyterian.

In the closing days of the Eighteenth Century the eighth child, and fifth son, of John Morgan II and Jane was born at Cwmrhibin and named David. He was to become the progenitor of our branch of the Morgan family. His birth marks the end of the beginnings.

1 The following description of the commons has been extracted and condensed from *The Encyclopedia Britannica*:

The Commons or common land is the term used for the lands held in commonalty, a relic of the system on which the lands of England were for the most part cultivated during the Middle Ages. The country was divided into townships, which were often, but not always, conterminous with the parish. Around the village in which the men of the township dwelt was the cultivated land. The poorest land of the township was left waste—to supply feed for the cattle and fuel, this waste land is the common of our own days.

The Morgan Family, 1866.

Ann Price Morgan, wife of the Progenitor.

The Progenitor.

Margaret Morgan and Little Johnnie — c. 1870.

David Morgan — c. 1870

Gelligaer Church.

Common rights are in most cases attached to or enjoyed with certain lands or houses. A right of common pasture usually consists of the right to turn out free of any payment as many cattle as the farm of the commoner can support in the winter, a most important limitation.

When the Newport Town Council purchased by Act of Parliament some of the common rights of the manor of Pencelli to build the Talybont reservoir, a meeting of the commoners was held in the village of Pencelli to deal with matters arising from the compensation for their rights. John Llewellyn Morgan, as owner of Pencelli Castle which carried with it the lordship of the manor of the Hundreds of Pencelli and as the owner of other farms carrying with them commoners' rights, was invited to take the chair at the meeting. After lengthy discussion as to how the money should best be used (suggestions ranged from building a village hall to the division amongst the commoners of the cash) John Llewellyn Morgan realized that there was little chance of any suggestion getting the approval of a majority of those present. He therefore suggested that more time be given to allow all ideas to be explored in the less formal atmosphere of a public meeting, and that until such time as an agreed solution could be found, the money should be invested in stocks. At this point a commoner rose to his feet and said, " That's all very well Mr. Morgan, but who is going to water the stock?"

2 Information given by William Morgan of Three Cocks, formerly of Llanbrynean.

17

3. The Progenitor 1799-1875

David Morgan was baptized in the parish church of Llanfechan at the turn of the century. His early boyhood was spent on the farm at Cwmrhibin sharing with his four elder brothers the many tasks which kept any boy busy on a farm. If he was lucky, he would be allowed to go with his father and mother on market day to Builth.

Builth was the centre of their small world. According to Malkin in his *Scenery, Antiquities, and Biography of South Wales, 1807*, it was not a very imposing centre.

Generations of Morgans lived within what is even to the present generation walking distance of Builth market. They went there not only for sale and purchase, but also for news and companionship. A man on a remote hill farm might go for days without seeing anyone but the occasional neighbour. The only sources of news were chapel on Sundays and the market place in Builth on market days.

In 1807 when David was nearly eight years old, his mother died. Cwmrhibin was her home before she married and the farm may have been passed on to another member of the Jones family. Shortly after her death John Morgan II left Cwmrhibin and moved to Bwlch farm in the neighbouring parish of Llanynis. To run a farmhouse and bring up a young family single-handed was a task beyond most farmers. A woman in the house was an economic necessity. A housekeeper was both an expense and, except for the elderly, a target for gossip. Marriage was the only solution. So, at the age of forty-nine years, John Morgan II remarried in 1809. His second wife was Elizabeth Lloyd, by whom he had four children. By his two wives John Morgan II fathered thirteen children. He died on 25 April, 1829, at the age of sixty-nine, while visiting his daughter Elizabeth (Mrs. Philip Jones) at the Greyhound Inn, Builth. The weather was so bad that the conditions of the road made it impossible to take his body back to Bwlch Farm, so John Morgan II was buried in the churchyard at Builth.

The progenitor, David, had before him exceptionally hard times. He was fifteen years of age when beribboned mail coaches, decorated with roses, and with horns trumpeting and flags flying, brought the news of Waterloo to the rural districts. The peace which followed the final overthrow of Napoleon brought in its trail a disastrous fall in agricultural prices. There followed a long period of appalling rural distress which lasted for thirty-five years of grave depression.

There could not have been a worse time for a young man to go out into the farming world to try to make a living. David Morgan had no advantages. His schooling was probably limited to being taught to read by his mother with the Bible as his primer, or perhaps one of the works of John Bunyan. Judging by the few examples of his handwriting in existence, he wrote with a firm clear hand very similar to that of his son David Morgan the Draper. What this progenitor of the Morgan family learned about farming from his father, John Morgan II, would be a repetition of the primitive impoverishing methods which had been handed down for generations from father to son and held them captive in their peasant poverty.

In 1830 Anne, the wife of John Morgan III the innkeeper, died at Garth Inn; and even though it was January, a month notorious for difficult travel in those parts, David would have made every effort to attend his sister-in-law's burial in the churchyard at Llanlleonfel. Either as an outcome of a meeting at this funeral or when they later met at a religious revival, David Morgan the Progenitor sought and won the hand of Ann Price, daughter of David Price[1], Maesllech.

She was the daughter of a remarkable man. He was a farmer and drover who organised the driving of cattle to distant places, such as London, the new industrial centres, and to farmers in Kent, who fattened cattle for the London market. He not only hired drovers to work with him, but took charge himself of the drives. He was responsible for the conduct of all the business connected with these operations, which usually included the transport of money, the carrying of messages to people who lived along the route and at the destination of the cattle drive, and above all he was responsible for the safe delivery and good condition of the cattle entrusted to him and to carry back the money earned by the sale. David Price was known for his trustworthiness and honesty and had a reputation for hard-driving energy, so much so it was said of him that he wore out three wives[2]. Most remarkable of all, he lived to be ninety-seven years of age. He was a vigorous and active man until very late in his life. His daughter Ann, born in 1807 when her father was sixty-two, inherited to the full his drive and purposeful energy. She would need it all her life.

The Price home, Maesllech, was a short walk over the fields from Llanlleonfel Church. David Morgan the Progenitor married Ann there on 9 March, 1832. Llanlleonfel Church appears a number of times in the Morgan family records. It was the scene of three marriages and several burials.

David Morgan the Progenitor and Ann found a tenancy at Cae Crwn, a farm of one hundred and twenty acres in the parish of Battle about four miles to the northwest of Brecon. It was part of the Penoyre estate owned by the Watkins family. The landlord at this time was Colonel Lloyd Watkins, one of the most distinguished of the landed gentry in Breconshire. Born in 1802, he became Liberal Member of Parliament for Brecon from 1832 to 1834 and again from 1854 to 1865, High Sheriff in 1836 and Lord Lieutenant of Breconshire from 1847 until his death in 1865.

The first impression a visitor gets of the farmhouse at Cae Crwn is of its smallness. Here in this small house David and Ann Morgan raised a family of five sons and one daughter. Their births are listed on the flyleaf of the First Volume of *Geriadur Ysgrythol*, a two-volume *Biblical Commentary and Dictionary* which is mentioned in the will of

David Morgan the Progenitor. It was a widespread family with nineteen years between the oldest and the youngest.

David,	born 28 October,	1833
John,	born 17 January,	1836
William,	born 30 July,	1838
Jane,	born 12 July,	1841
Thomas,	born 7 July,	1848
James,	born 29 Sept,	1852

An old friend of the Morgan family spoke of them affectionately to Kate Morgan of Llanbrynean as " Bachgen Bachi Caecrwn " which means " The little lads of Caecrwn ".

In the Census of 1841 the family was listed as follows:

David Morgan Caecrwn Farm Battle aged 41
Anne[3] Morgan his wife aged 30
children   David 7   John 5   William 2
servants   Charles Bevan agricultural labourer aged 15
          Mary Morgan female servant aged 15
          Hannah Price female servant aged 15

Cae Crwn was not the sort of farm that could afford to pay its help anything but board and infinitesimal wages. The ages of the labourer and the two servant girls indicate that, though there were two servants and a labourer, the farming was on the smallest scale and the three children were too young to contribute their labour.

Ten years later the Census of 1851 reveals some change at Cae Crwn. The entry was:

Cae Crwn 120 acres employing two men

Head of House	David Morgan	aged 51	
Anne		aged 43	
John Morgan		15	farmer
William Morgan		12	farmer
Jane Morgan		9	scholar
Thomas Morgan		2	

The first noticeable change from the 1841 return is the absence of the eldest son, David, who had gone to Newport as an apprentice. There was no longer room in the house for men who were employed, and the servant girls had gone.

According to the family records, Ann Price was born on 9 December, 1807. The ages given in the Census reveal that Ann had the traditional feminine weakness of taking years off her age, but not with consistency. She was thirty-four in 1841 when she gave her age as thirty, and in 1851 she permitted a certain amount of adjustment by allowing her reported age of forty-three to creep up to within one year of her true age of forty-four.

Some idea of what a struggle it must have been to raise the family and keep going at Cae Crwn can be gathered from an account of the state of agriculture from 1832, the year David and Ann Morgan started at Cae Crwn, to 1846, written by R. E. Protheroe in *Cassell's History of Social England.*

> In the first four years of this period the agricultural distress in which this country was plunged after the peace of 1815 continued with little or no abatement. Landlords with mortgages and rent charges on their estates were ruined; tenants farming on borrowed capital became parish paupers; bankruptcies, seizures, executions, imprisonment for debt were still universally prevalent. Rents fell into arrears; tithes and poor rates went unpaid; labour bills were reduced; improvements were discontinued; livestock dwindled. Tradesmen, innkeepers and shopkeepers who depended on farmers as their principal customers were involved in the same ruin. The failure of numerous country banks added to the distress of the rural districts.

The mills of traditional incompetence, inescapable poverty and grim despair were grinding David Morgan of Cae Crwn small. He had passed his fortieth birthday and had got nowhere, and worse was to come.

This devastating agricultural depression which reached its climax in "the Hungry Forties" struck both landlord and tenant, the difference being that for the tenant having no reserves the end of the road came more swiftly into sight than for the landlord. But with this long depression the end result was the same for David Morgan and Colonel Watkins. They both lost their homes.

David Morgan was plagued with asthma, a debilitating and depressing complaint, whose harassed victim will inevitably take any steps he can to avoid the onslaught of a violent attack. Little or nothing was then known about this affliction and its relation to allergies and pollen, though the words "hay fever" suggest some suspicion as to the real villain. Worry and tension also play their part. Anyone who has undergone a severe attack of asthma or witnessed the gasping for breath and exhaustion of one of its victims would understand the unwillingness of the sufferer to go out-of-doors if by staying inside relief or avoidance could be achieved. In the summertime David Morgan spent much time indoors at Cae Crwn, which was not conducive to effective farming. Not even the remarkable energy of his wife could make up for what appeared to be his reluctance to work. Though times were bad, the Morgan family still managed to hold on at Cae Crwn.

The first blow to strike them was a warning of things to come. The landlord decided to take away the two best fields at Cae Crwn and put them with an adjoining farm. This action must have been the result of David Morgan becoming increasingly behind with his rent.

The next blow was totally unexpected. When the eldest son, David, went to Newport to become apprenticed to a draper, John, the second son, had taken on more and more of the responsibility for working the farm. At harvest time when he was in his nineteenth year he led the line of neighbours who had come to help scythe a field of hay. It was the duty and privilege of the resident farmer to lead the line and set the pace and rhythm. In his father's absence, the duty fell on John. It is easy to assume that he set as good and as steady a pace as he could, one that would prove that he was an equal amongst his neighbours. At the end of the day, exhausted, hot and sweaty, he neglected to put on his coat and lay down on the grass, damp with the evening dew. He caught a chill, which revealed that he was a victim of tuberculosis[4]. The disease moved swiftly and he died that year, 1854.

This crippling blow hastened the ebbing tide of fortune for the Morgan family. William, the third son, was barely sixteen, an early age to have to take on the struggle against the odds of a severe agricultural depression and to try to catch up from being behind in the rent when the landlord himself was in financial straits.

The last and final blow came when they were evicted from Cae Crwn in 1855. Hampered by the loss of his two best fields and his second son, David Morgan would almost inevitably have been unable to produce even the reduced rent. And the landlord, himself in dire financial straits, would have no other choice than to evict David Morgan from Cae Crwn and find a tenant who might pay the rent for the farm.

The combination of the long agricultural depression and Colonel Watkins' generosity so crippled his own property that he was the last of his family to own Penoyre. He died impoverished at the old Bear Inn, Brecon, in 1865. Kilvert[5] visited Penoyre, which had been one of the great houses in Breconshire, five years after the Colonel's death.

> Everything overgrown and neglected, weedy walks, rusty gates, silence and the lonely deserted house and grounds.

The tower and glass-domed observatory gave the house such a grand look that Kilvert was surprised to learn that there were only twenty-five bedrooms.

> The hall is large and surrounded by a gallery and double staircase. . . The place was entirely unfurnished and had a dreary dilapidated look, the paper in some of the rooms waving from the walls in long strips.

It represented the ruin of the fortune of one of Breconshire's old county families.

Cae Crwn may have been poverty-stricken and a depressing failure, but it was all the Morgans had. It had been their home for twenty-three years. Now they were evicted. The situation had been desperate for some time; after the eviction it must have seemed hopeless. Destitution and the fate of becoming parish paupers was drawing near. Their resources were negligible. What could save them from the final disaster of bankruptcy, the poorhouse and the dispersal of the family? When John Arnott Lewis wrote to James Morgan the Solicitor about his ancestors, he added that his mother " also wishes me to tell you the family motto ' Owe no man anything ' ". They had lived up to that motto, and it saved them.

Fortunately for them the desperately-needed roof for their heads was found near at hand. A member of the Chapel at Pontfaen had an unoccupied house, Coed-y-genau, outside the very small village of Pontfaen. It was empty because the land was being farmed with another farm. Here in Coed-y-genau the Morgan family sheltered. Old David Morgan found odd jobs such as hedging at farms round Pontfaen. Ann and their daughter Jane, aged fifteen, earned badly-needed money by working as servants in nearby farmhouses. William went to work as a farm labourer for Mr. Edwards, Pontgwilym.

Ann Morgan never gave in, and with her customary determination set about finding a farm where the Morgans could start again. She was gifted with the legs of a good walker. Shanks' pony was the only transport she had, but what a good pony! Amongst the farms she investigated was Gethinog near Talybont; she walked there and back to Coed-y-genau, more than twenty miles, in one day. When David Morgan lost his two fields and saw he had little chance to make both ends meet at Cae Crwn he began to look round for somewhere to make another start. In 1854 he put in for the tenancy of a farm near Llanfrynach called Llanbrynean, but failed to get it. His record and health would not easily win the acceptance of a landlord.

In 1857 Ann Price Morgan heard that Llanbrynean was again vacant. It had had a run of bad luck. The tenant who had been the successful applicant in 1854 had found the deep depression of agriculture too much and had hanged himself. The children of William Morgan remember the stone weights of fourteen pounds, twenty-eight pounds and fifty-six pounds with which he had hanged himself lying in the farmyard at Llanbrynean.

The vicar then tried his hand at renting the farm and not the house. He soon called it quits and the farm once again became vacant. Hearing of this, Ann Morgan walked from Coed-y-genau to Llanbrynean to find out if it was true. Having learned that it was, she returned the same day, having walked a total distance of over sixteen miles. Application was made to the landlord, Mr. Allen of Hay. Before accepting the Morgans as tenants Mr. Allen went to Coed-y-genau to see how Mrs. Morgan kept house. She was a compulsive worker who was never satisfied with her own or other people's efforts. Her house was always immaculate. There can be no doubt that Mr. Allen was properly impressed, and the Morgan family moved into Llanbrynean. The event was of such importance to the Morgan family that every surviving grandchild remembered the date, 3 December, 1857. The farmhouse of the Old Llanbrynean to which they moved fell into decay and ceased to exist after the New Llanbrynean had been built by David Morgan the Draper in 1883.

Llanbrynean is a farm of 141 acres near Llanfrynach in the Usk valley. The fertile farmland of this valley and that of the Wye valley around Talgarth were the basis of Breconshire's reputation for good agriculture. It was these farms and their proprietors that enabled John Clark to close his report of 1794 with a final sentence of pride:

For let it be remembered that every improvement that has hitherto been introduced into South Wales, the County of Brecon has always taken the lead. Here the first turnpike road was made. Here the first society for the encouragement of agriculture was formed and a county to the West does offer annually a premium of ten guineas to any of their farmers' servants who will come and reside for three years in Brecknockshire and learn to hold a plough.

However, in spite of the greatly improved farming conditions, the first year at Llanbrynean was far from easy and the first year's rent was found not without some difficulty. No matter, the corner had been turned, and at last the long period of close on thirty-eight years of agricultural depression had taken a turn for the better.

According to *Cassell's Social History of England*:

The revival of agriculture set in before the beginning of 1835 due to the discoveries of gold in California in 1849 and in Australia in 1850. The Crimean War in 1854 helped to give a boost to the prices of agricultural products. . . Taking all things into consideration the period of ten years ending in 1862 were probably the most prosperous decade enjoyed by British agriculture. . . Up to 1874 the period of prosperity may be said to have prevailed with only one considerable intermission.

The fertility of Llanbrynean was a remarkable change after the rigours of Cae Crwn; above all, the eighteen years that old David Morgan lived and farmed at Old Llanbrynean were mainly times of agricultural prosperity.

William Morgan, the third son of David and Ann, left Mr. Edwards of Pontgwilym to join his parents at Llanbrynean. Undoubtedly William's natural gifts as a farmer were greatly enhanced by Mr. Edwards' training in more advanced methods of farming, which his father could not have given him. That pattern of unproductive, uninformed farming which had been passed down to him by two generations of ineffective farmers was broken. His remarkable capacity for work he had inherited from his mother, without acquiring her hasty impatience. He had that equanimity of temperament essential in a good stockman, together with his father's strong sense of fair play and honesty, which was to win for him a high standing in the opinion of his neighbours. Llanbrynean began to forge ahead.

Even though David went away to Newport, the three eldest children had experienced the fierce economies of Cae Crwn and the first taste of success at Llanbrynean. Their mother had sternly taught them the virtues of hard work. As they grew up they knew what failure could bring and that the route to security lay along the path of economy and saving. David, William and Jane were in many ways similar and had mutual respect and admiration for each other, and the marks of Cae Crwn showed from time to time in their long lives.

During these early years at Llanbrynean the Morgan family were blessed with a stroke of good fortune. William Hall of Pencelli Court

24

and Jane Morgan, the only daughter of Llanbrynean, fell in love. Their path was far from smooth because of the different backgrounds of the two families.

The Halls came of a long line of substantial yeoman farmers who, originating in the North of England, had come to settle in the late Seventeenth Century at the Manor House, Trewalter in the parish of Llangorse. They brought with them new practices of farming which enabled them to prosper. Towards the end of the Eighteenth Century a branch of the Hall family moved over the river Usk to the parish of Llanfrynach.

At the time that William and Jane met, William's father, with the help of his two sons, James and William, was farming Pencelli Court, where the Hall family lived, Pencelli Castle and Tynewydd—a total of 566 acres. On these good farms the carefully-bred stock of quality prospered on the lush river-bottom meadows. Well-bred, well-thought-of and comparatively well-to-do, the Halls justifiably thought well of themselves; so it is easy to understand their consternation when they discovered that William, their younger son, had become enamoured of a girl who had been a farmhouse servant and was in their eyes the daughter of a pinch-penny peasant, a man not only without position but a farmer who had undergone the disgrace of being evicted from his farm. Yet the courtship had been going on right under their eyes for some time. Perhaps the Hall family could not bring themselves to believe that William would be so foolish as to contemplate such an ill match. But that is exactly what he did contemplate.

At some date unknown he asked his father's permission to marry Jane, but his father angrily forbade such a match. His father died in 1860 and two years later, still against his mother's and brother's wishes, William Hall married Jane Morgan. To his dismay, his father's wishes were carried out and he was given Tynewydd to farm, the least valuable of the three Hall farms. Even so, Tynewydd was a good farm and under the hand of William Hall earned a high reputation as one of the best-kept farms in Breconshire. An award was several times given to him in recognition of this achievement. He also won prizes for his horses and cattle. These successes, together with the Hall standards of generous hospitality to all and sundry " be he Bishop or beggar ", gave an air of prosperity to Tynewydd, an atmosphere very foreign to the frugal austerity of Cae Crwn.

It was a tremendous step up for Jane, and she never quite made it. Jane Morgan brought to Tynewydd no worldly goods; what she brought was her way of life formed at Cae Crwn. She, of all the children born at that farm, most clearly bore the marks of that desperate struggle and the final ignomiiny of eviction. Accustomed to hard work without reward, she was driven to seek those petty scraping economies which were to her as gold to a miser.

The ancestral blood of those generations of hill farmers ran strong in her veins. Farming to her was the extraction of a living from the land and returning to the soil little but hard work, of which she gave unstintingly. Like her forebears, she could not bring herself to accept that to keep the land in good heart and raise or maintain the quality of the stock, a judicious return of some of the money earned is as important as manure. Her children remembered that to the end of her days she never ceased to deplore the extravagance of her husband, William Hall, when he spent two hundred and eighty guineas for a prize bull, forgetting the many cups won by William for his livestock.

She also brought with her the stern beliefs of Calvinistic Methodism, so different from the more comfortable doctrine of the established Church of England, to which the Halls belonged. Having suffered the Halls' slighting disapproval of herself and her family at the time of her marriage, she found compensation in the success of her brother David, whom she admired to the point of hero worship.

Her devotion to the Chapel was inherited from her father. Old David Morgan was constant in his attendances at the Chapel in the village at Pencelli. He listened with visible and earnest concentration to the words of the preacher. Sometimes he would feel sleepiness creeping over him. To avoid losing a word of the sermon he would overcome this by standing up; as he rose to his feet, with a gesture of humility in The Presence, he would remove all semblance of vanity by drawing his hand down from the top of his head over his face, dragging his hair over his forehead. Standing alone amidst the seated congregation, he would listen intently to every word of the sacred message. This somnolence was not likely to be the effect of toiling in the fields, but rather from long nights made sleepless by his asthma.

His quiet contemplative manner was in sharp contrast to the drive and energy of his wife, Ann. One day when Ann had returned from a visit to her daughter at Tynewydd, William Morgan heard his father call out: "Ann, come and sit down and talk to me", to which she replied, "There are plenty of people to sit down in the world". She then became even more energetic than usual and made a great deal of hustle and bustle about the house. They were undoubtedly an ill-matched pair. His lethargic calm could only have exasperated her nervous compulsion to work.

Something of the shadowy role the Progenitor played in the family's life is revealed by the fact that his eldest grandson, David Hall, who was eleven years of age when old Mr. Morgan died, could recall only one story about his grandfather. When a local man, having bought a bag of grain from David Morgan, complained afterwards that it was underweight, the old man immediately and without argument made up the claimed shortage. This story would have been told to David Hall by his mother. Knowing the feelings of her Hall relatives, she undoubtedly tried to present her parents to her children in as good a light as possible, yet apparently all she left in the mind of her son was this one story of her father's undoubted honesty.

David Morgan, borne along by the restless vigour of his wife and the skilled industry of his son William, moved slowly and quietly into old age. Times were better. Llanbrynean and its children began to prosper.

26

In 1873 Ann, exhausted from a life of overwork, died. She had been a difficult wife and a hard-driving mother, but she brought to the Morgan family an invaluable heritage, a tenacity of purpose and the will to advance in the world. David Morgan lived for two more years, watched over by his daughter, Jane. But he lived long enough to witness what must have been the climax of his life, something beyond any hope or expectation he may have ever had.

On 29 June, 1874, his eldest son, David, bought Llanbrynean from the estate of the late Henry Allen for the sum of £5,300, of which £2,000 appears to have been raised by a mortgage. This was a high price to pay. It had been forced up by competition from the de Wintons, who wanted to enlarge their estate around Llanfrynach. The draper had shown his financial muscle and outlasted the banker. To old David Morgan it must have been a triumphant moment; he would have thanked his Maker that he had been spared to see the day his son became a landed proprietor. He would still be a tenant, but it was his son who was the landlord. The Llanbrynean rent book carries the notation for September 1874: "David Morgan Senr and William Morgan in a/c with David Morgan Junr".

Less than a month after this great moment David Morgan Senior decided the time had come for him to put his affairs in order and on 9 July, 1874, he signed his last Will and Testament. He made his sons David and Thomas his executors. James, the youngest of the family, was then twenty-two years of age and was an articled clerk with Tudor and Cobb, solicitors in Brecon. His father was concerned that it would be three more years before he could earn a living as a solicitor. Special provisions were therefore made for his care and shelter in the instructions given to William, the heir to the estate, that he " shall allow to James the enjoyment of the same domestic comforts and privileges at Llanbrynean after my decease as he enjoys at present while in his present condition ". James was also to receive £450 and the interest thereon, " to be paid to him in half-yearly payments if he desires until the principle (sic) is paid up ". Possibly as a mark of old David Morgan's admiration of James's intellectual achievements there were also left to him what must have been treasured possessions of his father, two volumes of The Scriptural Dictionary[6] and a copy of John Bunyan's Pilgrim's Progress.

Except for an early reference in the will to " my dear children ", the only term of endearment was reserved for " my beloved daughter Jane " to whom a bequest was made of £320 " for her own use, will and discretion ". Even though she had come without dowry to the Hall family, she would now have her own money. It may have been in appreciation of the affection and care she had shown her father, especially after the death of her mother, that the best chest of drawers[7] and the best set of china were also given to her.

But it was on the sturdy shoulders of William that the burden was put of finding out of the estate the money to pay the legacies, which amounted to £810. He also had to pay his father's debts and funeral expenses.

William was very close to his father; because of his loyal, generous nature he would overlook his father's but slight contribution to the work of the farm. He had remained at home unmarried and had made Llanbrynean prosper. Being the farmer, William was left " the whole of the farming stock and all the instruments of husbandry, all the Brewing[8] and Dairy Utensils, with all the household furniture except the best chest and drawers ".

To William was given all the money and securities in the possession of his father at the time of his death. It would be of the greatest interest to know how much, or how little, was left to William to carry on at Llanbrynean after paying the legacies to his sister and youngest brother.

On 11 May, 1875, less than a year after creating this potential source of discord, David Morgan died. His son, writing from Pontlottyn to Mary Davies (the daughter of John Morgan II by his second marriage) in Australia said: " Father died in May 1875. He had got very weak and feeble for many years, but was out and about to within five days of his death ". At long last he and his wife came to rest side by side in the graveyard[9] of Pontfaen Welsh Calvinistic Methodist Chapel where they joined their son John.

1   The tombstone of David Price stands against the outside west wall of the porch of Llanlleonfel Church.

> In memory of David Price Maesllech in this Parish.
> He died Jan. 6th 1842 aged 97 years also of Ann his
> wife she died May 2nd 1835 aged 50 years

Four lines of Welsh verse follow in the form of an englyn:

> Y bedd yw diwedd y da call ár ffol
> Tran rhodio yma:
> Tyred oll o plant Adda
> Yr hwn ni rhed yno'ra.

Translation:

> The grave is (the) end (of) the good—wise and the foolish
> While dwelling here (on earth):
> Come all (ye) children (of) Adam
> To the one (who) does not run free (is constant) there will I go.

This gravestone was restored by David Price's great-grandson John Llewellyn Morgan.

2   Source of information on David Price of Maesllech, Willie Morgan of Llanbrynean.

3   According to the records the spelling of Ann Price Morgan's first name varies with or without an *e*.

4   Source, May Brummitt. Told her by the lady with whom she boarded when teaching at Pontfaen. The lady was a friend of the Morgans of Cae Crwn.

5   The Reverend Francis Kilvert, whose diaries tell of his walks around Clyro in Radnorshire.

6 The *Scriptural Dictionary* went with the rest of the Brynderwen library to Bernard. The copy of *Pilgrim's Progress* has disappeared.

7 Jane's chest of drawers went to James Hall upon her death, and was given to Aubrey by John Llewellyn Morgan after the death of James Hall.

8 May Brummitt translated this as "Small Beer Very Small Beer for the Harvesters".

9 In the back of an old rent book of Llanbrynean dated 1876 the expenses for placing a memorial "on Father Mother and John" are given in detail, amounting to £43-15-0. Each of the five surviving children is listed as having paid their share of £8-15-0.

4. David Morgan

THE FOUNDER: HIS YOUTH

The first child of David and Ann Morgan was born at Cae Crwn on 28 October, 1833. He was called David, the name of his father and his maternal grandfather, David Price, who came from Maesllech for the christening. Riding his pony, the old drover followed the long familiar trails over Mynydd Eppynt.[1] At eighty-eight years of age this vigorous old man held his new grandson in his arms[2], conferring on him not only his blessing but also the invaluable Price heritage of industriousness, tenacity of purpose and longevity.

David Morgan in his old age told very few stories of his home and boyhood to his grandchildren. When he and his brothers came together at Llanbrynean and old family stories were related, it was noticed that he was the only one who did not tell stories about his mother. There can be no doubt that his childhood was an unhappy time which he wished to forget. He used to say that he escaped many a thrashing by the quickness of his legs[3]; but there must have been a number of less fortunate moments because he added: " If I had not been able to escape her often, I think she would have thrashed me within an inch of my life ".

His mother, a hard-driving energetic woman, found herself married to a man who suffered from ill health and a consequent lethargy. Conscious of her husband's lack of drive, she sought to bring up her children in her own image of hard work. Times were very bad for the farmer, and Ann Morgan knew that only by very great efforts could the family keep their heads above the rising waters of agricultural depression. As a result she placed a premature burden of responsibility on their eldest son and expected too much of him. Too young and ill-suited by temperament to take on tasks usually done by older farm hands, David at times failed to come up to his mother's requirements. It was in the many small routine functions that he showed that farming was not his line. When sent to the fields to bring the cows in for milking he would often allow some to escape his attention and leave one or two behind[4]. His inexperience and lack of concentration infuriated his mother and she did not spare the rod in her efforts to teach him early in his life to be a farmer. It was undoubtedly a painful but fortunate failure.

However, one story, that of his earliest memory, when he was a four-year-old, he told frequently[5] and with pleasure. He was in bed at Cae Crwn when he heard his father returning from Brecon market. He noticed that the pony came into the farmyard at the trot, not the customary walk. As his father dismounted he called out to his wife upstairs; " Mae'r Brenin wedi marw! " (The King is dead!) It was the death of King William IV and the Accession of Queen Victoria in

1837. This earliest memory marks David Morgan as belonging completely and absolutely to that remarkable period of expansion and progress, the Victorian Age.

David and his brothers attended a one-room school over the blacksmith's shop in the small village of Cradoc beyond Battle, about a mile down the road towards Brecon from their home. Here they were taught English and made to speak English while attending school. The language of the home was Welsh, as young David's first memory shows. All the children of Cae Crwn spoke Welsh. David used it frequently in his shops at Rhymney and Pontlottyn[6]. Thomas when he visited Llanbrynean, often made his brother and sister-in-law laugh with amusing stories in Welsh, which none of their children could understand. When William and his wife wanted to keep something secret from their children they would speak in Welsh. Of the twenty-one grandchildren[7] of old David and Ann Morgan, not one could speak Welsh. David the Draper used to tell how, when he went to Brecon market with his parents, he would sometimes go round to the Duke of Wellington Hotel to watch the mail coach arrive and "listen to the foreigners talk". English spoken without a Welsh accent would sound a very foreign tongue in Brecon round about the year 1840.

Besides English, which was the compulsory language at the school, David was taught at Cradoc School to read and write and the rudiments of mathematics. This sparse schooling was all the teaching he ever received and it ended when he was fourteen.

The primitive nature of this school can be imagined from a story he told his grandson Aubrey. When the blacksmith in his shop below the schoolroom put a red-hot iron tyre onto the rim of a wooden wheel he would plunge it into a tank of water to shrink the tyre tight onto the rim and stop the wood burning. The resulting smoke and steam would pour up through the cracks in the floor of the schoolroom until it became unbearable and the teacher would order evacuation. David Morgan smiled as he told his grandson how the pupils ran down the outside stairway making as much fuss and noise as possible. He added with traces of reminiscent pleasure that this sometimes happened more than once in a day. His brother, William, remembered how the smell from the burning of a pile of hoof parings had a similar effect.

When he was twelve years of age some error of omission on his part exhausted his mother's very limited supply of patience. She packed his roll and sent him off on foot to go to work for a time with a relative who had a shop in Rhymney. He knew the way because he had been there before. On his first visit to Rhymney he had been sent there with his younger brother John. The journey took them past places the names of which would echo on throughout David Morgan's life. The two little boys set off from home on ponies with their father. The three riders passed through Battle, where the first Norman, Bernard Newmarch, conquered Breconshire. (David Morgan the Draper's first grandson was named Bernard after this Norman Conqueror.) Leaving Brecon, the three followed the Brecon to Newport Canal past Tynewydd, going

31

within a few hundred yards of Old Llanbrynean, and on past Pencelli Court, Pencelli Castle, until they reached Talybont, where they turned off the Canal. Their father parted with the boys, taking the ponies back with him. He warned his sons not to loiter but to walk on over the Trevil. Their route lay up the tramroad which started alongside the White Hart Inn; it climbed over the moors up one side of Glyn Collwng, over a shoulder of Llangynider Mountain, and on to a small cluster of quarry workers' cottages called Trevil, where there were limestone quarries, and then down to a point halfway between Rhymney and Tredegar. This tramroad delivered limestone to the ironworks and brought their output or coal down to the canal, by which it would be carried to Newport or Brecon. Travellers who used this moorland track to Rhymney spoke of " going over the Trevil ".

David and John did not heed their father's warning. They paused outside an inn up the valley to join some other boys in a game of marbles[8]. This all-absorbing game of boyhood caused too much time to pass, and it began to be late. When the two small boys inquired the way of the woman of the inn, she took pity on them and called out through the door of the inn: " Is anyone going over the Trevil?" A man who was washing his hands and face in the horse trough replied that he would be going shortly and would take the boys with him.

It was quite dark as they left Trevil on their way down to Rhymney. All of a sudden a furnace was emptied of its fiery molten metal and in a flash the black sky turned a bright and brilliant red. The two small boys, nurtured on the sin-conscious beliefs of Calvinistic Methodism, must have felt they were standing in the jaws of Hell, about to be punished for their marble-playing naughtiness. But for the steadying influence of their guide's presence they would no doubt have turned round and fled. It is difficult to say where they would have run because they were a long way from home, where the certainties of their mother's reception could be compared with the unknown terrors of the jaws of Hell.

After they had recovered from the shock, their guide led them on down to their destination in Rhymney. Whether because of this first and terrifying demonstration of the vast powers of the new Industrial Age or because he was to pass through Trevil later on one of the most important journeys in his life, to become an apprentice, the name remained fixed in David Morgan's mind. Sixty years later his third grandson was given the names John and, at his grandfather's request, Trevil.

It was in the employ of this Rhymney relative[9] as a handy-boy that David Morgan discovered that there were openings in life other than that of a farmer and experienced for the first time the rewarding pleasure of earning his own money. It was only six shillings, but he saved four shillings out of it[10]. This formative experience was probably short, but it was to have a long-lasting effect on David Morgan. When he was fourteen an all-important decision was made to send him away

32

Aberceiddon, Near Builth.

Cae Crwn.

Old Llanbrynean.

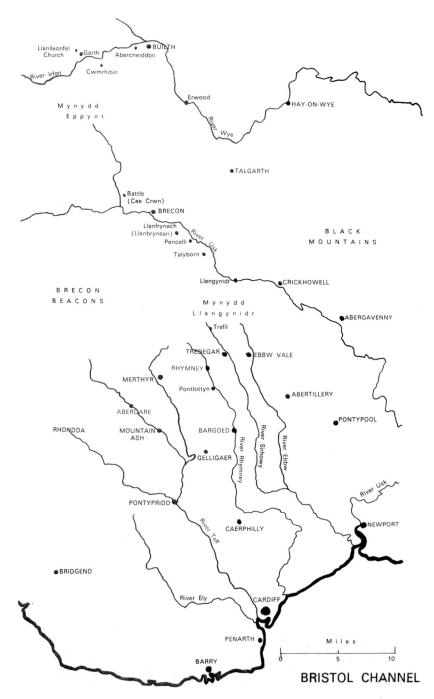

Map of Breconshire and Glamorgan.

from the farm and apprentice him to Mr. Philip John, a draper in Commercial Street, Newport.

David Morgan Senior accompanied his son to Newport. The journey was most probably made soon after David's fourteenth birthday, 28 October, 1847, before winter set in. They went " ride and tie ", which was the most economical and effective form of travel for two people evolved in the horse age. The two travellers would set off, one on foot and the other on horseback. After the horseman had ridden some distance ahead he would dismount, tie up the horse to some convenient gate or tree and proceed on foot. After a time the first pedestrian would come up, mount the horse and ride past his companion on foot. When he had gone a certain distance ahead, he would dismount, tie up the horse and proceed on foot. And so this procedure would continue to the end of the journey. By this method each of the two travellers would get the benefit of rides and the horse would get regular rests. The straightest and shortest way between Brecon and Newport was " over the Trevil " through Tredegar and down the Sirhowy Valley. So, for at least the third time, David Morgan passed through Trevil on the journey which was to take him to his start in life as a draper.

While doubtless the prospect of escape from the stern and sparse life of a farmer at Cae Crwn would act as a spur to do well as an apprentice, Cae Crwn was still his home and there was a certain amount of travel to and fro. His mother and sister came to visit him, making the journey from Brecon to Newport on a canal barge. Once when he was coming home for the holidays it was arranged that his father and his brother John should meet him with a spare horse at the town gate of Crickhowell. David would have been coming by barge or walking from Newport. Somehow he was late, and as he approached the rendezvous he saw his father and brother turn away and ride off towards Brecon. He was too far away to attract their attention and stood watching them go out of sight. He admitted that the feeling of disappointment and the longing for home was so great that he almost burst into tears. He spent the night at Crickhowell and early next morning walked to Brecon, where he found his mother in the market.

It was as an apprentice in Newport that he learnt a lesson about merchandising which he was to remember for the rest of his long life. A fancy waistcoat in the window of a competitor of Mr. Philip John caught his eye. The price on the ticket was more than his limited pocket money could afford. But the time of the sales, with their much advertised reductions, was close at hand and David decided to postpone his purchase, hoping no other customer would buy the object of his desire before the sales.

Early on the first morning of the sale the nose of young David was pressed against the glass. Yes, there it was with a big sales ticket on it. The red line, which customarily drew attention to the old price before the reduction, was drawn through the figure of an increased price and the new price was the same price which the waistcoat had carried before the sale. David was disappointed and furious; not only did he not buy

33

the waistcoat, but there and then he concluded that sales were a fraud on the public and swore that when he had a shop of his own he would never hold a sale. And, for the sixty-one years that he was in business for himself, he never did. This well-known family story is the first evidence of his interest in his own appearance. Photographs at various stages of his life almost always show that he wore clothes with a neatness, quiet distinction and a faint touch of elegance, not without a certain individualism.

While David Morgan was in Newport the railway came to South Wales from London through Gloucester, thus ending Bristol's reign as the Welsh metropolis. Immediately outside Newport Station on the Cardiff side there is a tunnel. When this tunnel was completed, but before the rails were laid, it was a popular Sunday " constitutional " for many citizens of Newport, of whom David was one, to take a walk through the tunnel to marvel at the preparations for the coming of the railway.

June 19, 1850 was the first day that trains ran between Newport and Cardiff. David Morgan bought a ticket to Cardiff on one of the cheap excursions that ran that day. After looking around he walked out to Llandaff, where he visited the Cathedral ruins, which were later restored by John Pritchard, who was also the architect of some houses in Llandaff, including one called Brynderwen. Once again as with David Morgan's first walk over the Trevil to Rhymney, we see the threads which were to weave the end pattern of his life appear early in his story.

After completing his apprenticeship in Newport he decided to gain wider experience by going to London. It has always been said that he went to work for a wholesaler in St. Paul's Churchyard in Dickensian conditions. He slept under the counter and his first duty of the day was to sweep out the shop.

He visited the Great Exhibition of 1851, which was held in the Crystal Palace erected in Hyde Park.

David Morgan bought at the Exhibition a Baxter print of one of the statues in the Crystal Palace and sent it as a gift to his mother[11]. Written on the mount in ink is the title of the statue: " The faithful messenger ". He paid ten shillings for it. This was a very generous gesture, which reveals that in spite of the experiences of his youth he was of an affectionate nature.

He was just nineteen when he went to the Horse Guards to see the Duke of Wellington lying in state[12]. The location of the wholesaler in St. Paul's Churchyard surely made it inevitable that David Morgan must have watched the massive funeral car with its vast ornate catafalque come to St. Paul's Cathedral, accompanied by the greatest military ceremonial seen in London up to that time.

The time had now come for David to look around for a likely place to start for himself in business. It was a decision calling for the most careful observation and judgement. Because of his very limited capital resources built out of hard-earned savings, he would have to find somewhere inexpensive, yet an area towards which trade was likely to flow and where conditions would improve and the value of the property would rise. The decision required a mixture of patience, courage and perception, together with some fifth sense about property and its future. David Morgan had these in abundance. Four times[13] he was to start a business on his own, and on each of them his judgement of site proved to be a good one.

He began by looking around in Birmingham, where he had become a shop assistant. There was a story in the James Morgan family that when John died in 1854 it took so long for the news to reach David Morgan and for him to make his way home to Cae Crwn that he was much too late for the funeral. That he was in Birmingham about this time is confirmed by a letter he wrote to his niece, Kate Morgan, dated 26 September, 1917. Referring to a holiday he had recently taken at Leamington he wrote: " I had been there one afternoon with a few fellow assistants when I lived in Birmingham more than sixty years ago ". Birmingham was a rapidly developing industrial town and had many of the things for which David Morgan looked when choosing a business site. The story of his stay in Birmingham according to the James Morgan family goes on to tell that he had already chosen a site for a shop (reputedly a part of the ground now occupied by Lewis's) when he was summoned home for his brother's funeral; his mother however was greatly disturbed by the time it took her eldest son to return home and she persuaded him to start nearer home. As a result he entered into partnership with a relative in Rhymney.

There is a story from the Hall family that suggests he did not go to Rhymney immediately after the funeral. Mrs. William Hall used to tell her children that the first time she saw Tynewydd was when she was walking across the fields to meet a canal barge to put on it some laundry for her brother David. This could not have taken place until the Morgan family had moved to Llanbrynean on 3 December, 1857, some three years after the funeral of John.

The canal goes nowhere near Rhymney, but goes to Newport, following the water level of the Usk through Crickhowell and Abergavenny. This leads one to believe that David Morgan returned once again to Newport to earn his living before going to join his relative in Rhymney as a partner.

1 My father when he told this story used the expression " The old man came over *the* mountain ".

2 My brothers, my sister and I can claim to have been held in the arms of a man who had been held in the arms of a man born in 1745 in the reign of George II.

3 This story of Ann Morgan's use of the stick on her eldest son was repeated in very similar words by his son.

4 All the members of the Llanbrynean family recalled this story.

5 I remember hearing this story from my grandfather, but I also heard it many times from my father and James Hall.

6   Morgan Price, son of John Price, grandfather's cousin, who bought the
    Pontlottyn shop from him, said that the speaking of Welsh with customers
    in the shop was common practice.

7   The twenty-one grandchildren were J. Ll. Morgan; the Hall children: Anna
    Maria, David, Anne, Sarah Jane, James, Lydia, William, Thomas, John,
    Frederick and Mary Frances (Nan); the Morgans of Llanbrynean: Kate,
    Agnes, David, May, Nellie, William; and the children of James Morgan:
    Wilfred, Arnold and Telford.

8   Kate Morgan, when telling this story which had been told to her by the
    previous generation, used the words " The naughty boys stopped to play
    marbles " which must have been the way the original story was told.

9   Believed to be David Price Morgan, son of John Morgan III the Innkeeper.
    D. P. Morgan kept the Albion Shop in Twyn Carno, Rhymney.

10 A story told in the Hall family.

11 This framed Baxter print is hanging in the living room at Brooklands, Three
    Cocks where Nellie and the late William Morgan of Llanbrynean lived.

12 David Morgan told this to his nephew William Morgan.

13 Cwm Shon Mathew Rhymney, Pontlottyn, The Pontlottyn Shop in Aber-
    tillery, and The Hayes Cardiff.

5. Industry Comes to South Wales

Along the edge of the high plateau of moorland just south of the Breconshire border, where the rivers Taff, Rhymney, Sirhowy, Ebbw and their tributaries scour their swift, precipitous way to the sea, there is a stretch of eighteen miles where nature laid the egg from which hatched the remarkable industrial development and prosperity of South Wales.

In this narrow strip the eight large ironworks were to crown the tops of the valleys with a diadem of iron: Cyfarthfa, Dowlais, Penydarren and Hill's Plymouth, all of Merthyr[1], Rhymney, Tredegar, Ebbw Vale and Blaenavon. Smaller works included Hirwaun, Sirhowy, Victoria, Beaufort, Blaina, Clydach, Varteg and Nantyglo.

In this remote, barren and empty area the bounty of nature had brought together the three ingredients essential to the making of iron: limestone, coal and iron ore. The iron ore was mined from the surface and the limestone quarried from the hillsides; coal was easy and inexpensive to extract from the northern limits of the fabulous South Wales coalfield where the saucer-shaped seams curve up close to the surface. In the early days in this area the coal was mainly gained by driving levels into the sides of the deep steep valleys. The costly drilling of deep shafts was therefore avoided. Added to these gifts of nature was an abundance of water which, because of the lie of the land, could be readily used for water power and washing the iron ore. Even the steepness of the valleys enabled the furnaces to be built close to the face of the hillside where they could be filled the more easily from terraces. The woods in the valleys provided the pit props. This cornucopia of natural resources lacked however two essentials: people to work them and adequate communications to the sea.

It was Anthony Bacon, a Londoner and Virginian planter, who in 1765 conceived this great development. He brought a Yorkshireman, Richard Crawshay, from London to Merthyr. Crawshay was the founder of the great iron dynasty of Crawshay, which included such eminent relatives as Crawshay Bailey and two sons-in-law, John Bailey and Benjamin Hall. When Anthony Bacon died in 1786 an obituary in the *Bristol Gazette* said: " Go to the mountains of Wales, view his deeds, what roads, what industry, what civilization, what sources of comfort and improvement he has opened to that once dreary and inaccessible district ".

These founders brought their drive, technical knowledge and, even more important, their access to capital in London, Bristol and many other places, such as Bath, Wells and Worcester. The successful ones rapidly developed large integrated industrial empires which owned the iron ore mines, the coal pits and limestone quarries essential to their works. Into these wild and empty valleys they brought from rural

Wales the great number of people needed to work these large operations. The ironmasters built for them stone houses which were similar to the small isolated half-door cottages in which they had lived in Mid-Wales. In these new towns the houses were assembled in continuous ranks, shoulder-to-shoulder, along the hillsides and were quickly blackened by industrial grime, which even the frequent rain could not remove.

Besides the ironmasters and the investors, the other great beneficiaries of this Golconda of iron were the owners of the land, who as a result of this surge of activity found that their previously almost worthless estates in this hilly region, which were at best poor sheep runs, had suddenly become sources of great wealth.

The industrial development at the tops of the valleys was only held back from its full potential by the extremely difficult terrain which lay between the ironworks and the sea. The seagoing vessel has always been and still is to this day unrivalled as an economical and efficient bulk cargo carrier. Between the furnaces and the sea there were only about twenty-four miles. But the mixture of high plateau and deep precipitous valleys made them an exceedingly difficult twenty-four miles to cross, especially with such a weighty commodity as iron. At first, teams of pack horses and mules carrying their burden in panniers wound their way down the sides of the valleys. Tramroads began to be developed, thus enabling horses to pull a number of wagons on rails.

It was the arrival of the canals that changed the whole scene. In 1794 the Glamorganshire Canal was completed between Merthyr and Cardiff. Newport was connected with its industrial interior by the Monmouthshire Canal in 1812. The building of the Glamorganshire Canal was a costly business. The swift fall of the Taff Valley called for the construction of forty locks[2]. The capital invested at the time of its completion in 1794 amounted to £103,600. But the economies effected by this change in transport were sensational. One barge with a load of twenty-four tons drawn by one horse and attended by one man and a boy brought down just as much as twelve wagons, forty-eight horses and twelve men and twelve boys[3].

Canals by their very nature are restricted to following the most favourable contour. Expansion by means of tributary canals was costly and rare. In fact the only addition to the Glamorganshire Canal was the Aberdare branch built in 1811. The canal companies extended the range of their canals by building tramroads to bring to the canal the products of the ironworks, coal pits and lime quarries not immediately alongside the canal. Those still further afield built their own tramroads to link up with those of the Canal Companies. Coal pits, lime quarries and iron ore mines were connected by tramroads with ironworks. Soon industrial South Wales was covered with a network of tramroads which, besides feeding the canals, became their competitors when, as a result of the gradual expansion of tramroads, it was possible to carry a load by tramroad all the way to a port. " Four tolerable horses would draw twenty tons of iron from Tredegar to Newport in one day, a distance of 23 miles[4] ". The four horses would be pulling a train of eight cars, each carrying two-and-a-half tons. However, this competition was slight and the canals flourished.

Because of their vital interest in improving their access to the sea, the large amount of capital needed to build the canals was mainly found by the owners of the ironworks. The chief shareholder in the Glamorganshire Canal Company was Richard Crawshay[5]. Yet there were frequent complaints from the iron interests. The management of the canal companies knew they had a good thing, in fact almost a monopoly, and were very conservative in the conduct of their business in spite of the pressing need for further development, quicker movement of consignments and reduced rates. A " Constant Reader " writing to the *Monmouthshire Merlin* said: " There is nothing like your mule for slow movement and dogged obstinacy save a body of canal proprietors[6]".

Due to the large number of locks, the canals were slow-moving conduits and their width limited the size of barges. Thus the cargoes could not be increased. The need to find a still better and swifter means of moving bigger and heavier loads economically remained constant. It is therefore not surprising that it was in South Wales that the first mobile steam engine[7] was developed. " In 1804 Trevethick's ' fire engine ' took a string of loaded wagons from Penydarren to the canal head at Navigation Abercynon, winning for Homfray a wager of one thousand pounds from Crawshay on the venture[8]".

The tramroads developed faster than the steam engine and by 1811 it was estimated that 150 miles of tramroad had been built in Glamorgan, Monmouthshire and Carmarthenshire to serve the iron, coal and copper industries[9].

But the great leap forward in transport was on its way. In 1830 " a steam engine drew fifty-and-a-half tons of coal from Blaencyffin Isha colliery to Newport and the empty wagons back to the colliery in twelve hours after being delayed for three hours by horse wagons. It accomplished in one day work which took six horses two days to perform, thus very considerably reducing time and transportation costs[10]".

Soon after this South Wales entered the Railway Age. The tramroads gave way to permanent way in a fever of railway building[11]. The problems of speed, size of load and high cost caused by the difficult access to the sea had been finally solved. The railways could take full advantage of the steep gradients, running downhill with a full load, the engine acting as a brake, and having to pull only empty trucks uphill.

When steam took the place of the horse it unleashed the full potential of the ironworks at the top of the valleys and created a new and vast demand for rails; but the mobile steam engine also opened up new markets for the coal from the South Wales coalfields and so set them free from the domination of the iron industry, which had hitherto been the principal consumer of the coal product from these coalfields. The arrival of the railway not only in South Wales, but all over Britain, altered the whole distribution of coal, opened new markets in other countries and created in itself a new demand for coal.

The pattern of the next stage in the industrial development of South Wales was set by the completion of the Taff Vale Railway between Merthyr and Cardiff in 1841. Sixteen years later the Rhymney Railway[12] linked the Rhymney Iron Works and the collieries of the Rhymney Valley with Cardiff. What the Glamorganshire Canal started, these railways completed. They established Cardiff as the major port for the export of coal and iron from South Wales, indeed as " the premier coal port in the world[13]". In 1850 the total export of coal amounted to approximately 700,000 tons. Twenty years later in 1870 the combined export tonnage for domestic and foreign use came to 3,100,000 tons.

The industrial activity of South Wales in the first half of the Nineteenth Century was largely dominated by the iron industries, and towns like Rhymney were rapidly growing in importance by the mid-century. The second half of the Nineteenth Century was marked by the astronomic rise of the Welsh coalfield, with Cardiff the beneficiary receiving a great stimulus from each wave of prosperity.

David Morgan by some instinct perceived how the growth of industrial South Wales was developing, and followed that growth. He started business in Rhymney when that town was responding to the benefits that came with the arrival of the railway. Twenty-one years later when Rhymney was coming to its peak of prosperity he made the decision to leave the top of the valleys and set up a business in Cardiff, catching the flood tide of the prosperity brought by the coal rush of the Rhondda Valley. Twice he was right in his estimate of the trend of development. Twice he had the foresight to see where the flow of trade was running. Thus the pattern of his life was woven into the pattern of the growth and prosperity of South Wales.

1 By 1825 Merthyr had by far the largest population of any town in Wales. One hundred years later three out of four of its adult population were unemployed.

2 *The History of Cardiff*, William Rees.

3 *The Crawshay Dynasty*, by John Addis.

4 *Rhymney Memories*, Tom Jones.

5 He also advanced £30,000 towards the completion of the Brecon and Abergavenny Canal. *The Crawshay Dynasty*, John Addis.

6 *Rhymney Memories,* Tom Jones.

7 In 1813 George Stephenson built a travelling engine named " Blucher " for tramroads in the North of England. He built the "Active " in 1822 for the Stocton and Darlington Railway, later renamed " Locomotion " it was the first engine to pull a passenger train. It was not until 1829 that his famous " Rocket " won the trials staged by the Liverpool and Manchester Railway.

8 *The Land of Wales*, Peter and Eiluned Lewis.

9 *Industrial Development of South Wales*, A. H. John.

THE CHEAPEST HOUSE FOR DRAPERY.

DAVID MORGAN,
THE SQUARE,
PONTLOTTYN.

BROAD & NARROW CLOTHS, PILOTS, WITNEYS, MOLESKINS, CORDS, BLANKETS, QUILTS, SHEETS, CARPETS, CURTAINS,
DAMASKS, MUSLINS, PRINTS, FRENCH MERINOS, COBOURGS, ALPACAS, FANCY DRESSES, WINCEYS, FLANNELS,
SHAWLS, MANTLES, JACKETS, FEATHERS, FLOWERS, RIBBONS, HOSIERY, GLOVES, HABERDASHERY, SHIRTS, SCARFS,
HATS, CAPS, TIES, COLLARS, HANDKERCHIEFS, STAYS, UMBRELLAS, DUCKS, LINENS, TICKS, CALICOS, CARPET BAGS.

READY-MADE CLOTHING. BOOTS & SHOES.

The Cheapest House for Drapery.

David Morgan's Shop at Pontlottyn.

1 Suit 2.5/11. 3 Selvia 4	1	6	0
4 Tweed 3/h. 3 Twill 6.6	7	3	6
3 Bro Disky. 1 Tears 8	2	5	
1 Stating - 1 Shirt 4/. 6. 8	3	2	
	1	6	2
Feb 6 1 Overcoat 30/ 37/ 3	3	7	0
Oct 3 Lany 17/ Tie 6	5	7	5
1880		6	11
Feb 9 Credit By Cash	3	0	0
	2	17	8

Bill Heading: Pontlottyn Shop.

Bill Heading: Cwm Shon Mathew Square.

Cash Book, Cwm Shon Mathew Square:
February 1858.

Dr.   Cash

1858			Dist		
Feb 12th	To Capital (Vote)		200	-	-
do	„ Mr. Jn.				
„	„ J Morgan Loan				
„	„ J Morgan Loan		100	-	-
12th	„ E. E. Jr.		50	-	-
„	„ J.P Morgan		20	-	-
„	„ Old Creditors		230	16	-
18th	„				
Feb 1	Interest due to J Morgan Loan		5	0	0
12th	to E. E. Jr. J.P Morgan			13	4
			£ 606	9	4

over

Contra   Cr.

1858			Dist		
Feb 12th	By Stock as pr Book		524	7	9
„	„ Furniture		15	-	0
18th	„ Do Col R Biddeis		29	4	0
„	„ d°		50	0	0
23th	„ House Keeping		3	11	4
„	„ Private A/C Self		£	8	9
			£ 623	11	10

over

'The Pontlottyn Shop' at Abertillery.

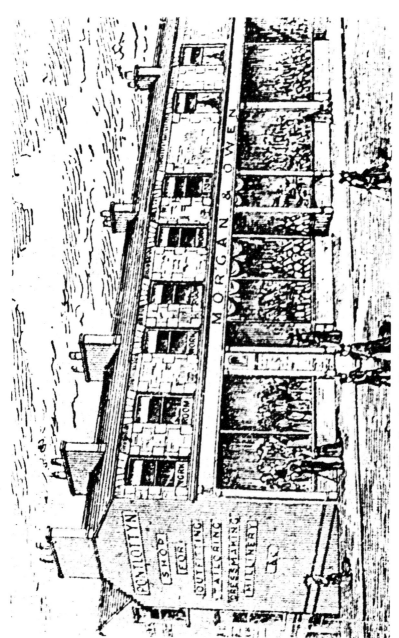

'The Pontlottyn Shop' (trading as Morgan and Owen).

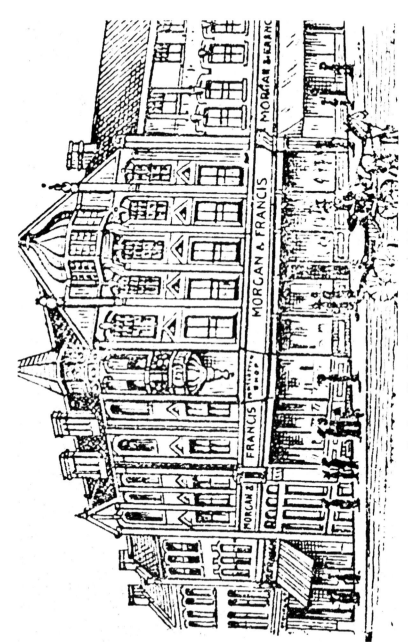

'The Pontlottyn Shop' (trading as Morgan and Francis).

DAVID MORGAN
DRAPER &c.

Pontlottyn,
September 9th 1879

Stuckey Esqr
Bristol & West of England Bank
Cardiff

Dear Sir,

I am about taking a Shop in
Cardiff & have been thinking of selling
or mortgaging some properties which
I have, but since I saw you the other
day, it has occurred to me that if
I became a customer at your
Bank. you may allow an overdraft
of £1000 or 1500. for a few years at £5 per
Cent & 1/8 Commission on monthly balance
which would enable me to take my
full discount

I have the following securities
by me any of which I could deposit

Letter to Bristol & West of England Bank, Cardiff: September 1879.

10 Ibid.

11 A railway map of South Wales dated 1883 lists twenty-three different railway companies on it.

12 " During the Crimean War when the Rhymney Railway Bill was being discussed in committee, Sir James Graham, First Lord of the Admiralty, stated that the supply of Cardiff steam coal was unequal to the naval demand and that any railway which could bring a new supply was an object of national importance." *Merthyr Guardian* 1854. Quoted in *The South Wales Coal Industry* by Morris and Williams.

13 *Cardiff, A History of the City*, William Rees.

6.   Rhymney and the Pontlottyn Shop

The first furnace at Rhymney was built in 1800 on land belonging to the Duke of Beaufort on the Monmouthshire side of the river.

Across the river on the Glamorgan side another ironworks was established on land belonging to the Marquess of Bute. The capital came from a group of Bristol Merchants. The ambitious plans for these works must have made them a striking and startling contribution to the landscape. The designs of the furnaces attracted widespread attention and drawings of them were exhibited in the Royal Academy. " The style was Egyptian and was adapted from the most striking part of the ruins of Dandyra in Upper Egypt[1]". The industrial achievements of the management did not equal their aesthetic aspirations, and the works were bought in 1835 by a new company, the Rhymney Iron Works, with capital of £500,000. Under the new management and with the injection of this large amount of capital, the works rapidly expanded and soon Rhymney began to count as a competitor of the neighbouring big works. By the time the Rhymney Railway connected the Iron Works with Cardiff in 1857 they were on their way to becoming one of the eight giants. It was about the time the railway came to Rhymney that David Morgan entered into partnership with a relative who was already established in business there.

The story of his partnership has been handed down in the family. It was said that he entered into partnership with a relative of his mother who had a shop in Rhymney. It is to be assumed that this was the relative he had visited with his brother John and for whom he had also come to work for a short time as a handy boy. The relative was a married man, and the inadequate housekeeping of his wife caused David Morgan to feel he was not getting fair value for the money he was paying for bed and board. According to this family story they quarrelled over this and soon after Christmas he decided to break away from the partnership and set up business for himself. He rented an empty shop in Cwm Shon Mathew Square and, after cutting ribbons, laces and all piece goods by the yard exactly in half and dividing equally the rest of the items of the stock, he put his share in a handcart and pushed it down the hill to Cwm Shon Mathew Square.

Like all " tales oft told ", this legend needs careful examination. One interesting point is that no one seems ever to have mentioned the name of the partner. If he was a relative of David Morgan's mother it would be a reasonable assumption that his name would be Price. The only relative so far discovered who had a shop at this time in Twyn Carno at the top of Rhymney was David Price Morgan, son of John Morgan III the innkeeper and Anne Price of Llwyn-y-brain. John Morgan III the innkeeper was the eldest brother of David Morgan the Progenitor of Cae Crwn. His son D. P. Morgan was always known by his initials, and he would have been more properly referred to as a cousin of David Morgan the Draper.

If the partner was D. P. Morgan there is every evidence that there was no quarrel. D. P. Morgan lent David Morgan money at interest several times when he needed it during the early days of his venture, and other business transactions occurred between them. Many years later David Morgan travelled to Builth to attend his cousin's funeral and was an executor of his will.

As to putting all David Morgan's share of the stock in one handcart, it seems most unlikely that one-half of the partners' joint stock in trade could be put into one handcart, even though the event took place in January when, according to the practice of the trade, it is always hoped to have the stocks at their lowest. While no doubt David Morgan would have had no need for a pantechnicon, the handcart must have made many trips or it was used as an advance party to take the small items to the new shop to be followed by the more bulky merchandise in a horse and cart. The handcart was apparently an embellishment indulged in by David Morgan to dramatise the smallness of his beginning.

In the opening lines of another story told by David Morgan the Draper to his grandson Aubrey, there is an indication that when he first went to Rhymney he lived at the top end of the town. He recalled that there was a public house at the top of the town on the edge of the moor which was much frequented by puddlers. These were highly skilled workmen who stirred and worked the molten metal with a long-handled rabble. First the impurities would be released; then, as the liquid iron thickened, the puddler would as quickly as possible work the metal into round lumps, a process called balling, in which state the red-hot metal would be brought out of the furnace. These men had to be real craftsmen, for upon their skill, judgement and dexterity depended the quality of the bar iron. They worked through a small door in the side of the furnace in conditions of great heat. It called for men of exceptional physique. It is not surprising that these men had thirsts commensurate with their immense strength.

There was a puddler, a patron of this public house, who was a giant even among puddlers. He was renowned for his fighting abilities in a district where the saturnalia of Saturday night were often a continuous drunken street brawl outside the many public houses. Aware of his prowess, strength and reputation he was a bully, and used to take a gulp out of the beer mug of any man in the pub without fear of reprisal. No one dared to take offence from so brutal a mauler.

One day a stranger came to this public house, sat down by himself at a table near the door and ordered a pint of beer. Soon after he was served, the hulking bully loomed through the door. Spying the stranger, he decided to initiate him into the local customs right away and took a gulp from his mug. The stranger leapt to his feet and threw the remainder of the beer in the bully's face. The challenge had been made and the crowd began to shout "Fight! Fight!" with sadistic expectations. The sawdust-covered floor was cleared by putting the tables back against the walls, making a ring for the fighters and a grandstand for the spectators. David Morgan said he found a good perch on the shelf that ran around the big fireplace. When the two men stripped to the waist he noticed that the smaller of the two was well-proportioned and in excellent shape, but he was so much smaller that none of the spectators gave him a chance against the local champion.

The fight started as expected, the big man pushing the little man all over the room and the audience were awaiting with blood-thirsty expectation the final slaughter. The quick footwork and the cool head of the stranger enabled him to avoid much of the punishment the giant was trying to administer in the rushes. Time passed and gradually the pounding of the midriff of the puddler began to take its toll. The puddler began to slow up noticeably, and gradually the small man began to get on top. Suddenly the fight came to an end; under a fusillade of hammer-like blows the bully sank to the ground unable to rise to his feet again. The stranger put on his clothes unmoved by the applause from the astonished crowd. He turned to go out; as he put his hand on the latch of the door he looked back and said: " I'm your new blacksmith ".

As he finished telling the story, David Morgan smiled, put his hands on his knees and leant forward to give emphasis to his words: " That was the best advertisement I ever knew ".

The shop that David Morgan rented was No. 6 Cwm Shon Mathew Square. An agreement was signed on 1 February, 1858, between David Williams the owner, a grocer, and David Morgan, described in the document as " a draper of Rhymney in the Parish of Bedwellty in the County of Monmouthshire ". This is the only factual evidence so far discovered that David Morgan was already living in Rhymney and trading as a draper before he set up shop at Cwm Shon Mathew Square. He was twenty-four years and three months of age when he signed this agreement by which David Morgan rented a dwelling house and shop and premises " situate " in Cwm Shon Mathew. He agreed that the shop be used for " a Drapery Shop, only, for the term of Ten Years from the date hereof at the yearly Rent of Twenty Pounds ".

There is a grocery shop today at No. 3, the owner of which produced an advertising leaflet of his shop when it was owned by Daniel Evans. The leaflet consists of a picture of the shop giving the customary well-stocked and prosperous appearance of such advertisements. Printed under the picture is

Daniel Evans
Tea Dealer
Grocer and Provision Factor
Cwmshone Mathew Square
Rhymney

Daniel Evans later acquired No. 6 from David Morgan.

With his limited capital, which according to David Morgan's entry on the first page of his Cash Book in February 1858, amounted to £370,

44

the choice of site was a good one. Number 6 was on a corner. Even though it was towards the lower end of Rhymney at that time, it was at the nearest point to the ironworks and at a road junction, which afforded an open space to the front of the shop.

Rhymney, when David Morgan came to it, was an enlarged village of about eight thousand people. The majority of the inhabitants came from the hill farms of Breconshire and Radnorshire, to whom were added the Irish immigrants who supplied the cheapest and lowest forms of labour. These uprooted peasants from the isolated farms of Mid-Wales had left behind them the old established routines and customs of a primitive rural life and had entered into an entirely new way of life, that of the Industrial Age. They had severed themselves from their traditions and had yet to find new customs and modes of civilized living. The concept of regular weekly pay was entirely novel to them and they were totally unaccustomed to living in close proximity with one another. They became rough, tough people, brutalized by the nature of their heavy work, the long hours and the squalour of their surroundings.

" Carlyle visited Merthyr Tydfil in 1850 and wrote ' Such a set of unguided fierce and miserable-looking sons of Adam I never saw before. Ah me! It is like a vision of Hell, and will never leave me, that of these poor creatures toiling all in sweat and dirt amid their furnaces pits and rolling mills. The town might be one of the prettiest places in the world. It is one of the sootiest squalidest and ugliest; all cinders and dust mounds and soot![2] '." This despairing description of Merthyr's " dark satanic mills " and their denizens would apply equally well to Rhymney, where David Morgan built up his business by understanding the needs of these people.

His background was very similar to that of the majority of the townspeople who had come mainly from Breconshire and Radnorshire farms. He had one great advantage—the fact that he had lived and worked in Newport, London and Birmingham before coming to Rhymney. This gave him a breadth of experience extremely rare amongst the inhabitants of this new town. However, like most of them he had, from his earliest boyhood, learnt to stretch every rare penny to its limits. He therefore fully understood that to serve the inhabitants of Rhymney and keep their custom it was essential that he should quickly establish a reputation for giving them good value for their money.

Rhymney was a typical company town where, besides operating the works, " The Company not only employed over ninety per cent of the population and owned most of the houses; it owned the local brewery and all the public houses; it employed the doctors and paid most of the vicar's stipend. It ran a ' company shop ' a large departmental store[3]".

The Company Shop was an essential part of a number of the swiftly growing new towns springing up round the new industries which came to South Wales at the end of the Eighteenth Century. By establishing these shops in those remote and inaccessible places the Companies were performing a public service by making a wide variety of merchandise available to their workmen. However the Company was also motivated

45

by that simple rule of Victorian conduct, "When your duty and your self-interest coincide it is no reason for not doing your duty". While there was always a temptation to make undue profits from a monopoly, by either raising the prices or lowering the quality, there were enough examples to show that after the earliest period this was not common practice.

The employer's self-interest was beyond the natural desire to make a proper and adequate profit. It really lay in the fact that the system of the Company Shop tied the worker to the works. The Company Shop was the main competition that David Morgan had to meet; strong and powerful competition not only because of the size of the operation, but also because it could extend credit, being assured of payment from the wage deductions. Its financial resources also enabled the Company Shop to extend credit in bad times.

Cautious as many of the wives were of spending the money that reached their hands from their husbands' wages, the men tended to be a turbulent and spendthrift lot. Drunkenness and fighting were the outlet for such energy as remained after the long hours of strenuous labour. Saturday nights were always rough, but on "turnbook" days, when the money which had been retained by the Company from the regular weekly wage payment was balanced against the debts owed to the Company Shop and the remainder, if any, was paid to the workers in cash, the state of drunken disorderliness reached the level of an orgy.

The Chapels of Nonconformity[4] were the civilizing influence which wrestled with the devil for the souls of these people. Their need was obviously great and there were many of them bearing names favoured by the Welsh: Ebenezer, Zion, Penuel, Tabernacle, Goshen, Brynhyfryd, Moriah, Jerusalem. Added to these were the English Chapels, such as Wesleyan Methodist, Baptist, Independent, Presbyterian, Congregationalist and others. A very short walk down the hill was the growing village of Pontlottyn, where another sizeable group of Chapels had sprung up. The Irish were ministered by a Roman Catholic Church in Lower Rhymney.

It was appropriate that the established Church of England in Rhymney should be endowed by the Company. The building of the Church was not achieved without a struggle. Some militant dissenters among the shareholders, offended by the spending of the Company's money by the directors for such a purpose, took the matter to court to seek an injunction. "It was argued that should this building of a Church be allowed, the successors of the directors might be Jews who might apply £4000 to the building of a synagogue[5]". The application for an injunction failed, but the Company took the precaution of petitioning Parliament for leave to bring in a bill for the purpose of building a Church and schools. "When it came before the House one M.P. said that he was reluctant to divide the House but where was it to stop? If a Church this year, it might be a Chapel next year and then perhaps a theatre[6]". However, in spite of this opposition the Third Reading was passed by seventy-one-votes to eight.

The Chapels, the Church and the schools battled valiantly to create, organise and educate the forces of decency. From the Chapels emerged "a valuable system of theological education for children and adults through small theological colleges, through the pulpit, through Sunday Schools and through periodical literature[7]". This effort bore fruit and it became a matter of importance for a man, if he wished to gain the respect of his fellow citizens, to be a member of a Chapel or attend Church.

A little more than a year after he had opened his shop David Morgan paid a subscription of two shillings and sixpence to Jerusalem, a Chapel a short way up the Tredegar Road from Cwm Shon Mathew Square. It was a most natural thing for him to join a Chapel; he had been brought up in a religious home and he would want to establish himself in the eyes of the community as a sober and serious businessman. Admittedly in the adhesive circle of the Chapel there was a materialistic and hypocritical side, but there can be no denying the extraordinary force that the Chapels were in mobilizing religion for the furtherance of honest goodness, decency and education.

Yet with all the abundant intensity of religious concern, the task of those who were trying to convert and educate the neighbouring masses was a frustrating one. The Headmaster of the Upper Rhymney School wrote in his diary in 1873[8]: "Influx of workboys who only purpose remaining as long as strike continues or they are driven to work elsewhere. Most of them are as wild as the 'untaught Indian brood'". Nearly a month later he noted: "School noisy. The uncouth savages from the mines do not appear to know simplest forms of decency". What better could be expected of children who were taken by their parents to work underground at a very early age? "The youngest children, up to the age of eleven generally, look after the ventilation doors, opening them for the trams and hauliers to pass through. 'With his solitary candle, cramped with cold, wet and not half fed, the poor child deprived of light and air passes his solitary day'. Other young children might help their fathers but their work was usually light as they did little more than pick up a few coals in loading the carts and handing and looking after the father's tools. Where thin seams were worked young children might often be employed in hauling trams as the making of roadways high enough for older workers or horses was expensive[9]". It was revealed in evidence before the Children's Employment Commissioners in 1842 that it was no unusual thing for children to be employed in collieries at the age of four. For these children there was no education.

Victorians tended to be self-centred optimists, who with a buoyant confidence believed that all things new were evidence of progress and all progress was good. Fortunately for their consciences they had a blind eye for the human casualties left in the wake of advancing progress. David Morgan was a typical Victorian. He attended to his own business, believed in what he was doing, took good care of his staff and did not concern himself with matters of social conscience. However, he showed

47

all his life a belief in the importance of education. Conscious of his own exceedingly limited education, he purchased in the first year at Cwm Shon Mathew Square a *History of England* in a series of volumes each costing seven shillings and sixpence and a map of the British Isles costing sixteen shillings. These were considerable sums when his other outgoings were so severely restricted to payments to wholesalers and minimal personal expenses. Looking some way ahead, it is interesting to note the only example of public service in the twenty-one years he spent in Rhymney and Pontlottyn was his acceptance of the office of Treasurer of the School Board of the Pontlottyn Schools. He also became treasurer of two Friendly Societies.

On 6th October, 1858 David Morgan took over a shop in Pontlottyn on the corner of Merchant Street and Chapel Street facing the Square. He paid Mr. Davies £5 for "part of lease and fixtures Gommorah (*sic*)" and five days later paid D. Davies £5-10-0 for balance of lease and fixtures. On the Cash side of the Cash Book the first week's takings of the Pontlottyn Shop of £16-14-0 are entered for the week ending 23rd October, 1858.

This decision to open another shop was made within eight months of opening at No. 6 Cwm Shon Mathew Square. Two months' rent for Gomorrah amounting to £2 was paid at the end of October. Two months' rent, the cost of " part of lease and fixtures ", when added together, came to the sum of £12-10-0, which was all that was necessary to start this new venture. On the last day of this month under " Expenses " the more respectable title of Pontlottyn takes the place of Gomorrah. This Biblical name, so redolent of hot ash, pillars of salt and sin, appears for the last time in the Cash Book in November 1858.

Trade at No. 6 Cwm Shon Mathew each year had been almost double that at Pontlottyn. Yet David Morgan decided to make his headquarters at Pontlottyn. Entries in the accounts showed that he started making alterations and improvements there soon after he took the lease in October 1858, while there was no record of any expenditure on No. 6.

It was not long before David Morgan began to show that the Company Shop " possessed no monopoly ". Some years after David Morgan had moved to Cardiff an old man came into the Pontlottyn Shop and, reminiscing about the old days, told of how often the women waiting for the slips in Company Shop Pay Office would be carrying the millinery bags of David Morgan. The millinery bag[10] was a large paper bag with David Morgan's name on it and " Pontlottyn Shop " in large letters over a picture of the shop front. It was the ancestor of the modern shopping bag.

1 *The History of the Iron, Steel, Tinplate and Other Trades of Wales* by Charles Wilkins, F.G.S. 1903.

2 *The Land of Wales,* Eiluned and Peter Lewis.

3 *The Life of the People,* by Tom Jones. *The Times* 1932. One of a series of articles later published in book form " Fifty Years Memories and Contrasts, A composite view of the period 1882-1932 ".

4   For the facts about religious life in Rhymney as with many other aspects of life in this town I am entirely indebted to the remarkable picture given in *Rhymney Memories* by Tom Jones.

5   *Rhymney Memories*, Tom Jones.

6   Ibid.

7   Ibid.

8   Ibid.

9   *Report of Children's Employment Commissioners 1842.* Quoted from *The South Wales Coal Industry* 1841-1875, J. H. Morris and L. J. Williams.

10 Morgan Price kindly presented Aubrey Morgan with an old millinery bag from the days when his father ran the Pontlottyn Shop of New Tredegar.

7. The Cash Book

The limited and unexpanded facts contained in the first Cash Book[1] of David Morgan are almost all we know of the first few years at No. 6 Cwm Shon Mathew and the start in Pontlottyn.

In the top right-hand corner of the fly leaf of this Cash Book is written

David Morgan

Cwm Shon Mathew

Rhymney Mon

in very clear, firm and well-formed letters, noticeable for their balance and evenness. The accounts are kept in this legible, neat, cursive handwriting. The figures are well-formed and carefully finished. The orderly appearance of the columns of figures and the ruled lines under the monthly totals bear the hallmarks of a competent man of business who got satisfaction from the keeping of his own books.

On the first page under "Cash" he listed his assets, or perhaps a better description would be the liabilities of his new business. First, opposite the date 1858 February 12th he has entered "Capital (self) . . . £200 ". This must have been the savings David Morgan had made while working as a shop assistant. When the meagre wages which were customary at this time are taken into account, this was a remarkable feat in the approximately six years he had worked for wages since completing his apprenticeship. These savings had been achieved by strict self-discipline and stern self-denial. He himself would pay his first assistant, James Griffith, whose name appears in the Cash Book on 16th March, 1858, a monthly salary of £1 with the customary bed and board. Wages in London and Birmingham would have been a little better, but not by any great amount.

What profits he had made in the Twyn Carno partnership would also be part of his savings. But after the equal division of the stock and the accounts outstanding in the bought ledger, there was not likely to be any substantial amount of cash to be divided between the two partners if the scale of David Morgan's own early operations was any yardstick.

When the history of the Morgan family up to February of 1858 is taken into account, the next entry is a complete surprise. Under the name of "David Morgan Llanbrynian" there is entered alongside the date 12th February 1858 "By cash bearing interest at 4 per cent per annum from this day £50 - -". One can only be left with a clear impression that when the tide of David Morgan Senior's adversity was at its lowest ebb he was somehow or other able to find £50 to invest in his son's start in business.

The next line in the list entered on 12th February 1858 is " E.E. pr D. P. Morgan £20-0-0 ". In the opposite column dated 2nd June 1858 " To Old a/c received at Twyn Carno Mr. D. P. Morgan to receive the sum of the a/c due to me £21-0-0 ".

This transaction could well be the nearest we shall get to proving that David and D. P. Morgan were partners. It is also of considerable significance that the name of D. P. Morgan appears fifteen times in this Cash Book between February 1858 and July 1865. There are also two other entries which must refer to D. P. Morgan: " 1858 August 31st carriage from T.C. 5/-"; " T.C." can fairly be assumed to be an abbreviation for Twyncarno and this entry may represent the last movement of stock belonging to the partnership down to No. 6 Cwm Shon Mathew. Again on 31st March 1859: " Recd from Twyncarno Settlement of old a/c £3-0-0 ".

All of which, while short of absolute proof that D. P. Morgan was the partner of David Morgan, is a fair indication that this was so.

The remaining item of importance on the Cash side of the first page of the Cash Book is the entry on 12th February alongside Old Creditors of £230-16-. On the Contra side is entered " Pd Old Creditors £29-4-0 ". These two entries together with the £524-7-9 of " Stock as pr Book " represent his share of the dissolved partnership.

Trading at No. 6 Cwm Shon Mathew started in mid-February 1858 and the takings by 1st March amounted to £51-4-3. By the end of March the takings came to £73-17-6. In March a bill for £14-1-6 was paid to J. & N. Philips & Co. This was the first firm to be entered into the cash book, forming a trading connection which was to last nearly one hundred years until that long-established house was absorbed into a big amalgamation.

David's sister, Jane, came to visit him in March 1858. A payment of two shillings and sixpence was entered against her name. Many years later her eldest son, David Hall, in a letter he wrote to John Llewellyn Morgan, after seeing the Cash Book for the first time, suggested that this may have been her train fare. But it was not until a year later, 1st August, 1859, that the Brecon and Newport Railway was opened. He may have asked her to come and see what life was like at No. 6 and tried to persuade her to stay permanently as his much-needed housekeeper. At first there was an entry each month entitled " Housekeeping ", which seemed to fluctuate between a little under £2 to about £7 per month, but these entries ceased after October 1858. There were a few items recorded which related to housekeeping; for example, in April David Morgan indulged himself with a feather bed which cost him one pound, and in July 1858 " Wages (Elizth) 18/6 " marked the first entry for the payment of domestic help. It could be that in his desire to keep his costs down at the start young David looked after himself and his first assistant, relying on those simple satisfactions of bread and jam, cheese and eggs, and that infallible basis of the bachelor's culinary art, the frying pan.

51

There was an entry in May 1858 which indicated that he was not too busy to visit Old Llanbrynean.

May   D. Morgan Llan. fr Phaeton 10/-
   ,,   ,,   ,,   Self   15/-

" Phaeton " suggests something grander than the farm trap. It is possible that Llanbrynean had not yet been able to afford one, so something had to be hired for David.

" Expenses to Aberdare 1/6 " is an interesting entry for August 1858. David Morgan could have gone to Aberdare for the same reason as he went to London, Birmingham, Rhymney and Cardiff. To use a modern phrase, he liked to be where the action was; he may have wanted to look at the possibilities of Aberdare as a place of business.

That he was searching around for an opportunity to expand is revealed by an entry one month after his visit to Aberdare: " Sept. 30th 1858 Gommorah (*sic*) 5/9 ". Gomorrah was a name used for an area in Pontlottyn, the village at the southern end of Rhymney. It was on the Glamorgan side of the river Rhymney. According to Tom Jones in his " Rhymney Memories ", Sodom and Gomorrah was an area where there were a number of public houses. At a time when the forces of respectability were entrenched in the Chapels this was a likely name to be given to such a place.

Certainly the location at Pontlottyn was a good one. It was situated on the corner of Merchant Street, the main street of the town, and Chapel Street, and faced the square, a large open space with buildings on three sides and the railway viaduct forming the fourth. The square was the natural centre of the town and a short distance from Lower Rhymney. The new railway station was just off the square in Picton Street.

All his life he was a great believer in the possession of freeholds, and his instinctive sense of property may have led him to believe that his future interests would be best served by acquiring property in Pontlottyn. There is also the possibility that when the revival of trade came it was the Pontlottyn shop that went ahead quicker. With a small expenditure its living quarters would be a considerable improvement on No. 6. Finally, he may have found it to be advantageous to be a little further away from his large and powerful competitor, the Iron Works Company Shop.

When David Morgan cast up his accounts at the end of 1858 he found that when he subtracted the total of the Contra Column of £1,850-18-4 from the total of the Cash Column of £1,879-7-5, the Cash exceeded the expenditure by only £28-9-1. When arriving at this meagre profit it should be remembered that, besides the takings, the Contra column includes the cost of opening the Pontlottyn Shop and his own capital and the loans listed on the first page of the Cash Book; David Morgan, after not quite one year's trading, had used up nearly all his capital, except for his stock in hand. This in no way unnerved him. He wound up the year with a burst of purchases; he paid bills in December 1858 to the extent of £298-4-0. Only in one month previously had he exceeded £100. These payments at the end of the year included the buying for the Pontlottyn Shop.

David Morgan told his niece, May Morgan, that before he opened in Pontlottyn he went on a buying trip to Manchester. When he returned he found a large bale of goods waiting for him on the pavement outside the Pontlottyn Shop. A working man came up to him and asked if David Morgan could sell him a suit of clothes: " Yes," was the reply, " if you will help me get this bale into the shop ". In this manner he made his first sale in Pontlottyn.

The first full year's trading in both shops in 1859 showed takings :

Cwm Shon Mathew	£1,668 - 16 - 0
Pontlottyn	£ 944 - 19 - 6
	£2,613 - 15 - 6

In April 1859 his sister, Jane, came to work for him at No. 6 Cwm Shon Mathew Square as his housekeeper. David Morgan all his life was very conscious of the costs of doing business. Even in the last year of his life, when he had become the owner of a large business and a man of considerable wealth, he showed he had not lost his concern for the details of expenditure when in a letter to his niece Kate Morgan he revealed that he was fully aware of the rapidly mounting cost of twine and paper. While his employees lived under his roof he took good care of them and believed in having them properly fed, but with that ever-watchful eye on cost and a determination to eliminate any waste.

He would have complete confidence in his sister's ability to take charge of the housekeeping, something which either by mismanagement or carelessness could become an expensive item in his overheads. Jane greatly admired her brother, and he could be sure that she would attend to his interests with unstinting devotion. He knew how well she had been trained in frugality and hard work by their mother. David Morgan from the very beginning impressed on his sister the need for care and economy by giving her a salary of only ten shillings a month to be his housekeeper at No. 6 Cwm Shon Mathew Square.

Jane Hall told her children that one of her daily duties was to clean the wax off the big iron candlestick that lit the shop window. On the frequent cold blustery wet evenings the little shop windows of Rhymney and Pontlottyn would do little to attract the customer; but, although the lighting inside the shops by candle and oil lamp would also be modest, there would always be the glowing comfort of the fireplace at the end of the shops to attract the customers. Coal in Rhymney was cheap and plentiful.

In January of 1859 David Morgan gave a subscription of five shillings to an Eisteddfod—a somewhat larger sum than one would expect from a man just starting in business, and especially a man so careful of expenditure as David Morgan. Eisteddfodau and Chapels went hand-in-hand and both played an important part in the life of the town.

Entertainment for the people of Rhymney was a rare and very limited luxury. Public attendance at sporting events was unknown except for prize fighting and, if one chooses to include it in the same category, street fighting. The Welsh fervour for Rugby football, with its national and local heroes, was still to come. Theatrical performances in Rhymney were rare, primitive and frowned upon by the Chapel Community. Most probably the greatest event on the entertainment calendar was the annual visit of Studt's Circus.

With such restricted resources for entertainment, music had little or no competition. It was the great outlet. Eisteddfodau, a competitive competition for the arts, of which singing and the writing of verse were the most prominent, and Cymanfa Ganu, organised congregational hymn singing, were held in Chapels. The Eisteddfod became a form of local, regional and national competition. Rhymney had its full share of triumphs. The Chief Choral Choir won the National Eisteddfod five times, three times in succession.

In an article published in *The Times* in 1932 written by Tom Jones, an almost exact contemporary of John Morgan, entitled " The Life of the People ", he gives a description of life in Rhymney when he was a boy. In the article he writes of the wide appeal made by music. " The Chief Choral was led by the School Attendance Officer, the Male Voice by a miner, and the Ladies' Choir by a young woman who ran a bake house—all three would be preparing for some Eisteddfod. Women sang the Handel choruses at the washtub ". John Llewellyn Morgan remembered some women in the back yards behind the Pont-lottyn Shop singing together passages from *The Messiah* as they hung their washing on the clothes lines. The first performance of *The Messiah* in Wales was given in Rhymney in 1864. Tom Jones closes his article with a glowing and sonorous description of the new exciting industrialism which in prosperous times was the life pulse of Rhymney.

> In good times a symphony of cheerful noises filled the air from hissing shears, pounding hammers and puffing engines. When the pits were winding coal, when the furnaces were in full blast, when night after night the hills were flooded with sudden light from ' the Bessemer ' and then plunged into sudden darkness, when rails, sleepers and tin bars flowed red hot from the rolls to the bank all day and all night, then the chapels, the friendly and assurance societies, the shop and the brewery flourished and ' everyone burst into song '.

By March 1859 entries began to appear in the Cash Book that showed that alterations were taking place at the Pontlottyn Shop. Amongst the entries was one for a cast iron pillar: cost £1 carriage 2/6. The pillar still stands today in the centre of the shop, the sole central support of the floor above. Nothing of the nature of an alteration or an improvement at Cwm Shon Mathew ever appeared in the Cash Book. It was in the Pontlottyn Shop that for the first time he found an opportunity to indulge in that enthusiasm for building, which was going to stay with him for the whole of his long life. Many years, and buildings, later he told his niece, May Morgan, that if he had his life over again he would be a builder. When May related this she added with a smile: " But then again, when he started the Refreshment Room at The Hayes and it proved to be so remunerative, he thought he should have been a restaurateur ". His enthusiasm as a builder took him up the highest scaffolding and he was often seen on the roof top watching the men work.

His personal expenses as revealed in his accounts were extremely limited: once a pair of trousers, never a suit in the first two years, a pair of boots and occasional repairs of them, and rarely a very small sum of cash for himself. After one year in business he bought himself a necessity—a Constantine Hug timepiece for £1-10-0—and in the same month he allowed himself to indulge in the luxury of buying some pictures; however, not without some serious soul-searching and self-criticism, because after the word " Pictures " he has added as penance " fool money ".

After July 1859 the entry " Jane wages 10/0 " disappeared. Her loyalties by this time may have become divided and her affection for her brother surpassed by a longing to see William Hall again.

The following year, 1860, which was the third year David Morgan was in business for himself, the figures of the takings were:

| Cwm Shon Mathew | £1,735 - 17 - 0 |
| Pontlottyn | £ 882 - 7 - 0 |

1860 could not have been an encouraging year. The £67 gained over the previous year in Cwm Shon Mathew was offset by a fall of £62 at Pontlottyn. Possibly due to the trading figures, he had resisted the urge to continue alterations in Pontlottyn.

1861 was the year of the Census, and from the return it is possible to get an impression of the household at No. 6 Cwm Shon Mathew. David Morgan, a bachelor, was a young man of twenty-seven. He lived at No. 6 with three young apprentices and a general servant. The three young apprentices living over the shop, aged nineteen, eighteen and sixteen, came from Cardiganshire. 1861 was not a time of prosperity in Rhymney. When David Morgan took stock of his position at the end of the year he must have been disappointed. It was the end of his fourth year in business. In later years he used to say that when a man set up in business for himself the test came after three years, because by that time the shopkeeper may have used up his capital and from that moment on he would be completely dependent on the daily takings to meet his expenses. It would then be a case of make or break. He spoke with long-remembered personal experience, for that was exactly what had happened to him. The takings for 1861 marked a real recession from the previous year:

	Cwm Shon Mathew	Pontlottyn
1860	£1,735 - 17 - 0	£882 - 7 - 0
1861	£1,347 - 18 - 0	£657 - 3 - 0
Minus	£ 388	Minus £225

At the back of the Cash Book at the top of the page there is a notation " 1860 Feb 1st Peace & Plenty "

„ May 1st Just & Generous "

1861 would prove a stern test for these worthy precepts. The 1861 takings were down £613 from those of the previous year. Times must have changed for the worse in Rhymney. When people became unemployed there were very few savings to tide over the lay-off. Customers would beg for credit and debts would be hard to recover. The only credit which could safely be given was to be obtained in limited quantities at the Company Shop, which with the large financial resources behind it and the future wages to provide guaranteed deductions could afford to extend some credit. But in hard times the small shopkeeper with his negligible capital could not afford to be generous. David Morgan was receiving an education that was going to last him his life-time.

David Morgan lost faith in neither Rhymney nor himself in the face of the adverse trading conditions. During 1861 he paid off the debt of £115 to William Jones and also paid his father £55, which involved £52 in cash and the rest in goods.

A surprising new entry, considering the times, appeared on the Contra side of the Cash Book, which had so far been confined to the payments of the bills of the wholesale houses and a few personal and business expenses.

Aug 15th 1861 Sent to Rees Rees, Mountain Ash
Subscription to Building Society   £15 - 3 - 9

Oct 14th pd Miss Rees Mountain Ash
2 months subscription to Building Club   £ 2 - 0 - 6

Dec. 31st pd. Miss Rees 3 Mo. Sub
to Mountain Ash Building Club   £ 3 - 0 - 9

This comes to a total of £20-5-0.

While trade was on a definite ebb tide David Morgan decided to start accumulating some more capital.

He had now lasted one year more than the critical first three years. Unfortunately it is not possible to trace the struggle David Morgan must have made to achieve financial security, because after January 1862 the cash takings were no longer kept in this Cash Book, but only the expenses. The situation at the end of 1861 is however made quite clear in the records of the Cash Book from February 1858 to December 1861:

	Cash	Contra
1858	1879 - 1 - 5	1850 -18 - 4
1859	2613 -15 - 6	2574 -10 - 0
1860	2618 - 4 - 0	2665 -19 - 5
1861	2005 - 1 -10	2007 -12 - 1½
	9116 - 2 - 9	9098 -19 -10½

While his expenses include the staff's bed and board and his own clothing, together with the repayment of money lent to him and his Building Society Savings, it should be remembered that the Cash account included his own capital of £200. It was not a very encouraging start. His total increase was £17-2-10½. This figure was coming uncomfortably close to that bare margin of solvency enunciated by Mr. Micawber.

Without further loans and with no more personal capital and no accommodation by a bank, the cash takings became an exacting form of stock control. The payment for the purchases of new stock would now be entirely dependent on whatever was in the till. As can be seen in the listed figures, the decline in 1861 was matched by an almost equal reduction in expenditure.

There was no record kept in the Cash Book of takings in 1862 except for January, but the record of expenses was maintained. If these were an indication of the cash takings it could be seen that the downward curve continued:

1860	£2665 -19 - 5
1861	£2007 -12 - 1½
1862	£1871 - 5 - 9

1862, the fifth year of business, must have been a disturbing one for David Morgan. However there is some evidence in the expenditure for that year which shows he had not lost his confidence or his courage. He early showed that his was not a nervous disposition. Besides depositing £5-0-0 in the Post Office Savings Bank, he maintained his quarterly payments to the Mountain Ash Building Club of £3-0-9. Then on 29 September, 1862, he made his first of many investments in gas. He paid £30 on the first call of £1 per share. He thus became an original holder of 30 shares in the Rhymney Gas Works, the building of which was not completed or production started until three years later in 1865.

That David Morgan should make this decision to invest this money, with further calls to come, in this entirely new and untried venture when the state of his business is taken into account, was a measure of the man.

The Cash Book runs out of space in October 1863, so unfortunately there are no further entries extant from which it would be possible to draw a picture of the emergence of David Morgan from the downward thrust of this cycle of declining figures.

The first ten months of 1863 were even more difficult than any previous year. The last entry was on 25 October, 1863. No matter how carefully costs and overheads were watched, no matter how tight the screw was turned on purchasing, it must have occurred to David Morgan that the spectre of bankruptcy could come rushing over the horizon very soon if it was not already in sight. It might not be enough to cut his expenses to the bone and exact the maximum economy in every way down to the food on his table, and keep his purchases within the limits of his decreasing takings; he would have to borrow if he was to survive until conditions took a turn for the better.

The iron industry traditionally moved in cycles between feast and famine, and by the end of 1863 tradesmen would begin to fear the mention of the latter. Yet, in this year of depression, 1863, David Morgan managed to find the money to increase his holdings in the Rhymney Gas Works by buying ten £1 shares from a Mr. Jones of Picton Street Pontlottyn, and paid the second, third, fourth and fifth calls on his gas shares, which amounted to a total investment of £170. He certainly proved his faith in gas. He also maintained his quarterly payments to the Mountain Ash Building Society.

At the back of the Cash Book some loans are entered with the dates of their repayment, which tell a little more about how he survived this lean period. In 1863 David Morgan borrowed on interest at five per cent per annum:

June 22	Mr. Prosser near Brecon	£100
July 11	Anne Powell, Tredegar Rd. Rhymney	£ 15
July 11	D. P. Morgan, Twyncarno, Rhymney	£ 25
August 14	D. P. Morgan, Twyncarno, Rhymney	£ 15

When one takes into account the narrow margins between profit and loss within which David Morgan managed to exist, a transfusion of £155 must have provided a much-needed and welcome assistance.

Again in 1864 another helping hand from Twyncarno:

Jan. 1st Henry Parry T'Carno signed note jointly with D. P. Morgan for £160. £80 of which I have at £4-10-0 per cent interest —£80.

This agreement was dated 1 January, 1864, which leads one to believe that by the end of 1863 David Morgan was in need of further help if he was to start the New Year with some hope of keeping his incomings and outgoings in balance.

On 7 August, 1864, Anne Powell increased her loan by £5 and on 1 December William Morgan of Llanbrynean lent his brother £20, which at that time must have been his life's savings. During 1864 David Morgan received some more capital in the form of loans to the amount of £105; in July 1865 he received yet another loan from D. P. Morgan of £100. In the two years of 1864 and 1865 he had been lent £180 by D. P. Morgan. If, as seems most likely, D. P. Morgan had been his original partner, these loans are solid evidence that, after the partners separated, they remained good friends and D. P. Morgan retained his confidence in David Morgan. There were two other loans written at the very end of the list. In 1865 James Morgan, who was thirteen years of age at the time, invested £2 in his eldest brother's business; an investment that was going to bring in returns in various ways many times over in the coming years. Lastly, in 1867, when Thomas Morgan was learning his trade as a draper from his brother, he lent David £10.

This review of David Morgan's first Cash Book reveals that a considerable crisis had been undergone, testing all David Morgan's confidence, resolution and level-headedness. The sums of money involved seem today very small and give little indication of what was at stake. It was indeed a case of make or break, and David Morgan had not broken.

With the incomplete records that remain, it is not possible to say when the corner was turned after 1863, but it must have been soon because in five years, by 1868, David Morgan was sufficiently sure of his financial position to contemplate getting married.

1   The Cash Book is in the possession of the family and kept at David Morgan, Limited, 26 The Hayes, Cardiff.

8. Marriage

On Union Street in 1867 there lived a well-to-do butcher named John Llewellyn who, besides the shop over which he lived, owned two farms. He was born in 1820 at Mardy Farm in the parish of Gelligaer. Like many other farmers' sons, he had found his way to the new industrial development at the top of the valleys, and practiced the trade of butcher in Tredegar.

In 1843, when he was twenty-three years old, he married Eliza Williams, the daughter of a blacksmith in Caerphilly, in the parish church at Eglwysilan[1]. Eliza was two years older than her husband and, according to their wedding licence, had made her living as a seamstress[2]. The young couple moved to Pontlottyn where, on 9 December, 1850, seven years after their marriage, their first child, Margaret, was born. There is an attractive photograph of this family. Margaret, at about nine years of age, is standing between her seated parents. Mrs. Llewellyn possessed the typical dark eyes and looks of a Welshwoman. The neatness of her appearance, the well-made dress with ruching and pleats, the good fit around the neck and shoulders all reveal her skill as a seamstress. Mr. Llewellyn and his stylish way of wearing his hair, his high and flowing stock, the quality of his suit and his watch chain complete the air of middle class prosperity which pervades this picture. In the middle little Margaret's lively face appears between her parents, an attractive child.

Another photograph exists of Margaret standing beside a seated man of powerful build who is believed to be her uncle. It is a picture of a more mature young girl of about thirteen years of age. She is fashionably dressed, and wears a pair of bracelets. In the three photographs that exist of Margaret Llewellyn the feature that stands out is her eyes.

Her parents had waited seven years for the arrival of their first-born, and it often happens that the long-awaited child is especially cherished and grows up accustomed to the constant expression of affection. A governess[3] was engaged for Miss Margaret, which must have been a very rare occurrence in Pontlottyn. Such was the concern of Mr. and Mrs. Llewellyn for the good education of their daughter that they decided to make the sacrifice of sending her away from home to a school in White Ladies Road, Clifton, near Bristol. Considering the times and where they were living, they must have been very enterprising people to have taken so unusual a step, and it is evidence of the importance and high esteem in which they held education. Margaret was accompanied by another young lady from Pontlottyn, her cousin May Croft.

The Llewellyn family spoke both Welsh and English. At first Welsh would be the language in the home. A Welsh Bible was given to Margaret by her father when she was four years old. The school in Clifton would ensure tnat she spoke correct English, as well as give her a very much better education than anything obtainable near her home.

As a result of this education and the position of the Llewellyn family, Margaret would be outstanding among the eligible young ladies of Pontlottyn by the time she had reached the age of seventeen. She inherited from her mother a bent for needlework. There are in existence two embroidered pictures[4] which are her handiwork. One has " Margaret Llewellyn 1862 " worked in black cotton. She would have been twelve years of age at that time. The other is a larger sampler with " Rebecca at the Well " at the top. It portrays two people in the presumed dress of Biblical times and at the bottom is inscribed with the words " John and Elisabeth Llewellyn ". This appears to have been worked at a later date than the one of 1862. Her sister Jane, who later became Mrs. Gething Lewis, gave it to her nephew, John Llewellyn Morgan, because it was worked by his mother.

The needles of Mrs. Llewellyn and her daughter and the appetites of David Morgan and his staff of young men would provide opportunities for the exchange of custom between the drapery and the butcher's shop on Merchant Street. The gregarious Thomas Morgan was the natural connecting link. Judging from remarks he made when he was much older, that he had kissed David's wife many times before David had, Thomas had been welcomed into the Llewellyn family with the customary warm hug and a kiss with which their friends, many of whom would be called in the Welsh fashion " Uncle " and "Auntie ", would be greeted.

What with the making of her own dresses and the clothes for her two daughters, Margaret and Jane (Jane was eight years younger than her sister), and also using her needle to furnish the rooms of their home with curtains, valances, lampshades, table and mantlepiece covers, throws, cushions, coverlets and all those multitudinous frills which helped create the cozy clutter of a genteel Victorian home, Mrs. Llewellyn was an ideal customer for the shop on the corner of Merchant and Chapel Street—someone David Morgan would like to attend to himself. If one day he was asked round for a cup of tea, he would enter an entirely new world; one very different from his boyhood at Cae Crwn or his bachelor establishment at No. 6 Cwm Shon Mathew.

The soft comfort of the furnishing, the air of ease and gentility, the femininity of the household and the openly expressed affection of the Llewellyn family to one another must have made David realize that something had been missing in his life.

In 1867 in the sewing circles of Pontlottyn David Morgan at thirty-four years of age would be considered a most eligible bachelor. In contrast to his careful way of life, the world of Miss Llewellyn was an exciting discovery. The attractive young girl in the family photographs had grown into a well-educated, petite and chic young lady of seventeen. Her schoolmate and cousin, May Croft, became engaged to the other outstanding bachelor, Mr. Henry Valentine Trump, Manager of the Rhymney Iron Works.

The easy-going charm of Thomas, who was nineteen, would have made him an agreeable companion for Margaret; but when his brother, the established business man, began to show serious intentions, it was David who carried all before him. Thomas may have opened the door, but it was David who walked in.

For David to be able to offer his hand in marriage at this time there must have been an improvement in his business. It was in keeping neither with his character nor with the custom of the times for him to propose marriage to a young lady of position without having the means to provide a suitable home for her.

There are still in existence some things which show what the standards of the Llewellyn way of life were likely to have been. Mrs. Gething Lewis, sister of Margaret Llewellyn, gave Aubrey upon his marriage to Elisabeth Morrow, a silvered teapot which she said belonged to his grandmother before she married his grandfather. Mrs. John Llewellyn Morgan frequently used at tennis parties, when a larger than usual teapot was needed, a large silver-plated teapot which belonged to Margaret. There is in the possession of her granddaughter and namesake, Margaret Morgan, a white china tea service edged with gold which belonged to her grandmother, together with a wooden tea caddy bearing a plaque " Margaret Morgan 1868 ". The caddy is a mahogany box containing two lined receptacles for tea and a central space for a missing sugar bowl, with a lid that could be locked. This tea caddy represents the only thing she was likely to have had in common with her mother-in-law, Ann Morgan, who dearly loved a good cup of tea. There are also six silver teaspoons with " M.Ll." engraved on them, which shows they were in her possession before her marriage. Jack gave to his daughter-in-law, Mary, the wife of Bernard, the plate which was used for his parents' wedding cake. He asked her never to use it and it never has been used.

There is a quality in these possessions of Margaret Llewellyn which shows that her family made an effort to surround themselves with those finer things of life which would be far removed from the austerity that necessity had imposed on the Morgans of Cae Crwn.

The Llewellyn family was an example of the new Middle Class, the small tradesman, that emerged as a result of the Industrial Revolution. Education was, for them, " the open sesame " to a better way of life and new opportunities. The Great Exhibition held in the Crystal Palace in 1851 made a deep impact on their life style and possessions. Their aspirations produced a civilized gentility, which did much to lift them out of the savage and brutal way of life so common in industrial towns. This new class was the bedrock upon which the Victorian era rested.

David, under the influence of this romantic moment, responded with some gifts in an effort to emulate the Llewellyn standards. He gave the two sisters each a plated cake slice. The one he gave to Jane Llewellyn had her initials engraved on it[5]. The cake slice he gave his fiancée[6] remained without engraving because it was thought to be unlucky for a young man to have the future initials of his bride engraved on a present before they were married. He also bought for Margaret an engagement ring of emeralds set in gold[7].

They were married 20 October, 1868, in the parish church of Gelligaer by the Reverend Gilbert Harris. Margaret gave her age for the wedding licence as seventeen. She was a little less than two months from celebrating her eighteenth birthday on 9 December. David was almost thirty-five years of age. The difference of seventeen years was considerable, but not so very unusual in Victorian times. While early marriages were frequent among the working classes, men who sought to better themselves accepted the necessity of a lengthy bachelorhood.

After the honeymoon in London[8], David and Margaret went to live at the Pontlottyn Shop. There was a private entrance on Merchant Street, which led into the downstairs parlour, a room alongside the shop, which occupied the rest of the ground floor. At the back on the ground floor were the kitchen and dining room, and upstairs there was a bedroom for the newly married couple and an office for the master, in which to this day there is the dresser which contains a desk, bookcase, cupboards and pigeon holes for papers. It is a large piece of furniture which fills the length of the wall on one side of the room. David Morgan had it made for him by the local carpenter, Robert Davis. The carpenter's name, the details of the cost and the total of £11-15-0 are written underneath the bottom of the desk drawer in David Morgan's handwriting. The rest of the upstairs was given over to rooms for apprentices and assistants.

Today the shop has been extended into the downstairs parlour. Behind the fixtures can still be seen the boarded up fireplace and the old wallpaper of roses etched in black on an off-white background.

It was a sizeable establishment and one worthy of the young bride. She would bring with her the sense of style she had inherited and learnt from her mother. With her mother's help, the new home would be furnished and equipped after the fashion of the Llewellyn home, to the delight of David, who would feel he was entering into a new and very different world of comfort, elegance and love. Sternly self-disciplined though he was, the hard shell of his exterior would be broken by the soft tenderness and wholehearted admiration of his young wife.

The joy of their first Christmas together as husband and wife would be intensified by the knowledge that Margaret could expect a child to be born in the coming summer. Margaret was a petite young woman and she may always have been of a delicate constitution. It is not possible to tell when she became a victim of that dread Victorian disease, tuberculosis. The customary pattern of the disease is for it to progress at first unnoticed, without showing any symptoms or warning signals. Modern methods alone could detect the very early stages. Pregnancy however would bring with it a rapid acceleration and the first symptoms would soon appear, exhaustion and a depressing feeling of not being well. But the symptoms would be masked by the expected effects of the pregnancy, and it would be considered likely that the mother would feel better after the baby had been born.

On 16 August, 1869, at two o'clock in the morning, Margaret was delivered of a son. She may well have had a difficult labour. Her son was always conspicuous for his large and impressive head. This large head could have caused a problem at the time of his birth with the result that Margaret would have been greatly fatigued.

The baby was christened wearing a robe worthy of his grandmother's needle. The robe has been used for the christening of all his five children and a number of his grandchildren. He was given the names of John Llewellyn. His father gave considerable importance to names. It would have been easy for David and Margaret to agree on John. It was the name of her father, and David must have known it would give pleasure to his parents because it was also the name of their son who had died fifteen years before. The addition of Margaret's family name, Llewellyn, was an affirmation of David's deep affection for his wife.

That they were deeply in love is revealed by a story told by David Hall, the eldest of David Morgan's nephews. As a small boy he went on a visit to his uncle in Pontlottyn. He found his uncle standing in the street outside the shop and was talking with him when out ran Margaret, who threw her arms around the young boy's neck and kissed him. Young David had not reached the age when the kiss of a pretty young woman was something to be treasured, and Margaret was a stranger to him. Reared in the harsher clime of his mother's severity, he responded to this unaccustomed display of affection with the usual reaction of small boys, an expression of disgust. David Morgan, seeing and understanding his nephew's reaction, drew his wife to his side where he stood in the street and kissed her saying: " Don't mind, David— see how Uncle loves Auntie[9]". In the strict, unsentimental upbringing of David Morgan a demonstration of affection would be no matter for public display; indeed, in his case, an almost unknown occurrence. But the tender affection of his wife had already acclimatised him to the gentler airs of human love.

Alas, the blissful days of happiness were already numbered. The expected recovery from the birth of the baby did not come, and anxiety took the place of happiness. Margaret, instead of feeling better, began to feel increasingly unwell and the more positive symptoms of her illness began to appear.

One of the few relics of this brief and poignant period in David Morgan's life is a sheet of blue notepaper in a matching envelope, on the outside of which is written " Little Johnnie's Hair ". Inside are some clippings of hair which is still of an auburn colour today, over one hundred years later.

The notepaper has a printed heading   " PONTLOTTYN

TREDEGAR 186..."

Written underneath is " Saturday July 30th 1870

The Hair enclosed in the paper is the
first cut from the head of little Johnny

64

when he was eleven months 14 days old.
The operation was by his mother with his
father's scissors ".

How characteristic is the mention of " his father's scissors ". They
were the tools of a draper's trade, something David Morgan was never
without. Many years later he told an apprentice who had misplaced his
scissors: " No scissors—no draper ". As an old man he was seen by
one of his grandsons using his scissors, which he always kept in his
waistcoat pocket, to trim paper to fit round the apparatus he used to
take his asthma cure; also he used the closed scissors to spoon out
the powder which he set alight and from which he then inhaled the
smoke.

A little later that year a photograph was taken of Margaret Morgan
with little Johnnie on her lap. It gives a very pertinent picture of the
change that his wife had brought into David Morgan's life. For the
photograph Margaret dressed with an awareness of style, wearing a full
crinoline skirt without the hoop for the convenience of the pose for
the picture. The skirt and arms of the dress have the sheen of quality.
She is wearing over her dress a smart zouave jacket with epaulets which
are emphasised by elaborate braiding. The coat is also edged with
braid. At the neck and at the opening where the zouave jacket is cut
away to reveal the waist an undercoat is shown, which is fastened with
clusters of minute brass buttons. In her ears she wears pendant earrings. It is a picture of a young lady of fashion; a fashion, however, of
about ten years behind that of London. The quality and air of distinction that this attire of Margaret portray were very different from the
style and dress in the pictures of her mother-in-law, Ann, and her sister-
in-law, Jane, which were taken four years before at the Brecon Agricultural Show. The very great difference was not caused by the passage
of time. It was her personality, her awareness of fashion and the means
to gratify it that made the difference.

No matter how proud David Morgan must have been of the admiration of the neighbours for his pretty well-dressed wife, he would be
already heavily burdened by anxiety. In the photograph taken in 1870,
Margaret's face is the face of a sick woman. Her mouth is slack and
her eyes are devouring her face. She holds in her lap her son, whose
head is resting against her breast. He is wearing a very elegant dress,
doubtless the work of his mother's or grandmother's needle.

The second Christmas of their marriage was a time of great sadness.
The dread verdict of phthisis (tuberculosis) had been given by the
doctor and now it was only a matter of time. There had been a plan
to take Margaret to the South Coast in an attempt to restore her health.
But it was too late. She was rapidly getting more exhausted. Until she
was too weak to leave her bed she was carried up and downstairs in
her husband's arms[10]. A pathetic reminder of her terrible emaciation
is the woollen thread woven round her engagement ring to keep it on
her finger.

There was little David could do to sustain his wife. When not engaged in his business, he would spend as much of his time as possible in the oppressive, ill-ventilated and overheated bedroom, keeping the fire going in a vain attempt to keep her warm. It was a very cold winter and nothing would have kept out the cold she would feel. As the days passed it became obvious to even the most hopeful that nothing could delay the rapidly-approaching death. According to tradition it comes most often in the early hours of the morning when the life force is at its lowest ebb; so it was with Margaret Llewellyn, who died at 3.30 a.m. on 27 March, 1871.

She was buried in the graveyard of Hengoed Chapel on 31 March. Her tombstone has engraved on it:

> In memory of Margaret wife of David Morgan (draper)
> of Pontlottyn
> Born December 9th 1850
> Died March 27th 1871

The insertion of the word " draper " on her gravestone was as if he had made a proud pledge to her memory.

A long-awaited death, with its painful and wracking climax leaves the survivor numbed and exhausted. The crushing emotion of the death of a young beloved wife inflicts deep wounds which, though healed, leave their scars forever. David Morgan never fully overcame the loss of his wife and the memories of those two years of her companionship. He did not marry again.

When his brother William married four years later, David said to him on his wedding day: " Take good care of her. I had a wife once and lost her ". In a letter written from Pontlottyn on 18 October, 1871 to Mary in Australia, the daughter of the second marriage of John Morgan II, he said: " Three years ago I was married to a young person from this place, but it was my misfortune to lose her seven months ago nearly. She was a loving and affectionate wife to me and I miss her very much ".

From time to time he made pilgrimages to her grave. On one occasion he was accompanied by his two nephews, William and Wilfred. Another time, before 1914, he took Aubrey as a small boy with James Hall to Hengoed to visit the graves of his wife and the other members of the Llewellyn family[11]. Aubrey remembers him, still and silent for some time, his two hands resting on his ebony-handled walking stick in front of him, his white beard held high above his stiff collar. He was standing sideways to the graves and looking off into the valley. James Hall moved away to look at some of the other tombstones. Aubrey found a large colourful clover flower growing in the grass and picked it. When James Hall returned he accused him of picking flowers off someone's grave, whereupon, to Aubrey's astonishment, his grandfather turned on him and rebuked him angrily and at length. The six-year-old boy was filled with a sense of injustice. Years later he realised that his innocent flower-picking had released a high degree of emotional tension in the old gentleman who was still mourning his bride of long ago.

When a daughter was born at Brynderwen, Llandaff, on 21 November, 1913, Jack suggested to his wife that the first girl should be named after someone in Edith's family. He much favoured Catherine, the name given to many generations on her mother's side of the family. Edith felt that Catherine Morgan was a harsh sounding name. Next morning a note came from Bryn Taff saying: "I am calling to see Margaret tomorrow"; this decided the matter. So fifty-two years after his wife's death David Morgan ensured that the name Margaret[12] should be carried on in the family.

After his death there were found in a drawer in his bedside table the emerald and gold engagement ring with the wool thread still woven round it and a pair of very small kid gloves. He had never forgotten her.

1 The curate who officiated was the Rev. Edmund Leigh, a member of the same family as Dr. H. V. (Bunny) Leigh.

2 There is a sampler which was in the possession of Miss Margaret Gwendoline (Gwen) Lewis, a granddaughter of John and Eliza Llewellyn, which has worked on it "Eliza Williams 1829". She would have been eleven years of age at that time.

3 My sister, Margaret, has a white porcelain mug which has inscribed in gold on it, "Presented by her Governefs, A. J. to Mifs M. L.".

4 Both are now in the possession of my sister, Margaret Morgan.

5 Now in possession of her grandson Kenneth G. Hughes.

6 Now in possession of my sister, Margaret Morgan.

7 Now in possession of my sister, Margaret Morgan.

8 The honeymoon was spent at Ridler's Hotel, Holborn Hill, London. The receipt stamp was signed by E. Morgan. There may have been some Welsh connection with this hotel which may have brought it to the attention of David Morgan.

9 Told to Mrs. D. N. Hall by her father-in-law, David Hall.

10 Told to my mother by David Morgan, according to my sister Margaret.

11 The Llewellyn family graves where John and his wife Eliza are buried with two of their three daughters, Margaret, and Elizabeth (who died aged three years in 1865), are in the graveyard of the Old Welsh Chapel at Hengoed founded in 1710. The two gravestones which are of the type called "gabled ledgers" are along the east boundary wall about ten yards from the south wall of the Chapel.

12 Besides my sister, the name of Margaret was carried by Miss Margaret Gwendoline (Gwen) Lewis, daughter of Mrs. Gething Lewis who was Margaret's sister Jane; by Mrs. Gething Lewis's granddaughter Margaret Llewellyn Lewis OBE, Headmistress of Howell's School; and by my youngest daughter Margaret Constance Eluned Morgan and my grand daughter Margaret Reed Hutchins.

9. The Seventies

It is rarely rewarding to speculate on what might have been; it only opens up limitless vistas of the unanswerable. Yet it is not without interest to contemplate what might have been the effect on the descendants of David Morgan if Margaret Llewellyn Morgan had not contracted the fatal disease of tuberculosis.

Would David Morgan and his wife, a happily married couple with a growing family, have wanted to leave Pontlottyn? What would have been David Morgan's way of life if his wife had lived until her husband's death in 1919? From what we know of Margaret, it is reasonable to assume she would not have countenanced for herself and her children the lonely austerity with which David Morgan surrounded himself as a widower.

In a letter dated 20 November, 1970, May Brummitt wrote: " I feel sure he would have loved a large family", and goes on to describe how one morning at Llanbrynean: " Mother heard a great noise in the upstairs front rooms, so she went to enquire and find fault with Kate, Agnes and David for making such a noise and disturbing Uncle. She was told ' Uncle is here with us '. The three were playing conkers when Uncle joined them ".

Four or five children would have been a modest size for a Victorian family. By the time of his death there could have been many more grandchildren to be included in his last will and testament. It would have been a very different document.

After Margaret's death two things stood out demanding his attention: his son and his business. The future lay with his son. His immediate concern was his business, which would ensure that future. By the time Margaret died David Morgan had spent twenty-three years of his life in the drapery business. Having learnt his trade in Newport, London and Birmingham, he had a wider and more varied experience than his competitors in Rhymney and Pontlottyn. There he had to find customers from a public which demanded as much value as possible for the penny spent. He had also undergone the tempering experience of bad times. He knew how to survive on a narrow margin between profit and loss.

He told May Brummitt some years after he had left Pontlottyn that he had always made as little profit as possible on each item so as to win and maintain a reputation for giving good value. His policy as regards advertising conformed with this view. He had a contempt for " puffs " and sales. To him the best way to get a customer into the shop, which is of course the whole purpose of advertising, was the cut price line or loss leader.

A story is told that one day in the Pontlottyn shop, when David Morgan was offering a cut line in calico being sold at a farthing[1] a yard less than what it cost him, a competitor, Mrs. Croft[2], sent someone across from her shop on the other side of Chapel Street to make an unusually large purchase. A shop assistant, Tom Samuel, recognising the source of the purchase, came to David Morgan to ask if he should make the sale. " Go ahead ", was the reply, " We might make a customer of her some day³". This anecdote is an illustration of David Morgan's business methods, both as regards price cutting and also the minute scale in which he was prepared to operate, and the calm with which he approached all business problems.

Shortly after the death of his wife David Morgan gave up his business at No. 6 Cwm Shon Mathew Square and sold the remainder of his lease to his neighbour, Daniel Evans, the " Tea Dealer Grocer and Provision Factor ". From the profits of his business and the proceeds of the sale of No. 6 he began to make investments in property around the Pontlottyn Shop. He eventually acquired the leases of four shops and twenty-four cottages. As well as these investments in " bricks and mortar ", he gradually expanded his holdings in the Rhymney Gas Company.

In 1874 he made his first investment in land in Breconshire. He bought old Llanbrynean, which was the family home, for £5,300. This, more than any other investment, must have brought home to his family that David had become a very successful business man.

Though he had sought solace in a concentration on his business, he had not in himself responded to the stimulus of success. Feeling run down, listless and depressed, he went to see the doctor, who prescribed for him as a tonic a well-known remedy of those days, stout. David Morgan had been brought up in the strict discipline of the Calvinistic Methodists. Within the proverbial stone's throw of the Pontlottyn Shop were four Chapels of various denominations of Nonconformity. David Morgan fully appreciated the importance to his business of the opinion and respect of the people who attended these Chapels. Careful of his reputation, he gave the most careful instructions, when he ordered a barrel of stout from the Rhymney brewery, that delivery should be made after dark at the trap door in the pavement near the side door on Chapel Street, which was off the busy square.

The brewery was famous for the quality of its cart horses, the pride of the draymen in their turn-out and the high polish of the wagons. So, to David Morgan's consternation, his barrel of stout arrived with considerable flourish. He was waiting at the open trap door in Chapel Street, where bulky consignments were delivered into the cellar. His main object was to achieve a speedy delivery and see the brewer's dray on its way as quickly as possible. After lowering the barrel by ropes down the smooth sides of the steps into the cellar, the men asked if they could come down and tap the barrel for him. Anxious to remove the brewery's advertisement from his door, he answered " No! No! On your way!" Closing the cellar trap door behind him, he placed the barrel on end, put the candle on it and proceeded to undertake an operation of which he had absolutely no experience whatsoever—the broaching of a barrel. By the pale candlelight he located the bung, picked up the tap in one hand and a hammer in the other and tried to drive in the bung with the tap. Unfortunately he failed to drive the tap home. The upended cask, shaken by its journey, spouted like a true whale. A jet of stout hit the ceiling, doused the candle and drenched the amateur tapster. Realising the scale of the disaster he placed both hands over the bung hole, thereby saving himself from a heavy loss of stout.

Time passed; at closing time there was no sign of Mr. Morgan to carry out his customary duty of shutting shop. Unfortunately he had deliberately avoided telling anybody what he was doing or where he might be. A search was made upstairs, the street was scanned, and there was still no sign of the master. It was well after closing time when David Morgan surrendered to the inevitable. From the cellar came the high-pitched voice of the "Guvnor" shouting "Somebody fetch a light". The door inside the shop at the top of the cellar stairs was opened, and the rescue party was met with as rich a bouquet as if the great Andrew Buchan himself was brewing in the cellar. The "Guvnor" was relieved of his guardianship of the stout and, without too much loss, the barrel was placed on its side and properly tapped. David Morgan went upstairs to remove his clothing. It took some days to remove the all-pervasive smell of stout in the shop. James Hall used to say, when he told this story with much relish, that if David Morgan had taken a front page advertisement in the local newspaper saying that he was taking stout the story could not have got round Pontlottyn any quicker.

The relations between the master or "Guvnor" as he was called and his apprentices and shop assistants were exceptionally good. These young men became a substitute for the family he might have had.

In 1875 ten admirers, who had at one time or another served on his staff, presented him with a framed illuminated address and a gold watch[4]. The testimonial expressed their appreciation of his care and training and their deep sense of obligation to him. In part it said:

> Those of us who spent under your guidance, the opening years of their business life will never be able adequately to express the gratitude which they feel to you for your constant attention to their domestic comfort; your uniform forbearance with the shortcomings to which they, as beginners were liable, the genial encouragement which their efforts at improvement met from you, and above all the endearing influence of your precept and example upon their moral character and welfare.

Real admiration and warm-hearted affection underlie the formal utterances of this testimonial.

It is interesting to note that, at a time when the usual fare provided for the staff who "lived-in" was not renowned for its plentitude and the word *comfort* would hardly describe the customary living quarters of the apprentices, the first expression of gratitude in this testimonal referred to the "domestic comfort" provided by David Morgan. He had

70

not forgotten the nights spent sleeping under the counter when he first went to London, or the sparse meals of his apprenticeship days.

The first signature was appropriately that of James Griffith, whose name appears in the Cash Book on 16 March, 1858, as the first employee of David Morgan. The next name is David's brother Thomas. Amongst the other names is David Morgan Davies, who became the partner of Thomas Morgan in Morriston and, despite " the precept and example " of David Morgan, ran away to New York leaving his affairs in a state of bankruptcy. Another was David W. Davies, who was for a few years a partner of David Morgan in a drapery business first at Trealaw[5] then at Tonypandy.

Though not included on this list, a young apprentice named John Price had come to the Pontlottyn Shop in 1873. He was a first cousin of David Morgan. His father was the brother of Ann, David Morgan's mother.

On a cold, wet wintry day in 1873 John Price was very miserable, doing the dirty job of cleaning turnips in the field at his family's home at Cwmdu near Crickhowell. So intense was his dislike of his task that he decided, there and then, to seek some other way of making a living and asked his father to find him work of a different sort. It was decided to apprentice him to his successful cousin in Pontlottyn. John Price was put on the Brecon and Newport Railway at Talybont. He was met at the station at Fochriw by David Morgan, who helped carry his bags over the short walk to Pontlottyn.

David Morgan would have remembered his own boyhood as he listened to his young relative tell of his unhappy experiences with farming.

Although there were twenty-four years between them, there grew up a close bond between these two cousins. John Price was joined by Thomas Samuel and later by John Arnott Lewis. These three young men were the successors to the band of signatories on the testimonial. They lived over the shop and must have brought an air of gaiety so lacking in David Morgan's life.

They came to David Morgan to learn their trade not only because he was one of the best known of the valley drapers, but also because all three were related to him. They were all descended from John Morgan I of Abercneiddon.

John Price, besides being a nephew of Ann Price Morgan, was also descended on the female side from Elizabeth, a daughter of John Morgan I, she married Rees Price of Llwyn-y-brain. Thomas Samuel was the grandson of Jane, an elder sister of David Morgan the Progenitor, and therefore an aunt of David Morgan of Pontlottyn. Tom Samuel eventually set up in the drapery business in Ferndale in the Rhondda Fach. He was known as " Uncle Tom " in both the Price and the Lewis families. The youngest of this trio of apprentices was John Arnott Lewis, the grandson of another Morgan aunt of David Morgan. She was Elizabeth, daughter of John Morgan II of Cwmrhibin. She married Philip Jones. After farming at Poityn this couple kept the Swan Inn and later the Greyhound in Builth. Lewis was brought up in Bristol. His mother had married a saddler, Morgan Lewis, who lived on Bridewell Street. Lewis was a gifted youngster and made good use of the education he had received at the Coleston School, Bristol. After working for David Morgan both at Pontlottyn and Abertillery and later at The Hayes, Cardiff, he became one of the first students when the University was opened in 1893. He started in business for himself in Tongwynlais, with his sister as his sole assistant. He eventually moved to Whitchurch where, like his mentor David Morgan, he acquired a reputation for the quality and good value of his merchandise.

Fortunately John Arnott Lewis took a keen interest in the genealogy of his Morgan forebears. In 1904 in answer to an enquiry by James Morgan the Solicitor about the Morgan family history he wrote an amusing but also most informative letter[6]. In it he tells of his last meeting with D. P. Morgan when " D.P." reminisced about John Morgan I of Abercneiddon and John Morgan II of Cwmrhibin.

John Price was not only the senior of these three assistants; he was also the one most trusted by David Morgan. Early in his apprenticeship he used to accompany David Morgan on the walk over the moors when the weekly cash takings were carried to the bank in Merthyr. John Price remembered one time, when they were passing through a railway siding on their way to Merthyr, David Morgan was so overcome by a severe attack of asthma that he had to lean against one of the railway trucks for some minutes before he recovered sufficiently to proceed. This memory of John Price is the first evidence that David Morgan was, by 1873 at the age of forty, a victim of asthma as was his father. However he inherited a large share of his mother's determination and never allowed his affliction to interfere with his work; indeed, such was his fortitude, no one seems to recall hearing him complain of his asthma.

After a time the cash was carried by John Price to the bank in Merthyr in a locked pouch, David Morgan keeping one key and the bank the other. Nearly forty years later David Morgan was in Merthyr and decided to draw a cheque on this account, which he still kept open at that bank. When he presented his cheque at the desk it was referred to the Manager in his office, who came out and said: " Mr. Morgan may I shake you by the hand? The managers who preceded me while your account has been here never had the pleasure of meeting you ". Somehow this amused him and he told James Hall about it when he returned home to Bryn Taff.

It was to John Price that the task was given of collecting the rent of the cottages owned by David Morgan.

The eighteen-seventies were passing by and the businesses at Pontlottyn and Abertillery were prospering. Evidence of the sizeable accumulation of capital appears in the first letter dated 27 February, 1877, which James Morgan wrote when he set up as a solicitor in Cardiff. It is an enquiry sent to another firm of solicitors whether Blaenant, the farm of 193 acres adjacent to Llanbrynean, was for sale. With that customary care with which David Morgan approached his property purchases, his name was not mentioned in the letter, which said that the " client has a considerable sum lying in the Bank at low interest, before seeking an investment would like to know if the property is likely to be on the market shortly ". It was not until 1888 that Blaenant came onto the market, when David Morgan bought it.

In 1874 he had paid £5,300 for the 141 acres of Llanbrynean. He could expect to pay a comparable sum for the 193 acres of Blaenant. Yes, the client had a considerable sum at his disposal to contemplate such a purchase with equanimity.

1   At that time there were four farthings to a penny, twelve pennies to a shilling, and twenty shillings to a pound.

2   Mrs. Croft was the sister of John Llewellyn and the mother of May Croft, who went to a school in Clifton with Margaret Llewellyn. May Croft married Henry Valentine Trump.

   Mrs. Croft's son was the Reverend Jack Croft, who performed the marriage service for Lillie Lewis (daughter of Mr. and Mrs. Gething Lewis) and Griff Hughes, the parents of Kenneth Hughes.

   John Llewellyn Morgan, his cousin John Llewellyn Lewis, and John Llewellyn Croft were all related and were all born in Pontlottyn.

3   Story told to Morgan Price by Tom Samuel.

4   David George Oxford Morgan, great-great grandson of David Morgan the Draper, now has the watch.

5   The following notice of the dissolution of the Partnership is the only existing evidence of this Partnership:

   " Take Notice, that the Partnership hitherto existing between us, the under-signed, DAVID WILLIAM DAVIES and DAVID MORGAN, trading as D. W. DAVIES and CO., carrying on Business of Drapers, etc., (formerly at Trealaw,) but now at Tonypandy, near Pontypridd, Glamorganshire, was this day dissolved by effluxion of time, the Business in future will be carried on by the said D. W. DAVIES alone, who will still trade under the same style. All debts owing by the said Partnership Firm will be discharged by D. W. DAVIES.

   TONYPANDY, May 1st, 1878."

6   Letter now in possession of David Norman Hall. It was found in the papers of Dr. Telford Morgan, son of James Morgan.

10.   Little Johnnie

While the businesses were growing so was the other great responsibility of David Morgan, his only child.

When his mother became desperately ill little Johnnie was inevitably moved up the street for his Grandmother Llewellyn to look after him. After his mother's death he would spend most of the time in his earliest years in the Llewellyn home rather than with the housekeeper, who would be looking after the domestic side of things at the shop. He would be petted and spoilt by his grandparents and Aunt Jane Llewellyn. He was their sole consolation for the loss of Margaret. He was so much their pride and joy that one day before a group of admiring friends John Llewellyn, in a state of exaltation, lifted his little grandson above his head and exclaimed, " The richest little boy in Pontlottyn! [1]"

When Grandmother Llewellyn died in 1876 little Johnnie would lose a great deal of that comfortable world in which he was surrounded by a glow of admiration. His Aunt Jane would still help to look after and comfort him, but she too would soon be leaving the Llewellyn home on Merchant Street to marry Samuel Gething Lewis, bringing to an end what must have been a source of great happiness to little Johnnie.

Fortunately another family home welcomed little Johnnie into their midst. David Morgan had begun sending his son for the holidays to the Halls at Tynewydd, where his sister Jane already had a family of six of her own. The members of the Hall family used to claim that their mother gave more attention to her motherless nephew than to her own children. Nevertheless, it is likely that the numerous Hall children would prove a healthy corrective to the adulation of the Llewellyn family. The Halls had a capacity for reducing the ego of any favourite.

There is a photograph of James Hall, Maria Hall and Johnnie Morgan. The Hall family favoured the use of abbreviated names, such as Will, Lyd, Tom, Fred. So, for those in the photograph it was Jim, Rie and Jack; and Jack he became for the rest of his life to his family.

The photograph was taken in about 1875 when Jim and Jack (as we must now call Johnnie) would be six and Rie eleven years of age. The two boys were almost the same age, Jack being two months older than Jim. Standing on either side of Rie, who is seated in a chair, they are dressed in rather similar suits, brand new judging by their pristine condition, an unnatural state for the clothing of small boys. The photograph may perhaps have been taken to record the first occasion on which they changed from the dresses of infancy to the more mature attire of suits. They are wearing trousers and double-breasted jackets outlined in braid, with a corner of a handkerchief showing in the breast pockets, narrow bow ties with the ends carefully draped over the lapels of their jackets, and each is carrying a straw sailor's hat. Jim looks serious, Rie calm, and Jack a trifle cocky. Jim shows the good looks which were to remain with him all his life. Jack is noticeably curly-headed. This photograph is the first record of a close and lifelong friendship between the three.

Because of the abundant companionship of the prolific Hall family at Tynewydd, where games of cricket and tennis were played and visits made with his father to Llanbrynean, Breconshire always had happy memories for Jack and became a much more formative influence in his life than Pontlottyn. In comparison with the pleasures of Breconshire, Pontlottyn would seem a much more subdued place for a small boy. However, during his early boyhood Jack formed a close friendship with the boys of the Trump family. Mrs. Trump, who had been Miss Croft, had gone to the same school in Clifton as Margaret Llewellyn, which would have given rise to the friendship between the Trumps and Margaret's son Jack. Henry Valentine Trump was general manager of the Rhymney Iron Company. Rhymney was still a company town, and the general manager was very much its first citizen.

By the time Jack was seven he was attending a school in Pontlottyn. In 1876 the Gelligaer School Board awarded a colourful blue, red and gold Certificate of Merit to Jack Morgan for regular attendance. David Morgan, with his great respect for education, may have earned a share of this award, for he was not one to allow malingering or loitering to interfere with the education of his son.

If David was to fulfil the pledges he would have made to Margaret, the education of their son would be of prime importance. Margaret had come to David as a bride fully conscious of the benefits of a good education. David Morgan, aware of his own lack of early education, throughout his life made constant efforts at self-education. He now set about bringing up his son as a member of the middle class, preparing him to fulfil the high hopes and expectations that rested on him. Though his father and mother had been brought up speaking Welsh, Jack was brought up speaking English. It was the language of his home and the compulsory language of his school. When his oldest surviving cousin[2] on the Llewellyn side was asked whether Jack learned to speak Welsh as a boy he replied: " Oh no! He was evacuated too soon "; he was referring to the removal to Cardiff of Jack at the age of ten when his father set up business on The Hayes.

Fortunately Jack had inherited from his mother's side a taste for the intellectual and artistic side of life, which made him a good pupil, and he soon established himself as a winner of prizes. These gifts of the mind were at first to be a source of pride and satisfaction to his father, but in the end were to underline the great difference of temperament between father and son.

1 Information provided by D. N. Hall.

2 Jack (John Llewellyn) Lewis, oldest son of Mr. and Mrs. Gething Lewis.

11. Abertillery

THE FIRST EXPANSION

" By the year 1876 the Rhymney Works achieved its maximum growth. To accommodate the boilers there were ten chimneys 195 ft. high. The Works contained 50 miles of railway on which ran 10 locomotives. There were 181 coke ovens, 11 ore furnaces, and 21 lime kilns besides machines, presses, saw pits, trams and waggons for all purposes. The Iron Works employed 4,000 to 5,000 men[1]".

Upon this hive of industry depended the prosperity of Rhymney and Pontlottyn, and prosper they must have until the late 1870's, when due to foreign competition many of the ironworks closed. David Morgan chose this period to look for opportunities for expansion elsewhere than Rhymney.

In 1875 he decided to establish in Abertillery, Monmouthshire, another drapery business. This must have come as a surprise to many of his old apprentices, when the attractions of the prosperous Aberdare Valley and the rapid growth of the Rhondda Valleys were to be considered. Possibly the absence of competition in Abertillery at that time was an incentive. By 1875 Abertillery had grown from a coal mining village to a small industrial town dependent on two collieries. David Morgan showed considerable foresight and courage when he decided to open in Abertillery in 1875, for it was not until after 1880 that the town really began to develop, " the period 1875-1914 witnessing the most extensive development of coal mining and housebuilding. Six new mines were sunk and the population of the urban area between 1891 and 1911 rose from 10,846 to 35,425[2]".

Abertillery was far from the boom conditions it was ultimately going to enjoy when John Price[3] was sent over from the shop in Pontlottyn to open up the new shop on the corner of Somerset Street and Commercial Street. David Morgan, aware of the reputation he had already earned of giving good value, called this new shop *The Pontlottyn Shop*; the goodwill associated with this name was evidently not confined to the small town of Pontlottyn. The Abertillery shop is still known by this name today. A manager from London was appointed, and it must have reminded David Morgan of his own early experience when John Price, after only six months, asked to return to Pontlottyn because he was unhappy in Abertillery, chiefly because the manager's wife was such a bad cook.

Evidently the London manager did not prove satisfactory, because by 1877 David was thinking about some other arrangement for the Abertillery shop. A letter of that year from James Morgan the Solicitor refers to drawing up terms for a partnership in Abertillery, and soon the business took on the title of Morgan & Owen. The man   David

76

Morgan chose as his partner was John Owen. He was described[4] as a man well known for his honesty and trustworthiness. There was something about his style of dress and manner that made him seem more like a preacher than a man of business, and at times he gave the impression that his mind was rather more on spiritual than commercial matters. Results proved him to be a good partner.

There exists an engraving[5] of the Morgan & Owen premises, which occupied the same site as the present business on the corner of Somerset and Commercial Streets. The main front was on Somerset Street and consisted of shop fronts let into a row of two-storey cottages. It is believed that David Morgan put in these shop fronts.

In 1879 the business had grown enough by its fourth year to justify carrying a stock valued at £1,800[6], while the long-established shop in Pontlottyn was carrying a stock to the value of £2,300.

As the town of Abertillery grew, so did the business. So much so that on 16 June, 1896, David Morgan took a lease of the land on the corner of Somerset and Commercial Streets for a term of 99 years from 24 June, 1894, at a ground rent of £9-4-0 per annum. In the lease David Morgan agreed to spend at least £1,000 on rebuilding. This he did, and more in 1897 when he instructed Turners of Cardiff to build a new building on the site of the old one. It was a major undertaking and must have called for a considerable financial outlay. It stands unchanged to this day. The exterior is ornate and impressive and has a basement, a ground and first floor, with a second floor in the roof. Amongst the rest of the shopping district this large and imposing building must have stood out unchallenged as much the biggest premises in Abertillery. Its unique status was later challenged by the Bon Marche, which was built on the opposite corner of Somerset and Commercial Streets. These two large shops, standing together in the middle of Abertillery, were symbols of the ultimate prosperity of that town.

The corner of the Pontlottyn Shop on Somerset and Commercial Streets is surmounted by a curved, decorated, projecting tower. On it is a plaque " D. M. 1897 ". When David Morgan built this new shop Abertillery had reached the beginning of its era as a boom town. Housing was very short and people responding to the rapidly increasing opportunities of employment had the greatest difficulty in finding living accommodations. David Morgan met this problem by devoting a large space (4,500 square feet) in which staff could live. There were at one time as many as eighty members of the staff who lived on the premises, which is some indication of the scale of business. The housing and feeding of this staff was in itself a big undertaking, a reminder of which is a frying pan so constructed as to hold 36 eggs separately at one time, which the present management[7] found in the abandoned living quarters when they took over.

After the death of John Owen, Benjamin Francis succeeded as the other partner and the names on the fascia boards became " Morgan and Francis ", though the shop retained the name of The Pontlottyn Shop. According to an active nonagenarian from Abertillery, both Owen and

77

Francis were really only managers and David Morgan was the power. Apparently David Morgan came only occasionally to Abertillery, but there was no doubt who was the boss. Francis had been a buyer at The Hayes. Possibly to keep an eye on Francis and as a test to prove his own metal, Jack Morgan was sent to Abertillery, where he lived over the shop in approximately 1890. This experiment lasted only a short time and then Jack started coming up to Abertillery for only a couple of days a week. This dwindled to coming up only for the day, and finally ceased. Cardiff had its attractions, and Jack was to marry Sarah Edith Jones in 1898.

Many years later Jack was invited to Abertillery to speak before the Chamber of Trade. In this speech he reminisced about the time when he lived in Abertillery and greatly amused his audience when he referred to Mrs. Titus Philips, Mrs. Henry Philips and Mrs. Dr. Williams as pillars of Abertillery society when he lived there, ". . . ladies before whom you had to pull up your socks and be on your best behaviour[8]".

It would appear that the Pontlottyn Shop at Abertillery was not held on a very tight rein as long as the figures were satisfactory. Judging by a photograph[9] which appears to be taken before 1914, there are posters on every window announcing a sale. Word could hardly have reached David Morgan's ears of such a total disregard of one of his basic business principles. If it was brought to his attention, he must have turned a Nelsonic blind eye. Likewise, it is very difficult to associate him with the Pontlottyn Ball[10] organised by the shop and held annually at first in the Abertillery Market Hall and later at the Institute.

The Pontlottyn Shop had a high reputation as a good-class shop doing a better class business than its rival the Bon Marche. Good times continued through the 1914-1918 war until 1920, when the decline of the coal trade began.

In 1922 David Morgan's estate sold the property.

John Rawlings in his thesis on Abertillery lists five significant dates in the development of Abertillery: " 1840 preindustrialisation; 1880 end of period of moderate industrialisation; 1901 period of most rapid growth; 1920 end of growth, eve of decline; last twenty years final running down of coal mining " (1970).

It is interesting to compare the period of David Morgan's investment in Abertillery from 1875 to 1922 with these dates. With remarkable courage and foresight he had chosen a place and a time to start a business when trade was beginning to develop in what was to become a prosperous area; but he made his decision so early in that upswing that few would have believed in the wisdom of opening a business in the small mining town of Abertillery in 1875.

He survived the grave economic slump which came at the end of the seventies. In 1876 he wrote to his aunt in Australia: " Trade is getting very bad here now, never was worse since I have known the hills."

1 *Hanes Rhymney a Pontlottyn*, Rev. D. S. Jones, Haverfordwest. Transl. by G. M. Harries, B.A. Published by Gelligaer Historical Society, Vol. 9, 1972.

2 Extract from *The Growth and Decline of the Mining Valley Town of Abertillery with Particular Reference to Housing Standards and Conditions,* by John Rawlings, who gave me the greatest possible help in my research in Abertillery.

3 Source of references to John Price, his son Morgan Price.

4 Mr. Sam Rogers, a remarkably alert nonagenarian, gave me the benefit of his memories of Abertillery from his early youth. He personally knew both Owen and Francis. I am much indebted to him for details about The Pontlottyn Shop.

5 Found and photographed by the Abertillery Museum Society whose Secretary, Mrs. Andrews, was most helpful in matters of research.

6 These figures taken from a letter David Morgan wrote to a bank manager in Cardiff in 1879 listing his assets. To bring these figures up to March 1974, they should be multiplied by 9.55 (from a conversion table furnished by Lloyds Bank). See also footnote 2 on page 84.

7 This information given by Alexander Rawlings, one time manager of the store, now owned by Rivlins. It is still called The Pontlottyn Shop, and trades under the name of Morgan & Francis.

8 I am indebted to Mr. Sam Rogers for the information about Jack Morgan's speech.

9 Photograph discovered by Mrs. E. Andrews, Secretary of Abertillery Museum Society, who was most generous of her time and help.

10 This information, as with much of the other information about the early days of Morgan & Owen and Morgan & Francis, was given me by Mr. Sam Rogers of Llanerthil, Llandenny, near Usk, whose lively memory and sturdy vigour belie his many years.

12. The Great Decision

In 1877 James Morgan started on his career as a solicitor in Cardiff. Like his brother David, he had a strong sense of property values and immediately began to develop the mortgage side of his practice. He quickly saw the great possibilities in the rapidly growing town of Cardiff.

However, not unmindful of the influence of his brother David and the business it could bring him, James kept an office in Pontlottyn and made regular visits there. He wrote to a client on 7 May, 1877: "About, four o'clock at my office at Pontlottyn would suit me ". It was quite likely that the office was a room over The Pontlottyn Shop lent to James by his most important client, his brother David. In those evenings the two brothers spent together, the conversation of James would be concerned with the growth of Cardiff and the opportunities that it presented. James used to say in later years that " It was I who found Cardiff " and claimed that he had opened the door for David to come to Cardiff.

Be that as it may, James was not the only person to discuss with David Morgan what was going on in Cardiff. The commercial travellers, who were the eyes and ears of the retail trade, who passed every rumour or exaggeration over "the grapevine ", would not underplay the sensational rise of Cardiff. The products of the Rhymney, Rhondda and Aberdare valleys were pouring down to the sea at Cardiff. Its docks, coal exports and shipping companies were making Cardiff known throughout the world. Someone as alert as David Morgan to the development and potential of trade was bound to be attracted by events in Cardiff.

Sometime in the spring of 1879 ideas which had been passing through the mind of David Morgan began to take shape and during that year he finally came to a major decision. He would sell the Pontlottyn Shop, move to Cardiff and start up in business there once again.

He picked the site where he would open his business at the bottom end of The Hayes, a triangular open space, surrounded by slums, that lay between the docks and the business centre of the town. He revealed the capital resources with which he was going to back his new venture in a letter he wrote to the manager of the Bristol and West of England Bank, with whom he had discussed his possible need of support from the Bank on one of his visits to Cardiff.

Stuckey Esqr
    Bristol and West of England Bank
        Cardiff

Dear Sir

I am about taking a Shop in Cardiff and have been thinking
of selling or mortgaging some properties which I have but since
I saw you the other day it has occurred to me that if I become a
customer at your Bank you may allow an overdraft of £1000 or
£1500 for a few years at £5 per cent and ⅛ commission on monthly
balance which would enable me to take my full discount.

I have the following securities by me any of which I could
deposit.

137-¾ Shares £10 fully paid in the Ystrad Gas & Water Co. present market price 20 to 21 per share.

  77   Shares Rhymney Gas Co. £5 fully paid Average dividend
        from commencement 12 per cent and shares not changing
        hands.

  86   Shares Blaenavon Gas and Water Co. £5 fully paid in 1878
        divided (sic) 9%, this year 6%, they had expended more
        than 4% in renewals, extensions & repairs.

  20   Shares £10 fully paid Brynmawr and Abertillery Gas &
        Water Div. pd 5%.

  25   Shares Taffs Well Gas and Water Co £5 all paid, new
        works.

   5   £5 Shares Hengoed Gas Works all paid, new works.

  20   £5 Shares Caerphilly.

Second charge on new draper's shop at Pontardulais £200.
Leases etc. of 4 shops and 24 cottages at Pontlottyn cost me at
        low times most of them built ten years ago fully £4000.

  10   £50 shares Rhymney Iron Co. Ltd.

   1   6 per cent Debenture Bond Rhymney Iron Co. £250.
        The two last about six weeks ago.

I have also a Freehold Farm near Brecon which cost me £5300

                            but there is a charge of £2000
                                                      ————

                                          Bal.   £3300
My stock here is about   £2,300 - 0 - 0
    Book debts good   480 - 0 - 0
                                ————————————
                                 2,780 - 0 - 0

81

less trade liabilities about	150 - 0 - 0
	2,630 - 0 - 0
Stock at my shop at Abertillery is about	£1,800 - 0 - 0
No book debts	
Trade liabilities less than	250 - 0 - 0
	£1,550 - 0 - 0

I shall not open for six weeks or two months and shall not require overdraft until beginning of New Year.

Kindly let me know if you want to entertain the subject.

Yours faithfully,
David Morgan

He could not have written this letter without some feeling of pride. It was a record of his remarkable achievements in his first twenty-one years in business. Starting in 1858 with £200 of his own capital, he had by 1879 accumulated a sum of capital of at least £17,000[1]. Assuming that it is necessary to multiply by 9.55 to get an approximation of what this sum would be in modern times, he arrived in Cardiff with £162,350 at March 1974 values[2].

He was forty-six years of age, a time of life when most men are presumed to have reached their zenith. Everything around him confirmed his wisdom in making the decision to come to Rhymney. The Iron Works in 1875 entered one of its most prosperous epochs[3]. His own business prospered. He had acquired property in Pontlottyn and considerably expanded his holdings in gas, that profitable new source of light and heat. He was an established and respected citizen of prominence in Pontlottyn, holding the position of Treasurer of the Gelligaer School Board. To most men of his age the financial position would appear very secure and the future assured, and offer little temptation to make a complete and drastic change.

It is interesting to note that the Bristol and West of England Bank did not jump at the opportunity to accommodate this new customer, as is indicated by the following letter:

Bristol and West of England Bank Ltd.
Cardiff 19th of Sept. 1879

Mr. D. Morgan
Pontlottyn

Dear Sir:

Your application I have laid before my directors but they decline to pledge themselves to make a loan of £1500 for two years.

82

Can you see your way to realise some of your securities so that a temporary loan of £500 to £700 would answer your requirements. If so I shall be very pleased to take your account on the terms mentioned in your note or if you wanted £1500 for say twelve months only, I think it would be granted.

You will probably be down here tomorrow when if you will favour me with a call I daresay we shall be able to arrange matter on this satisfactorily.

Yours truly,

Geo. P. Stuckey

Mgr.

Mr. Stuckey, who had already met David Morgan, seemed to have more confidence in him than the directors and gave a broad hint that the door was wide open. David Morgan in his usual calm manner did not hasten down to Cardiff as the manager expected, but wrote him another letter dated five days after the one from the Bank:

Sept. 23rd 1879

Dear Sir

In reply to yours of the 14th I could easily dispose of some of my securities but as I have never parted with any property I would prefer holding for the present.

It is quite reasonable that your Directors decline to pledge themselves for any fixd time & I would be quite content with say £1500 for about twelve months as you suggest, but I hope that I shall not require as much, however I named the maximum sum so that I should not for any time go beyond that amount. In about 12 months from commencement of overdraft shall hope to get it reduced to quite half if not less.

I am yours faithfully

D.M.[4]

This letter has about it an air of calm confidence. While there was a sort of compromise, he got what he wanted. Four days after he wrote this letter, the Bank Manager replied saying he had arranged Mr. Morgan's overdraft with the directors.

When reading his two letters to the Bank one feels that he was drawing on all the experience he had gained since he first started at No. 6 Cwm Shon Mathew Square. He knew what it was to be under-capitalised and he had been through very hard times, but what he had saved he had managed to hold. " I have never parted with any property ". Now that the matter with the Bank had been settled and the shop on The Hayes chosen, all that was left was the decision as to what should be done about the Pontlottyn Shop. David Morgan had not entered any price for the sale of his shop in his list of assets for the Bank. He had already made up his mind as to what he should do about that.

John Price had become his much-trusted right hand. David Morgan was an acute judge of character and undoubtedly had his eye on John Price for a future manager. Satisfied with the progress of his apprentice, David Morgan made the very generous offer to John Price that he take over the shop and pay David Morgan for it out of the profits. David Morgan knew his man and the potential of the Pontlottyn Shop.

The correspondence with the Bank and the business letters he received from his brother James[5] prove that David Morgan was living in Pontlottyn and actively engaged in the drapery business there right up to the time he moved to Cardiff. This disposes of a legend that he sold the Pontlottyn Shop and retired to live in the new substantial farmhouse he had built at Llanbrynean. After about six months (so goes the legend) he became bored with his rural retreat and set up in business once again in Cardiff in 1879. The new farmhouse was not built until 1883.

The only particle of truth in this legend is that at one time he did contemplate retirement. Owen Owen, one of the few intimate friends of David Morgan, said that David Morgan used to tell him that he would retire when he had made £20,000; but, when that figure had been reached, he said he would retire when he had made £30,000. After that figure had been passed, no more was heard of retirement[6].

Many years later E. A. Hughes[7], the son of a Pontycymmer draper, sought David Morgan's advice on some problem concerning the family business. The draper's son used to relate how David Morgan, having listened to the problem without interruption, then delivered a reply which was brief but much to the point: this experience was likened by E. A. Hughes to an appearance before a judge of the High Court.

The calm and restrained manner illustrated by this story concealed his strong ambition, that determined drive for greater success and the fortune which would be its reward. He must have felt that his achievement in Pontlottyn did not suffice and Cardiff would fulfil his ambition. Due to foreign competition, the Rhymney Iron and Steel Works finally shut down in 1891[8]. David Morgan's farsightedness may have given him some warning that those great works had reached their peak of success and his future lay with Cardiff.

1 A conservative estimate made by an accountant from the facts given in this letter.

2 Conversion table supplied by Lloyds Bank. In May 1977 the value of the £ dropped to 5½% of the 1879 value so that the appropriate multiplier would have been just over 18. The value of money has halved between 1974 and 1977.

3 *History of the Iron, Steel and Tinplate Industry*, C. Wilkins, p.192.

4 From the use of the initials and the absence of a letterhead, this letter appears to be a copy of the original letter.

5 A number are found in the first letter book of James Morgan, addressed to David Morgan, Pontlottyn. This book is now in the possession of James Morgan & Co., 33 St. Mary Street, Cardiff.

6 Told to David Morgan, son of William Morgan, Llanbrynean, when he was working in a bank in Swansea, by Owen Owen.

7 E. A. (Ted) Hughes, Senior History Master at the Royal Naval College at Dartmouth, told this to my brother Trevil. Ted and Mary Hughes, together with their brother Trevor and their sister Margaret (Mrs. McVeagh), were close friends of Jack and Edith, and used to visit Brynderwen. Gifted singers and musicians, they would spend evenings round the piano, much to the pleasure of James Hall, who joined in with his fine bass voice. They gave the Morgan family a very thorough grounding in the light operas of Gilbert and Sullivan.

8 *Western Mail,* 13 July, 1907.

13.   The Creation of Cardiff

The statue of John Crichton Stuart, Second Marquess of Bute, stands at the foot of St. Mary Street. Born in 1793, he died in 1848. He faces his Castle, an ancient and historic representation of his vast feudal possessions of 22,000 acres in South Wales. Behind his back lies his great creation, the Docks. The marriage that he brought about between these two gave birth to modern Cardiff.

By the beginning of the Nineteenth Century the medieval town of Cardiff had become little more than a fishing village on the banks of the River Taff with three hundred odd houses and a population of just over one thousand. The Taff flows into an estuary of the Bristol Channel formed by its mouth and that of the River Ely. This natural harbour, used by small sailing vessels, was restricted by its shallow, silted waters and by the tidal extremes of the Bristol Channel.

The opening in 1794 of the Glamorganshire Canal, which linked the iron of Merthyr and the coal of the Taff Valley with Cardiff, started this small port on the road to its great destiny.

The primitive facilities at Cardiff for handling cargo soon proved inadequate to deal with the continuously expanding iron and coal business which was coming down the canal. This problem was further increased when an extension of the canal, built in 1811, served the rapidly developing Aberdare Valley.

The solution lay in the hands of the Second Marquess of Bute. The Bute family by marriage, inheritance and purchase had become the owners of large estates, which by 1800 were becoming the seed bed[1] of the industrialisation of South Wales. Cardiff was their particular domain. It would not be difficult for Lord Bute and his advisers to see that it would greatly benefit his interests if he could open the bottleneck to the industrial development of his properties and the rest of South Wales by solving the inadequacies of Cardiff's harbour. The solution may have been obvious; but the cost of building a dock which could overcome the extreme tides of the Bristol Channel, allow for much more efficient loading of cargo and provide facilities for larger vessels, would tax to the utmost limits the financial resources of even so wealthy a man as the Marquess of Bute.

The decision to build a dock was a great gamble. It took every penny the Marquess possessed or could raise from other sources; a total of £300,000 of which £220,000 was in hard cash, and the remaining money was found by the sale of limestone and timber from the Bute Estate[2]. As a result of these huge commitments, the Bute West Dock was opened in 1839.

> If the Dock had been a failure, if Lord Bute's foresight had not been justified by subsequent events, he would have been—great noble that he was—an absolutely ruined man; and as it was he died, so far as his personal estate was concerned, utterly impoverished if not insolvent[3].

When John Crichton Stuart, Second Marquess of Bute, died in 1848 he was succeeded by his infant son; and the affairs of the Bute Estate were placed in the hands of trustees, with the new dock still in the first stages of its development. Fortunately for Cardiff, the trustees were an able body of men, imbued with the ideas and determination of the late Marquess to make the dock at Cardiff the leading port on the Welsh side of the Bristol Channel.

Lord Bute had backed his determination to make Cardiff the dominant port with a degree of ruthlessness which only a landowner of vast properties could have brought to bear. An example of this forceful attitude appears in a letter he wrote: " It is my clear rule not to grant facilities for carrying any materials to Newport which might be brought to the Bute Docks[4]". One of the most important effects of Lord Bute's decision to build his dock in Cardiff was the impetus it gave to the building of the Taff Vale Railway, which in 1841 linked Cardiff with the great ironworks of Merthyr and Dowlais and their collieries, and also with the pits which were spreading down the Taff Valley. It covered much the same ground as the Glamorganshire Canal, but served it much more efficiently. But in spite of Lord Bute's efforts to keep Cardiff ahead of Newport, the products of the Rhymney Iron Company at the time of his death were going to Newport over a tram-road on the Monmouthshire side of the Rhymney River.

The trustees then took the next essential step in carrying out Lord Bute's policy of establishing the dominance of the Port of Cardiff. They obtained in 1854 " an Act of Parliament authorising the building of a railway linking Cardiff with the upper Rhymney " and " made themselves responsible for raising the initial capital of one hundred thousand pounds[5]". The railway began to operate in 1858. During the first seven years the Rhymney Railway had a hard struggle to survive. The ironworks did not expand as expected and the coalfield of the Rhymney Valley was not being rapidly developed. It needed faith, perseverance and much needed loans from the Bute Estate to save the Rhymney Railway from collapse. Gradually the tide turned, and in 1871 came the great final achievement when the tunnel under the Caerphilly Mountain was completed and the route from the valley to the port shortened; this ensured for Cardiff the production from the Rhymney Valley and the other valleys of Monmouthshire. By 1879, the year David Morgan opened his shop on The Hayes, the total quantity of coal brought to Cardiff was 9,000,000 tons, of which the Rhymney brought over 1,000,000—an increase of 400 per cent in eight years.

In the late 1850's the increasing flow of coal and iron coming to Cardiff by the Glamorganshire Canal and the Taff Vale Railway, combined with the planning of the Rhymney Railway, called for an expansion of the dock facility of the West Dock. As a result, the Bute Estate built and opened the East Dock in 1859.

With communications between Cardiff and the industrial areas of the valleys well developed by 1860, the Bute Estate undertook the most important and rewarding development of all. Some of the hill farms and valleys of the Rhondda Fach and the Rhondda Fawr were part of the Bute Estate. There had been some minor development of coal mining, but until 1860 it seemed extremely doubtful that a seam of the essential steam coal existed in the Rhondda. W. S. Clark, the mineral agent of the Bute Estate, firmly believed however that it did and persuaded the Bute trustees to sink the deep shafts at Treherbert in the Rhondda Fawr. The exploration was successful and a seam of steam coal was found at these pits, known as the Bute Merthyr Collieries. Only then could the Taff Vale Railway Company be induced to build their lines up the Rhondda. It was considered such an important occasion that W. S. Clark accompanied the first trainload of steam coal to go down to Cardiff from Treherbert.

In 1860 David Davies of Hirwaun, one of the great coal owners of the Aberdare Valley, acquired a mineral property in the Rhondda Fach. After two years of anxious toil, the famous Aberdare four-foot seam was struck at a depth of 840 feet. With the finding of steam coal in the Rhondda, the last great coal rush was on and it resulted in the final quarter of the Nineteenth Century being one of almost constant growth in the mining and shipping of coal, and in the growth and prosperity of Cardiff.

The world-wide appetite for Welsh steam coal was well-nigh insatiable. Cardiff-owned vessels known as " colliers " shipped it all over the world. Some idea of the scope of the market for Welsh steam coal is given in an advertisement in 1905 of Lewis Merthyr Consolidate Collieries Ltd.:

> Proprietors and shippers of Lewis Merthyr Navigation Steam Coal, Uniform in Quality, Highly Durable, Free from Spontaneous combustion and unsurpassed in Evaporative Power.
>
> Used largely by British, German, Italian and Dutch Governments, Cape Government Railways; by the following large steamship companies, Cunard, White Star, American Line, P.O., Union Castle, Royal Mail, Orient, Pacific, Anchor Line, Hansa Line to India, Royal Hungarian Sea Navigation Co., Adira Ltd., The Compagnie General Transatlantic, etc. Lewis Merthyr is also extensively shipped to the principal Depots Gibraltar, Malta, Port Said, Aden, Las Palmas, Cape de Verde, Grande Canary etc.

By 1880, as a result of the opening up of the Rhondda and the growing coal trade of South Wales and Monmouthshire, there was a great need for additional dock accommodation at Cardiff. John Patrick Crichton Stuart, the Third Marquess of Bute, had been repeatedly approached to provide that accommodation, but the yield from the large capital expended on the docks by his father had proved so unsatisfactory that his lordship persistently declined to invest any more capital. Nevertheless, soon after his appointment as general manager of the Bute Docks and of the whole of the mineral properties and estates of Lord Bute in South Wales, Sir William Thomas Lewis was able to show so great an improvement in the revenue that he was able to convince Lord

Bute of the necessity for the construction of further docks. As a result the Roath Docks were completed in 1887, which permitted the loading of a much larger class of vessel and thereby preserved for Cardiff a very substantial portion of the coal trade of the district[6].

Of all the coal mining development in South Wales, none was so swift, so large, or had more bearing on the growth of Cardiff than that of the Rhondda.

> Tradition has it that at the turn of the century (1900) no bed in the Rhondda Valley was ever cold; as one man got up to go to the pit another came off shift to sleep . . . with a population around 170,000 and nearly 200 coal pits it was the most densely mined area in the world. Fourteen continuous miles of miners' cottages hastily thrown up by such large land-owners as the Marquess of Bute still stretch along the narrow valleys[7].

The crowning glory of Cardiff came in July 1907 when the Queen Alexandra Dock, which at that time was the largest walled dock in the world, was opened by King Edward VII accompanied by Queen Alexandra. It was a great occasion and a great day for Cardiff. With justifiable pride in their considerable accomplishments, coal and shipping magnates representing their various associations presented addresses[8] to Their Majesties, calling attention to achievements of the Cardiff Docks and the industrial areas they served.

Mr. W. J. Tatem (later Lord Glanely), as Chairman of the Ship-owners, reminded Their Majesties he was speaking for " an Association representing one-fourteenth of the shipping tonnage of the United Kingdom ". In the address of the Cardiff Chamber of Commerce, Sir Clifford J. Cory, Bart, M.P., referred to the Port of Cardiff as " the seat of the largest trade in the world for the export of coal[9]". Mr. W. W. Hood, Chairman of the Monmouthshire and South Wales Coal Owners Associations, called Cardiff " the principal coal shipping port of the world " and continued: " it may interest Your Majesties to know that in the South Wales coalfield there are 588 mines in operation employing about 174,000 workmen producing nearly 50 million tons of coal annually " and " that the capital expenditure in connection with these works may be estimated at 25 millions sterling[10]".

The shipping of coal was the barometer of Cardiff's prosperity, and it was still rising and set for fair until it reached its peak in 1913, when exports of coal reached a record of 13,676,941 tons and 8,980 vessels of 6,167,933 tons register were cleared from the Bute Docks. The cataclysmic war of 1914-1918 brought the feverish, unhealthy flush of wartime boom to coal, and especially to Cardiff shipping. This was the last great burst of energy and prosperity in the collieries and docks. After the war, the boom in shipping broke with dramatic and devastating suddenness. Many docksmen who were new to the business, attracted by the quick and large profits easily earned in the wartime conditions, found themselves bankrupt almost overnight.

This disastrous collapse, which destroyed the fortunes of many Cardiff magnates, did not directly affect the fortune of David Morgan. He had always looked to gas for the investment of such money as he did not need for the development of his business. Never during the forty years he did business in Cardiff did he invest in the prosperous worlds of coal or shipping. Indeed he never did in his whole life, except for some ten £50 shares and one £250 six per cent Debenture Bond in the Rhymney Iron Company bought in the Seventies when he lived in Pontlottyn under the shadow of those great works. David Morgan did not live long enough to see the collapse of the kingdom of coal, which must have seemed so secure and certain all his life. He died in 1919, before coal went into its prolonged decline as a result of oil and electricity taking over as the great sources of power and energy.

During the forty years David Morgan did business and prospered in Cardiff, Coal was King, his throne was in the Rhondda and Cardiff was his Consort.

1 By 1913 the harvest from the seed bed amounted to £100,000 per annum in mineral royalties alone.

2 *Syren and Shipping* 1940.

3 *The Illustrated Guide to Cardiff*, Daniel H. Owen, Howell & Co. Cardiff 1882.

4 *The Rhymney Railway and the Bute Estate,* Dr. John Davies, Gelligaer Historical Society, Vol. VIII, 1971.

5 Ibid.

6 Passage dealing with extension of docks and Sir William Thomas Lewis from *Western Mail* 15 July, 1907.

7 *Out of the Valley, A Survey of Wales.* The Economist, 13 July, 1972.

8 The names and the extracts from the addresses taken from the *Western Mail Special Number* celebrating the opening of the Queen Alexandra Dock July 1907.

9 In 1913 Barry deprived Cardiff of the title of the largest coal exporting port in the world when it exported 11.05 million tons of coal. That year (1913) Cardiff exported 10.6 million tons. Barry was the creation of David Davies of Llandinam, who was probably, after the Marquess of Bute, the man who had most impact on the development of the coal trade. Creation of Barry and its railway to the coal fields was his direct challenge to the monopolies of the Bute Docks, Cardiff, and the Taff Vale Railway.

10 When studying these resounding statistics, it is not without interest to note that " on Vesting Day Jan. 1st, 1947 (nationalization of coal) there were more than 250 collieries in South Wales; today (April 1971) there are 52. In the Rhondda alone there were 25, now there are three. Twelve years ago 110,000 were employed in the South Wales coalfield, today there are 40,000." *The Times*, John Clare, *Survey of Unemployment* 27 April, 1971.

14. The Great Coal Rush

That genie of steam which came out of the legendary kettle of James Watt created a world-wide demand for coal. King Coal was going to reign supreme for more than a hundred years, unchallenged as the creator of the all-essential power needed to drive the wide variety of machinery which was being designed to meet the demands of the new Industrial Age.

Without coal no steam, without steam no Industrial Age; and the best steam coal was Welsh steam coal, and Cardiff was its port.

Two Englishmen played a great part in changing the pattern of the South Wales coal trade. Though owners of collieries, their fame rests on their ability as salesmen to open new markets. The first was George Insole, a coal shipper who was the Cardiff agent for the famous woman colliery owner, Mrs. Lucy Thomas of Waun Wyllt Colliery, Merthyr, the mother of the Welsh steam coal trade[1]. In 1830 Insole at his own expense shipped to London a small cargo of Waun Wyllt steam coal. The smokeless quality and steam-raising power of this coal won for Insole a contract with a London firm of Wood & Co. for 3,000 tons of that coal in 1832[2]. This contract was the foot in the door of the London coal market. The use of this steam coal in the steamers plying the Thames and in Government Steam Packets at Woolwich advertised to a wider circle the advantages of using Welsh coal.

The next great salesman after George Insole was John Nixon. It was a Thames river steamer that introduced him to South Wales, where he became one of the greatest figures in the history of its coal trade. Nixon, a mining engineer, came from Durham and had become the manager of a colliery and iron works in France. Nixon himself told the story of his conversion to Welsh Steam Coal in a speech[3] he gave in 1860 at the opening of the Navigation Colliery at Abercynon. " When on a London steamer in 1840 I saw stokers throw continuously coal into the furnace and when I looked at the funnel I saw no smoke. This was a wonder to me ". His interest was still further roused after he had been permitted to stoke the furnace himself (a typical Nixon action). Making inquiries he learned that the coal came from Merthyr and was being supplied by Wood, a London coal merchant, who shipped about 150 tons a week from Cardiff, mainly for use on the Thames steamers. Nixon then went to South Wales, where he found Thomas Powell sinking the " Old Duffryn " pit. " I went to Mr. Powell and told him that if he wanted a market for his coal at Duffryn I was willing to enter into some arrangement with him so as to introduce his coal into France and that I was engaged in the trade of that country. After a great deal of negotiation we agreed that he should pay me so much a ton on all coal exported to France, that he should at first give the coal and pay the freight and I should go over there and give it away. I knew that was the only way to introduce it into that country ".

Nixon took his first cargo to Nantes, which was the beginning of a long relationship between that city and Cardiff. Nixon first got the sugar refiners of Nantes to use it and then the French river steamers; finally got orders from the French government. Now the battle for coal markets was on, a struggle in which the aggressive salesmanship of Nixon played so great a part. The outcome of this struggle was to have a profound effect on the progress of Cardiff. Already the coal exported from Cardiff had risen from nearly four thousand tons in 1840 to close on three hundred thousand tons in 1851. Cardiff was moving rapidly ahead of her rival ports in South Wales. The Northerners did not give up without a struggle and the coal masters of South Wales did not rest upon their laurels. Under the leadership of Nixon and Powell, they were possessed of a ruthless and aggressive competitive spirit and an absolute belief in the overwhelming superiority of their steam coal.

Potentially one of the biggest markets would be that of the British Navy, but the acceptance of steam power by the Admiralty did not come readily. The first attempt to introduce it into the Royal Navy came when Sir Marc Isambard Brunel, the father of the famous engineer of the Great Western Railway, proposed to the Lords of the Admiralty that steam tugs be used to take the sailing warships out to sea, thereby freeing them of dependence on a favourable wind. In spite of the great tactical advantage this would give the fleet, the Navy Board squashed this proposed innovation in a short minute.

> Their Lordships feel it is their bounden duty to discourage the employment of steam vessels as they consider the introduction of steam is calculated to strike a fatal blow at the naval supremacy of the Empire[4].

But the fast-spreading use of coal by the commercial Merchant Marine and the appearance of French ironclad men-of-war using steam overcame this traditional reluctance for change, and soon the doors of the Admiralty were open for bids for the supply of steam coal. The Admiralty set up trials to ascertain the best possible coal to fuel the new steam driven men-of-war, which were to be the essential safeguard of the nation. These trials formed the amphitheatre in which the great struggle between Tyneside and South Wales was to be fought out. The trials began in 1845 when the Admiralty launched its first iron steamship the *Birkenhead*. A wide range of 98 varieties of coal were tested, including 37 from Wales and 17 from the North of England[5]. The outcome was an overwhelming victory for Welsh steam coal.

> The best Welsh coals lit easily, blew steam up rapidly, produced fine clear fire and gave off very little smoke. The best Newcastle coals on the other hand all caked excessively, choking the draught and demanding constant attention, and gave off a dense black smoke[6].

The result of the trials was the winning of Admiralty contracts for the South Wales steam coal. So much so that on the occasion of a naval review in 1856 the *Merthyr Guardian* reported that " to obviate the chances of collision among such an immense gathering of ships an

Admiralty order has been issued directing the fleet to provide themselves with Welsh coals for the occasion and all other ships that may be present are to adopt the same precaution. Any vessel making a smoke will be requested to withdraw ". From this order it can be seen that thick black smoke was a considerable handicap to the handling of the fleet and made it very difficult to observe the essential signals; it also warned the enemy of the approach of warships, and interfered with the gunnery control, which was directed from the bridge, and made much more difficult the task of the gun layers dependent on good visibility to aim their guns.

The stakes involved, the coal contracts for the rapidly-growing steam-propelled Navy, were too high for the Northerners to leave the field to South Wales. For more than twenty years they fought back. A series of compromises were evolved for using a proportion of Northern coal to be mixed with a larger proportion of Welsh. All these efforts by the Tynesiders to get a share of this important and growing business were energetically opposed by the South Wales coal owners under the leadership of John Nixon and Thomas Powell. Their views were supported by the users. The Commander-in-Chief of the Mediterranean Squadron stated his opinion of the relative merits of the competitive coals in a report to the Admiralty: " I consider it my duty to point out to their Lordships that in the case of war North country coal is totally unfit for Her Majesty's service[7]".

The overwhelmingly favourable results of the Admiralty tests conferred the greatest possible prestige on Welsh steam coal. Shipping companies all over the world became customers for Welsh steam coal[8]. By 1870 the demand for steam coal had reached a stage when, of the total exports of coal from Great Britain, South Wales supplied 49.4 per cent of all the deliveries to France, 50.7 per cent to the Mediterranean and 63.3 per cent to South America.

Because of the Glamorganshire Canal, the Rhymney Railway and above all the Taff Vale Railway, Cardiff was the main beneficiary of this demand for steam coal. In 1839 the Marquess of Bute had initiated the growth of Cardiff as an iron and coal shipping port by building the Bute West Dock of 19$\frac{1}{2}$ acres. By 1875 the docks of Cardiff had been increased to over 97$\frac{1}{2}$ acres. Cardiff had become the headquarters of the shipowners, the shipping agents of the collieries and the representatives of the big purchasers of coal, as well as such ancillary activities as importing pit props from the Baltic and the various trades which met the needs of this great shipping activity such as the dry docks for repairs and the ship chandlers who supplied the ship's stores from rope to pickled beef.

1879, the year David Morgan made his move to Cardiff, was a year in which Britain was in the grips of a general economic depression. Cardiff did not suffer as badly as most cities[9], but since the great strike and lockout of 1875 the price of coal had steadily declined until it reached its lowest pit head price of eight shillings and sixpence per ton in 1879[10]. It was a year of great depression in the coal trade. Nevertheless, the momentum of Cardiff was maintained and the export of coal continued to grow and in 1880 showed a remarkable increase.

David Morgan's judgement and faith in the future of Cardiff was justified by the growth of the population and the new housing which was continuing to be built on Splott, Canton, Grangetown, along the Newport Road and in the suburbs of Roath and Llandaff. Cardiff was growing rapidly in all directions. Though it was a period of depression, the prospects for trade of all sorts were encouraging when David Morgan made his decision to locate his new shop on The Hayes. He selected for his business a position that put him between the burgeoning Docks and the growing retail business centre to the north and west of St. John's Church, which stands at the north end of The Hayes.

1879 was to leave its mark in the annals of history of the Welsh coal trade as the year of acute depression. Only if one accepts the old adage " when you are at the bottom there is nowhere to go but up " was 1879 the right year to start a business in Cardiff. Hindsight has confirmed that there could be no question that David Morgan's decision to move to Cardiff was the right one. The only question is: why The Hayes?

1   " Mrs. Thomas of Waunwyllt whose name will live in the history of the South Wales coalfield, for in sober fact she and not Nixon was the pioneer of the Welsh steam coal trade . . . She was the first person to bring steam coal into Cardiff."

2   *The South Wales Coal Industry 1841-1875*, J. H. Morris and L. J. Williams,

3   Ibid.

4   *Biography of Marc Isambard Brunel*, P. Clements. Publishers: Longmans, Green & Co. London.

5   *The South Wales Coal Industry 1841-1875*, J. H. Morris and L. J. Williams.

6   Ibid.

7   Ibid.

8   " Welsh Cardiff, the best Marine coal in the world was preferred by all navies ", *Sea Power in the Machine Age* by Bernard Brodie.

9   " Since 1874 the country has passed through a period of great depression but that depression has not been observed among the working classes at Cardiff to the extent that it has been felt by the same classes in other towns."
    Growth of Cardiff from 1875 to 1880, by Thomas Glyde 1880.

10 The price in 1873 was twenty-three shillings. Some colliery proprietors sold coal for as much as twenty-six and twenty-seven shillings a ton. These statistics and the price of coal in 1879 from *The South Wales Coal Trade and its Allied Industries*, C. Wilkins 1888.

15. The Hayes

The name of The Hayes is derived from the Norman-French " le heys ", meaning " the hedges "[1]. According to Speed's map of Cardiff made in 1610, what is now known as The Hayes was part of a large area of open ground to the south of St. John's Church lying within the town wall " largely consisting of gardens[2]".

An ordnance map surveyed in 1879, the year David Morgan came to Cardiff, shows the same area around The Hayes, between the Glamorganshire Canal and St. Mary Street as honeycombed by small open spaces and courts. Within the quadrangle formed by St. Mary Street and The Hayes and by Wharton Street and Caroline Street, lay Wharton Place, Baker's Row, Black Lion Court, Golden Lion's Court, Lewis Williams Court, Rising Sun Court, Union Buildings, Kettle Court, Green Gardens Court, Kingston Court and Gainor's Court. There were also a number of unnamed open spaces, some containing trees large enough to be marked on the map, and also three smithies in this area. Across The Hayes, outside the quadrangle, were Evans Court, Temperance Court, Rowes Square, the largest of these courts, and Carpenters Arms Court.

Small alleyways led into these courtyards, which were paved with flagstones. Round the sides of these courts were unpleasant and un-hygienic hovels of an unsavoury reputation[3]. There was usually a drain in the centre and sometimes there was a hand pump, and occasionally the flagstones gave way to small garden plots. In these courtyards, the old slums of Cardiff, flourished brothels and shebeens, where illegal spirituous liquor was sold and often distilled. Many of the inhabitants were impoverished Irish immigrants who had come to Cardiff to ex-change their native rural poverty and squalor for a similar but urban life, in the hope of finding employment for their unskilled labour, for which there was an increasing demand, especially in the docks, due to Cardiff's rapid growth. The gradual development of Cardiff eventually eliminated these courts. The ultimate acquisition by David Morgan of Kettle Court, Rising Sun Court, Union Buildings and Green Gardens Court removed these degrading habitations that lay between his shop on The Hayes and St. Mary Street[4].

In 1885 the Cardiff Medical Officer found a whole family stricken with typhus fever in a cottage in Carpenters Arms Court[5]. This alarming discovery was very close to David Morgan, for the court lay behind the Oxford Hotel, with its entrance nearly opposite David Morgan's shop on the corner of The Hayes and Barry Lane.

His niece, May Morgan of Llanbrynean, as a little girl visited David Morgan in 1888, staying with him in his living quarters over the shop. She remembered, on that and subsequent visits, how frightened she was by the blowzy, clay-pipe-smoking women with greasy caps, using sacks for shawls and aprons, who hung about Barry Lane, which was the entrance to several courts. Often drunk, they would stand about in groups shouting, swearing, spitting and quarrelling; May wondered why anyone ventured into her Uncle's shop.

When David Morgan bought some cottages to the rear of his premises, he learnt that one of the trustees of the estate from which he bought the property was then the Chief Constable of Cardiff. Shortly after he took over the property, he received a notice from the Chief Constable that if he did not forthwith remove the brothels on this property he would be served with a summons. As it was his intention to build on this land he was most willing to comply with this request. But he did notice that similar action had not been taken while the Chief Constable was one of the trustees of the estate which previously owned this particular hellhole[6].

From this picture of The Hayes and its surroundings, it can be seen that David Morgan needed all his courage, foresight and experience to have confidence in its future when he decided in September 1879 to take a lease from George Hopkins, a neighbouring grocer, of Number 23 The Hayes. He must have drawn on his early experience of the raw, brutal life of the iron workers and colliers of Rhymney and Pontlottyn when he decided to make his second start on The Hayes.

There is some uncertainty about the exact date on which he started business under the style " Morgan and Co." at 23 The Hayes. The only possible authority is David Morgan himself, who states quite positively in his first account book: " Opened shop at 5:00 pm, Friday, Oct 31 1879 ". He then proceeds to qualify this simple statement by the immediate following words: " first sale on Tuesday the 28th 2/7 & sold goods every day up to today and including this evening making total receipts £7-3-7¾ ". It should be noted that October 28th was his forty-sixth birthday, and, though not a man given to superstition, the inquiring tap on the window by a passerby while David was marking his goods, may have given him the idea that it was an auspicious date on which to serve the first customer of his new venture. As he continued his preparations, a few more customers must have taken the opportunity to slip into the new shop; but the combined sales up to and " including this evening " only amounted to a little over £7. The takings for the following Saturday, which was the first full day, came to £13-8-7. The first week's total was £97-12-9 and the first month's takings were £344-6-8.

Number 23 The Hayes was indeed a very small shop when compared with David Morgan's shops in Pontlottyn and Abertillery. Its size and surroundings would remind him of his very modest beginnings twenty-one years before at Number 6 Cwm Shon Mathew Square. His new shop had a frontage on The Hayes of only 17 feet and a depth of 50 feet. The two floors contained a total area of only 1,360 square feet. Number 23 was one of a row of five small shops doing business in this unprepossessing area.

It is difficult to imagine what were the factors that persuaded David

Statue of John Crichton Stuart, 2nd Marquis of Bute.

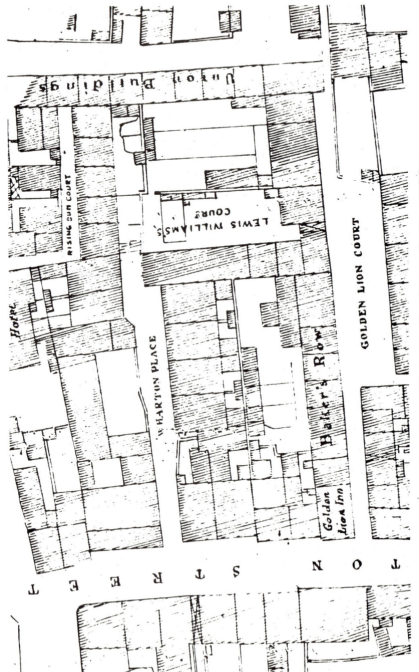

Ordnance Survey Map 1879, showing site of present Furniture Building.

Numbers 23 and 24 The Hayes, c. 1880.

On Completion of
my 60th Year
Oct. 28. 1893
David Morgan

David Morgan in Green Garden Court, subject of law suit: 1896.

David Morgan in Tabernacle Burial Ground, The Hayes: 1902.

The Hayes Front, c. 1900.

Entrance to Morgan Arcade from St. Mary Street, c. 1912.

Morgan to make his decision that The Hayes would be the place where he would start to build his new business. Most certainly he had not moved from Pontlottyn with £17,000 capital and the offer of a £1,500 loan from the bank with the intention of remaining a small draper. What did that remarkable mixture of judgement and foresight tell him about the future possibilities of this locality? Such surroundings would ensure the availability of low-priced property for future development. He may have been influenced by the presence of the Royal Arcade, an important artery of small shops which connected The Hayes with the approaches to the Great Western Railway station. However, when any of his old customers from up the Rhymney Valley came to shop with him, they would join the large crowd of shoppers who would come down Crockherbtown to Queen Street from the Rhymney and Taff Vale Railway stations, which served the densely populated industrial valleys.

There was on The Hayes near the shop, where he planned to start in business, the Tabernacle Chapel, which with seating for 1,200 must have attracted a large congregation, many of whom on their way to worship would pass his shop. David Morgan, having been surrounded by Chapels of various denominations at Pontlottyn, was fully aware of the importance of the Chapel connection to his business. Being a Calvinistic Methodist, he did not however attend the Baptist Tabernacle.

His choice of The Hayes would bring him within reach of the families of shipowners and sea captains, who in those days lived down near the docks in substantial houses in such places as Loudon Square and Bute Terrace. These would be customers with a much higher income than those in his immediate surroundings.

There was one other important advantage. In 1879 the newly-laid tramway system, of which one line ran from Roath past the Taff Vale Railway station and that of the Rhymney Railway, to its terminus at the docks, stopped at the door of David Morgan's new shop. Attention was called to this important fact at the bottom of every sales invoice.

In 1879 the drapery business of Cardiff was dominated by James Howell, who was already well established where St. Mary Street runs into the High Street. An *Illustrated Guide* published in 1882 described Howell's as " unquestionably the finest drapery establishment in South Wales and the elevation and general arrangements will favourably compare with the shops of its kind in any of our provincial towns ". James Howell first started business in Cardiff on The Hayes on the site of the Oxford Building, facing Hayes Bridge Road. He left The Hayes to go to St. Mary Street.

Samuel Hall built one of the leading drapery businesses of the town in High Street; and just around the corner two other household names in the drapery and clothing business of Cardiff, Evan Roberts and Charles Marment[7], started their shops on the north side of Duke Street[8] about the same time as David Morgan, whose choice of site put him somewhat removed from these developments and the main stream of shopping traffic. He must have had complete confidence in his ability to attract customers to The Hayes by his own efforts.

97

The area around The Hayes and between it and the docks was where his first potential customers lived. He would have to attract these people with his well-tried policy of giving good value for money; for it was mainly a working class trade, which he knew thoroughly through his previous twenty-one years' experience. He was not frightened by the looks and smell of the place, or its inhabitants. They were to be his customers.

Early in 1880 he occupied Number 24, the smaller shop between Number 23 and the corner of Barry Lane. It would appear that David Morgan also took a lease of Number 24[9] at the same time as he took Number 23. In the accounts drawn up in January 1881, David Morgan made the following notation:

> There was the sum of £151-18-5 paid for repairs of the premises which were subleased from George Hopkins[10] for 13 years from Sept. 1st at £180 per annum when taken they were in filthy and dirty condition.

This is the only reference in the accounts to rent and there is no mention of an additional rent for Number 24. This would suggest that the leases for both were taken in September 1879. The closing remark shows that there was something other than their condition which attracted David Morgan to The Hayes.

Largely due to his methods of bookkeeping, in which he included in his sales and purchases accounts the cost of repairing and fitting his two shops, the trading over the first fourteen months showed a loss of £344-18-6. However, the business must have grown rapidly because David Morgan found it necessary to increase the original staff of three to ten by mid-1880.

By 1884 David Morgan had evidently decided that his selection of a site on which to found a business was the right one and he began to undertake a major capital commitment for the development of The Hayes front. Between his original shop and the buildings of the Royal Arcade were Numbers 20, 21 and 22. These were torn down and the foundations were laid for a building with a basement and five floors. This was completed and occupied in 1885. The accounts show payments to the builder of £6,531. The new building had a frontage on The Hayes of 44 feet and a depth of 74 feet. There was also an entrance on the Royal Arcade with three shop windows. This new building, with its 16,320 square feet, dwarfed the 2,000 square feet of the original corner site on Barry Lane. It established the design of the facade of what was going to be, and still is, the major portion of The Hayes front. The top floor was given over to " living-in " accommodations for the men and larger dining room and kitchen facilities for the staff.

Edgecumbe House was still retained to house the overflow. The expenditure in 1886 of £78 for horse, trap, cart and truck, the start of a delivery service, showed that he had attracted customers outside the immediate area of The Hayes and probably of a better class. It was in 1886 that a lease in Harpur Street was taken for 99 years. Here the horses were stabled and the vans were kept.

David Morgan was developing laterally along The Hayes, but the greatest depth he could acquire was only 74 feet. Two years later in 1887 he set about rectifying this situation. He took on the areas behind The Hayes front, bounded by Barry Lane and Tabernacle Lane, and behind the shops in the Royal Arcade. In 1894 he built a large four-storey building with a basement on these areas. The original shop on the corner of Barry Lane was rebuilt in keeping with the rest of the new Hayes front. Unfortunately, owing to the assertion of "Ancient Lights"[11] by the owner of the Duke of Cornwall, a public house on the opposite corner of Barry Lane, he could only rebuild Numbers 23 and 24 to the height of their original two storeys. In the same year he strengthened his position on The Hayes by taking leases of the shops at that end of the Royal Arcade.

In his first fifteen years in Cardiff he had so extended his business that it had already become one of the major drapery shops in Cardiff. On The Hayes front, to the north of Barry Lane, were two public houses, which must have appeared as serious obstacles to any ambitions David Morgan had for developing along The Hayes to the north of Barry Lane. But when George Hopkins decided to move to much larger premises across The Hayes, David Morgan seized the opportunity to squeeze between the two public houses by acquiring Hopkins' leasehold shop and started to erect another building matching that of the rest of his shop on The Hayes. A strike of the Cardiff stone masons delayed the completion of the building for a year until 1891 or 1892. This addition was cut off from the rest of the business by the public house on the corner of Barry Lane.

News of the next development on The Hayes front appeared in the *South Wales Daily News* of 26 November, 1902:

> Messrs Morgan and Co. of the Hayes contemplate making an improvement in their property on a somewhat large scale during next year. Some time since they secured the Pavilion Hotel which intercepts their business premises and as the lease of this will be falling in next year they propose rebuilding it and at the same time to widen what is known as Barry Lane which leads from the Hayes to Morgan's Arcade. They will also probably raise the elevation of the hotel and that portion of their premises on the opposite corner of Barry Lane and if no objection is raised build over a portion of the latter.

From this news item it can be seen that the name of the public house on the north corner of Barry Lane had been changed from the Duke of Cornwall to the Pavilion Hotel, and by its purchase David Morgan had at last eliminated its claim to "Ancient Lights ". Permission was granted to build over the entrance of Barry Lane. The new building on the site of the hotel was thus connected with the original two-storey shop, now raised to the height of the other buildings. So did David Morgan finally complete in 1904 his long-planned continuous front, with one facade, on The Hayes, reaching from the Royal Arcade to the entrance of his other great venture, the Morgan Arcade. That year, to celebrate the completion of The Hayes front and to mark the twenty-fifth anniversary of the foundation of the business, a clock was hung from the tower over Barry Lane. It marked not only the boundary line between the parishes of St. John and St. Mary, but also the distance David Morgan had travelled from the small shop on Cwm Shon Mathew Square to the large imposing business on The Hayes.

Sometime in the early Nineties David Morgan had begun to plan his most ambitious development of his business, the Arcade, first called the New Central Arcade but soon and to this day known as the Morgan Arcade. While he was still to complete his building of The Hayes front, he embarked on a plan to extend his business to St. Mary Street, the thoroughfare on which his rival, James Howell, was so firmly established. The arcade would link his planned premises on St. Mary Street with his shop on The Hayes. This was a formidable undertaking, calling for a considerable outlay of capital and entirely dependent on the acquisition of the property lying between St. Mary Street and The Hayes. Some impression of how this was financed can be gathered from the bank manager's record book now in the keeping of Lloyds Bank Ltd.:

> 1896 July 1st   Mr. David Morgan (sole) called and said that there was £8/9000 in his a/c wh: until the Arcade was built wd. not be required. Shd he put a part of it on deposit or wd. we allow him something on current a/c. Told him that after deducting a sufficient balance to work the a/c free, we wd. allow him @ 2% (when overdrawn he pays 5%). He has some freehold property near his place, wh: he is thinking of developing. The land is worth infinitely more than the buildings on it.

> 1898 March 1st   Mr. David Morgan called and said that he had spent £12/13,000 on his Arcade and wd. want to overdraw £2/3000 but he has several thousands coming in shortly from Ystrad Gas & Water Co. sold to a District Council.

He acquired the site of the abandoned Royal George public house on The Hayes. One of the key properties he had to buy was a long court called Union Buildings, which had an entrance on The Hayes alongside the Royal George and ran back to Tabernacle Lane[12]. The back portion of this court opened up in an L shape, occupying the back one-third of the frontage on Barry Lane. Between Tabernacle Lane and St. Mary Street were a series of properties which had to be obtained at auction or by private treaty. David Morgan faced some serious problems.

May Morgan of Llanbrynean, who was at that time living with her Uncle David at Bryn Taff while she attended Howell's School, remembered discussions between her Uncle, his son Jack and James Hall, which revealed to her that there were periods of real anxiety over the task of carrying through this costly project. Among the many problems arising from acquiring possession of the various properties were two major obstacles.

The first was the reappearance of the old bogey "Ancient Lights ". After the arcade had got under way, starting at the St. Mary Street end, its progress reached the property that David Morgan owned on the west and nearer side of Tabernacle Lane; he then found himself faced with a claim that his planned three-storey arcade building would interfere with the "Ancient Lights " of Green Gardens Court. The landlord of this court was an estate administered for two minors by a trustee named Sam Hern. The purpose of this claim was possibly to force David Morgan into buying Green Gardens Court at an inflated price, even though it was not needed for building the arcade. If this was so, he would be faced with a difficult decision at a time when his capital resources were fully committed to the purchase of property essential for the arcade as well as to building costs. Should he incur the considerable further cost of acquiring Green Gardens Court; or should he risk an action for the infringement of "Ancient Lights " by continuing to build on the property adjacent to Green Gardens Court?

This problem, undoubtedly, brought pressure on David's usually steady nerves and patience. He was convinced that Sam Hern was motivated by his own selfish interests, not those of the minors for whom he was trustee. One evening at Bryn Taff, when a map and papers dealing with the arcade were being studied by David Morgan, he jumped to his feet and exclaimed " Sam Hern is a devil! "; then, stamping his foot and banging the dining room table with his hand, he repeated himself. This outburst from so quiet and reserved a man, whose strongest expression was " Gammon! ", was received by his son Jack and James Hall with amazed silence.

David's brother, the solicitor, James Morgan was consulted and advised a compromise[13], as he greatly feared a decision in a court of law would go against David. After the excavations had been made and the building started, an attempt was made to meet the claim of "Ancient Lights " by offering to make some alteration in the plans. But Sam Hern remained obdurate. This left David Morgan with the choice of abandoning his arcade, buying Green Gardens Court, or proceeding with building and facing a law suit. James Morgan, fearful of the disastrous effects on the future of the arcade if the case, as he believed, would go against his brother, tried to persuade David not to let this come before a judge and most strongly advised him to take any steps possible other than recourse to law[14]. But David had made up his mind. Conscious of what was at stake, knowing the amount of expenditure to which he was already committed and fully aware there could be no half measures, that the arcade must reach The Hayes from St. Mary Street or fail, he was determined to face " the Devil " in a court of law in the belief that the facts would prove his right to build.

In 1896 a law report was published in a local newspaper headed *New Central Arcade*: Motion for an injunction, *Rogers v. Morgan*:

Yesterday in the Chancery Division of the High Court of Justice Mr. Justice Sterling had before him a motion for an injunction restraining the defendant till the trial of the action from proceeding with the erection of the new arcade buildings so as to obstruct the access of light to houses in Green Gardens Court . . . the freehold of six artisan cottages situated on the Northeast side and three on the Southwest side of the court which is stated to be thirty-three feet in width. On the Baker's Row side buildings known as Morgan's and Turners were erected about ten years ago, the former about sixty feet and the latter thirty-three feet high the effect being it was said very seriously to affect the access of light to the buildings in the court. . . In August last excavations and buildings for the new arcade were being proceeded with on the Northwest side and some correspondence took place the result of which was that an alteration was made in the plans but the plaintiff (surviving trustee under will of Capt. Rogers) did not consider that it met his complaint and the writ in this action was issued on the 17th of October last . . . Mr. Graham Hastings Q.C. described the effects of the new building as practically to enclose the plaintiff's property in a well . . .

Mr. Justice Sterling directed a reference to a surveyor to report whether the buildings proposed to be erected by the defendant would materially obstruct the access of light to any and which of the plaintiff's windows as that access existed before the buildings formerly on the defendant's land were pulled down and if so whether any and what modifications of the defendant's plans would prevent that obstruction.

Presumably the surveyor's report satisfied the Judge that David Morgan's planned building would not infringe the "Ancient Lights " of Green Gardens Court because the building of the arcade proceeded.

The second serious obstacle was created by his rival, James Howell. He had become sufficiently aware of David Morgan as a competitor as to have no wish to see him gain a foothold on St. Mary Street. In order to stop him in his drive through to St. Mary Street, James Howell bought privately some property which lay across the route of the planned arcade. When David Morgan tried to obtain this property, he found out who the new owner was and that there was no hope of purchasing it. A little later Mr. Howell, an inveterate builder himself, found that some property he needed for the expansion of his business had found its way into the hands of David Morgan. Eventually an exchange[15] was made and each man went ahead with his own plans for expansion.

David Morgan was aware of the dangers of such opposition and of owners making him pay dearly for the property he must have. One precautionary measure that he took when a property came up for auction was to employ a secret representative to join in the bidding. When David Morgan dropped out of the bidding, the agent continued but the opposition relaxed when it was seen that David Morgan had dropped out, leaving his representative to acquire the property which to the discomfiture of the opposing bidders would find itself in the hands of David Morgan. He built a shop on St. Mary Street in 1898 adjacent to the entry of the Morgan Arcade. The St. Mary Street entrance to the Morgan Arcade was built in 1899, the year of the completion of the

102

arcade. That year The Hayes entrance to the Morgan Arcade was also completed and formed a major addition to The Hayes front. As if to mark the very special undertaking of the arcade, the front of this building was of an entirely different architectural design from the rest of The Hayes front. This building was originally designed to be an hotel. The upstairs room on the first floor was intended to be a billiards room. The two pillars in the centre of the room, now part of the shop, are so spaced as to allow a full-sized billiards table to stand either side of them.

The building of the Morgan Arcade was a big operation, taking three years and demanding a considerable backing of capital. In the end success rewarded David Morgan for overcoming the hazards he had faced. The scope of his operations and their success can be judged by the final reference in the bank manager's report on the arcade:

> Feb 10th 1899. Says he has spent £27,000 in the last 3 years principally in land (four or five farms in Breconshire) and acquiring ground and building the Morgan Arcade but all his deeds are " at home " (bank manager means there were no mortgages on David Morgan's property). All his shops and offices are let and he will now be building in the Hayes.

With The Hayes front accomplished, his presence in St. Mary Street established and the arcade successfully completed, it could now be expected that, at the age of seventy-one, his urge to build would be sated. But there remained a sizeable plot of land he owned on The Hayes front, to the north of the Morgan Arcade building, on which the buildings had been demolished. Here, behind a wooden hoarding covered with bill-posting, were the winter quarters of Studt's roundabouts and carnival. Studt's Circus used to travel around South Wales, and Rhymney was one of its ports of call. Possibly some acquaintanceship from those days qualified Mr. Studt as a suitable tenant. In 1911 David Morgan, at the age of seventy-eight, felt once again the urge to make his, final, addition to the large structure he had already erected, by building over this space.

This building is very different from all the others. The design has much greater claim to architectural distinction than any of the other structures of David Morgan. For instance, the windows above the street level were made into distinctive architectural features and the entrance was graced by two pairs of fine black marble pillars, which gave this building a more opulent appearance than the rest of The Hayes front. Money had been spent on appearance. This new concept was due to the influence of David's son, Jack, who had an interest in architecture and a definite feeling for standards of good taste. He was deeply interested in the planning of both the outside and inside of this building, because it was going to be devoted to the furniture department, which was his creation. He had developed this side of the business, indeed the whole furnishing side, without much support from his father. David did not approve at all of his son introducing the furniture business and was heard to complain that " he could not understand Jack bringing all

103

that dirty straw (with which the furniture was packed) into a good clean draper's shop ". He remained " very critical for a long time till he saw the change in the turnover figures which shut him up there-after[16]".

The building was completed[17] and opened in 1912[18]. It had a larger floor space than any other single building of Morgan and Co. and was distinguished by the openness of the floors, as the structure was carried on girders and narrow columns, without the heavy interior walls which were part of the structure of the other buildings. In the centre was a feature common to many department stores, especially the famous ones in Paris, a big well with a large skylight at the top bringing daylight to each floor. The use of skylights to bring light into the selling space was a very prominent feature[19] throughout David Morgan's premises. With his ever-keen eye on expense, he was willing to sacrifice space for savings in the cost of artificial light. To him the illumination of the shop by gas light was an expense needing careful watching. On one occasion when he was on his way through the shop with his grandson Aubrey to take the cab home that was waiting for him on The Hayes front, he paused at the foot of the main staircase and, looking down the department where material was sold by the yard, called out " What are all those lights on for? There are no customers there, so put out some lights ". Assistants jumped on counters and put out lights. What had been before a dark department, owing to the colours of the bulk of the stock in the high fixtures being black, dark blue, and brown, then became cave-like in its gloom. David Morgan left for Bryn Taff, undoubtedly feeling that he had effected some economies on a not busy day, and had taught his staff a valuable lesson.

With the completion of the Furniture Building, David Morgan at the age of seventy-nine was at last willing to rest on his record of building. This compulsive builder had, in the second half of his life, built almost all the external structures of David Morgan, Limited in existence today. The interiors of these buildings, however, have been greatly changed. He expanded into and occupied most of the area between the Morgan and the Royal Arcades. The only completely new building erected since his death is the one over Green Gardens Court, the top floor of which was the Counting House until 1977. (See Epilogue: The Portrait.)

One of David Morgan's rare weaknesses was to overbuild. It was as if he believed that, given the space, the business would fill it. He had not become aware of the modern statistic of trade per square foot, but if he had it is doubtful whether he would have allowed it to interfere with his determination to build one of the largest drapery businesses in Wales. The sole restraint would be money and, such was the success of his business that he did not have to wait long between the completion of each building for the till to fill up. He left to his future heirs a very large built-up area of business property which, because of the Royal and Morgan Arcades, Barry Lane and Tabernacle Lane, were a veritable nightmare of a maze when it came to dealing with the flow and directing of customers, or defining the areas of a department. Due to David Morgan's determination to bring daylight into the centres of his shop, the selling floors were wastefully planned; and as the various buildings were developed, a variety of levels were permitted, with numerous rises of three or four steps occurring throughout the upper floors. No matter the unsolved problems he left behind, David had accomplished what he had set out to do, build a very large shop; but it was not until about fifty years after his death that the trade of David Morgan, Limited began to justify the space with which it had been provided by its founder.

Nearly one hundred years have passed since David Morgan opened his shop at Number 23 The Hayes in 1879 and, while it is not possible to discover the reasons for this choice of locality, it is possible to view some of the results of that decision. The evident and visible success of his business shows that by his methods he was able to overcome any of the handicaps of his original surroundings and undoubtedly, by the presence of his shop, he made The Hayes an attraction to shoppers. It has been said that by building his business on The Hayes he pushed the dockland slums of Cardiff onto the other side of The Hayes Bridge, which marked the southern limit of The Hayes. Salubrious as this may have been for the general well-being of Cardiff, it did not make the area attractive to other important businesses. After the fire which destroyed the grocery of George Hopkins on the opposite side of The Hayes, no other big or growing retail business entered that area to help David Morgan bring the shopping public into The Hayes. The most active development of retail business in Cardiff has been along Queen Street, a quite separate location, when during his lifetime a large flow of customers walked or travelled by tram from the railway stations of the Rhymney and Taff Vale Railways or from the more affluent suburbs developing along Newport Road and to the east side of Cardiff, such as Roath. Even shoppers from Llandaff would find a convenient place to alight from their horsebus, or later their tramcar, outside the Castle Gate, much closer to the shops of Duke Street, High Street and Queen Street, than to The Hayes.

While the Great Western Railway Station would bring in passengers from Newport, Penarth, Barry and the Vale of Glamorgan to walk through the Morgan and the Royal Arcades, the growth of Queen Street was proof of where the major flow of shoppers was. His choice of site eventually enabled him to have a front with shop windows and entrances on both The Hayes and St. Mary Street, but on St. Mary Street, with the exception of Jothams, he was some distance removed from the shopping activity created by Howell's and the Market, Samuel Hall's and the other shops in High Street. One day, leaning against the wall of the bank opposite to the entrance of the Morgan Arcade and watching the people walking on the other side of St. Mary Street, he said to his grandson Aubrey: "The trouble with this street is that it is a one-sided street. People shop only on one side. This side is all banks and banks kill business". He did not expand his St. Mary Street front after 1899.

105

It was long after his death that Cardiff put its big central bus terminus outside the Great Western Railway Station, thereby adjusting somewhat the previous pattern of the flow of shoppers.

1 Cardiff Records.

2 Ibid.

3 Some indication of the reputation of this general area was given in a paper read to the Annual Meeting of Building Societies Association in Cardiff, 1912 " One infamous slum most damaging to the town's reputation was in close proximity to the Great Western Station." *Growth of a City*, by C. F. Saunders.

4 A *Western Mail* photograph of approximately 1873 shows the gardens in Green Gardens Court. Eventually bought by David Morgan, tenants were removed and buildings boarded up until 1924 when the Court was torn down to make way for building containing the Counting House. The flag-stones were presented to the National Museum of Wales by J. Ll. Morgan and used to make the floor of the Model Welsh Kitchen.

5 *Cardiff Records*. A photograph of the court shows it to be in existence in 1890.

6 Source: J. Ll. Morgan.

7 Samuel Hall started in 1880.
  Marment started in 1879.
  Roberts started in 1880.

8 North side of Duke Street, now demolished.

9 Ordnance Map surveyed in 1879 shows 23 and 24 as one shop.

10 George Hopkins, a grocer, had a business on The Hayes which was sand-wiched between two public houses, the Duke of Cornwall and the Royal George to the north of Barry Lane.

11 The phrase "Ancient Lights " describes in English law the right of an owner or occupant of a building to prevent the erection of an adjoining building which would obscure the light to his window provided the window had had 20 years of unobstructed light. It has been generally held it was no inter-ference if an angle of 45° sky light was left, but this is never conclusive.

12 Tabernacle Lane, as it came to be known, was an extension of Baker's Row, a right-of-way between Wharton Street and the back entrance of the Taber-nacle Chapel on The Hayes. It cut across the whole length of the back of The Hayes Shop crossing Barry Lane and had an entry on it to Union Buildings and was the sole entry to Green Gardens Court.

13 Source of Sam Hern story and James Morgan's advice, May Brummitt.

14 That James Morgan became the first occupant of a large suite of offices over the entrance of the new Arcade would not be without some satisfaction to David Morgan after his brother's advice.

15 A plan of the property involved is in the possession of James Morgan & Co.

16 Source of quotations was Will Hall, and quoted in letter from J. T. Morgan, May, 1973.

17 The building contractors were Turners of Cardiff.

18 The building narrowly escaped catching fire just after it was completed but before it was occupied when the building next to it, Howell's grocery department, was seriously damaged by fire, scorching the external woodwork and blistering the new paint on that side of the building.

19 Many of the wells beneath the skylights have been floored over and made into selling space.

THE HAYES

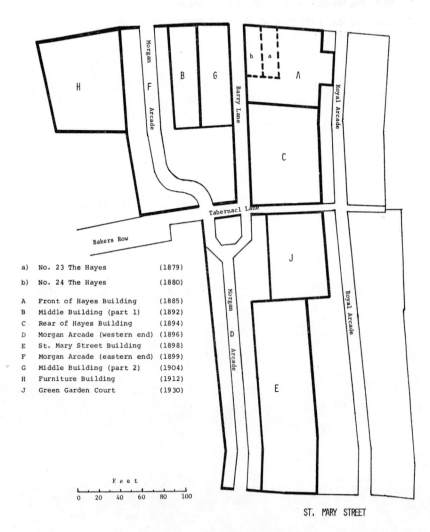

a) No. 23 The Hayes   (1879)

b) No. 24 The Hayes   (1880)

A   Front of Hayes Building   (1885)
B   Middle Building (part 1)   (1892)
C   Rear of Hayes Building   (1894)
D   Morgan Arcade (western end) (1896)
E   St. Mary Street Building   (1898)
F   Morgan Arcade (eastern end) (1899)
G   Middle Building (part 2)   (1904)
H   Furniture Building   (1912)
J   Green Garden Court   (1930)

ST. MARY STREET

PLAN OF DAVID MORGAN LIMITED

showing dates of main buildings

16. The Education of Jack

During his long life David Morgan repeatedly showed his strong belief in the value of education. Conscious of the inadequacy of his schooling at Cradoc, which ceased when he was fourteen, he strove constantly to improve his knowledge. One of the first purchases he made, other than goods for his business at Cwm Shon Mathew Square, was a *History of England*, which came in instalments. To this he added a map of the British Isles. His niece May Morgan Brummitt remembered him when he was well on in years reading the *Encyclopedia Britannica* to enlarge his knowledge.

When it came to the education of his son, his personal view of the importance of a good education was reinforced by the never-to-be-forgotten influence of Margaret, who had received a far better education than David. It would be an essential part of the trust she had left with him that he should make sure Jack had as good an education as possible.

Fortunately young Jack early showed a taste for scholarship and was a good pupil at Schulebrooks School[1], Cardiff. As evidence of this there exists an honour certificate from the University of Cambridge dated 1884 when Jack was fifteen:

> This is to certify that John Llewellyn Morgan
> of 23 The Hayes, Cardiff
> Son of David Morgan
> Index Number 620   age fifteen
> Was examined at Cardiff in December 1884 and
> passed the examination for Junior Students prescribed
> by the Regulations of the Syndicate for
> conducting the examination of students not
> members of the University and attained to the
> Second Class in Honours.
> The following were the subjects in which the
> above-named student satisfied the examiners:
>
> I   Subjects of Preliminary Examination
>
> > (1) Reading aloud from an English Prose Author
> >
> > (2) Writing from dictation
> >
> > (3) Rudiments of English Grammar
> >
> > (4) Elementary Arithmetic

II Subjects selected by Student. Five in number.

    Religious Knowledge

    Latin

    Mathematics

    Freehand Model Drawing

    History, Geography and Shakespeare

in the last of which he was distinguished.

It was not surprising that the young examinee chose mathematics as one of his free choice subjects. All his life he showed an unusual grasp of figures. With surprising quickness he could read a balance sheet and extract its strength or weakness; he could add up mentally and simultaneously four columns of figures. He would irritate his eldest son, Bernard, at board meetings by producing the answer to some problem in a few moments of thought, leaving Bernard to work it out on paper or with slide rule, only to find that his father had mentally calculated the sum to within but a fraction of the figure computed to a greater degree of accuracy, yet more laboriously, by Bernard.

Yet it was not in this that he was considered " distinguished ", but in history, geography and Shakespeare, much less precise areas of knowledge than mathematics. He had a natural taste for history, especially that of a local nature. With more application he could have made himself a good antiquarian. The books he read were always of substance, and as a schoolboy he would have read the plays of Shakespeare with pleasure. In the memory of his children he never displayed any skill that would suggest he would choose as one of the five subjects freehand model drawing. There was in the family's old private dining room in The Hayes a presentable copy of a Landseer drawing of a Scottish wolfhound done by Jack when he was a schoolboy, hung there no doubt by his father in a moment of paternal pride.

The record continues, and gives every indication that he was improving as a scholar:

July 28th, 1886

University of London

This is to certify that John Morgan matriculated as a student
in the University of London at the June Examination in 1886
and that he was placed in the

FIRST DIVISION

This academic distinction was a far cry from the rudimentary teaching of the schoolroom over the smithy at Cradoc. It would have given his father great satisfaction and it was what Margaret would have wanted.

After this certificate placing Jack in the first division, something happened. His intellectual appetite was satisfied. In 1888 he received the following certificate:

University of London

This is to certify that John Morgan passed the
Intermediate Examination for the Degree of
Bachelor of Arts in the year 1888.[2]

No marks of distinction here.

There is considerable evidence of his father's dissatisfaction. A letter was received, maybe from Jack's tutor, calling attention to his lack of effort, expressing disappointment in his failure to maintain his previous standards of scholarship and a hint that, unless matters improved, he might not achieve his final degree. His father took Jack away from the University, and he was sent to Llanbrynean to take a correspondence course and told to get on with it. May Brummitt remembered the time when this happened and recalled that, while Jack was a voracious reader and was never without a book in his hand, she never saw a work book opened. That David Morgan was angered by this waste of opportunity there can be no doubt. His brother, William, told of taking David and Jack in the trap. The journey was spent by David Morgan delivering a fierce lecture rebuking his son for his laziness. When William told this to his family he said that David was so unsparing of his son that he, William, felt very sorry for poor Jack.

Unfortunately there is no record available[3] of Jack taking a final examination at the University of London.

Besides his lack of application, there was another cause for Jack's decline in academic achievement. Like many another student coming from the strict confines of his home, he had found a new sense of liberty, the opportunity to seek the more pleasurable aspects of university life. He had discovered the attraction of the opposite sex and " sported with Amaryllis in the shade ". His intentions were serious and honourable. He wished to become engaged to a girl in London. Greatly daring, he asked his father's permission. David Morgan told his son that if he were ten years older he would not object, but at that time his objection was total and absolute, adding that he had not married again because he did not want to bring to his son a stepmother[4].

Possibly to remove Jack from this folly, David Morgan sent him to study at the Sorbonne in Paris, where he lived with a French family. No matter what the reason, this was a surprising move for David Morgan to make. One cannot help but wonder if it was not again the result of the Trump influence. Miss Croft, who became Mrs. Trump, had taken a great interest in her friend Margaret's son. Jack had become a good friend of the Trump boys. It is not without interest that their father, the general manager of the Rhymney Iron and Steel Works, had a talent unlikely to be found in most ironmasters, an ability to speak and write French[5]. As possible confirmation of this theory that the Trumps had persuaded David Morgan to send Jack to France, there was found in Mrs. Trump's family album a photograph of Jack taken in Paris.

Jack told May that at one time he had hoped to become a barrister.

111

Whatever the plans may have been for Jack to enter some field other than the business[6], his father was too keen a judge of character not to perceive that he was in danger of bringing up his heir as a dilettante. He therefore decided to keep him under his eye by putting him into the business. But first Jack was sent to do his apprenticeship in a big drapery shop in Sauchiehall Street, Glasgow. On completing his apprenticeship he returned to The Hayes and began to take an active part under his father in the management of the business.

The only story the Morgan children knew of their parents' romance was the one told to Margaret Morgan by Mrs. Henry Gethin Lewis of Porthkerry in the drawing room at Brynderwen. It was her own account of the first meeting of Jack and Edith. Nathaniel Jones of Danyrallt had come to Llandrindod Wells for a holiday with his daughter Edith, then aged about twenty. " In their hotel was another family named Llewellyn, with a daughter about Edith's age. The girls became friends and Annie Llewellyn told Edith that her fiancé, Henry Gethin Lewis, was coming up from Cardiff. Henry arrived, and of course called upon his fiancée, Miss Llewellyn, and her parents, and was introduced to Mr. Jones and his daughter at that time. Henry either knew or found out that his friend Jack Morgan was also at Llandrindod Wells, or perhaps met him in the town. Jack was staying at another hotel with his father, David Morgan. Games of croquet and strolls in Rock Creek Park took place. The young couples used to split up on the narrow path, and the fiancées were allowed to go a little ahead ". Mrs. Lewis of Porthkerry said to Margaret Morgan: " We never gave it a thought until one day we got to the end of the path without them catching us up, and when we turned back, we found Jack and Edith on our seat ".

When Jack had come to his father previously to ask about the possibility of becoming engaged to a girl whom he had met in London, David Morgan absolutely refused to give his consent, saying he would not however interfere if Jack were older. There was no objection in the case of Edith; indeed, there was approval.

Edith and Jack were married at Llangadock Parish Church on 7 August 1898. Jack asked his best friend, James Hall, to be his best man. The marriage of the only son and heir of one of the outstanding drapers in South Wales, who was described in the local newspaper as " a draper in a big way of business ", and the daughter of one of the most eminent farmers in the rich agricultural land through which the river Towy flows was an event of some importance in that locality. The description of the marriage in the local newspaper reveals that the importance of the occasion was fully recognised: " fusillades were fired from an early hour " and " triumphant arches spanned the route from the bride's home to the church ". In the eyes of David Morgan the education of Jack had been completed, and he was now in good hands.

1 Schulebrooks School, named after its headmaster, became Monkton House School.

2 There is a cutting from a Brecon paper in James Hall's scrapbook, date and origin unknown. " Llanfrynach. We are pleased to hear that Mr. John

Jan 5th 1881

Stock Taking

1st year of two months trading
at 23 & 24 The Hayes Cardiff

Dr. To D. Morgan —
for Cash & Goods but into the
Business 1559 11 5
To Trade Creditors 2577 17 9
Rent Taxes Gas
Salaries &c owing 200 9 3
£4337 18 5

By Goods in Stock 3649 19 1
Book debts (Club Books) 49 0 4
for Alterations .... 96 7 .
Fixtures & Fittings 129 14 4
Furniture Fittings 67 4 2
3992 19 11
loss on trading 344 18 6
£4337 18 5

There was the sum of 157. 18. 5 paid for
repairs of premises which were let.
Leased from Serg't. Hopkins for 13 years
from Sep 1. 1879 at £180. per annum
when taken they were in a filthy & dirty
condition.

David Morgan's Accounts for the first fourteen months' trading at The Hayes.

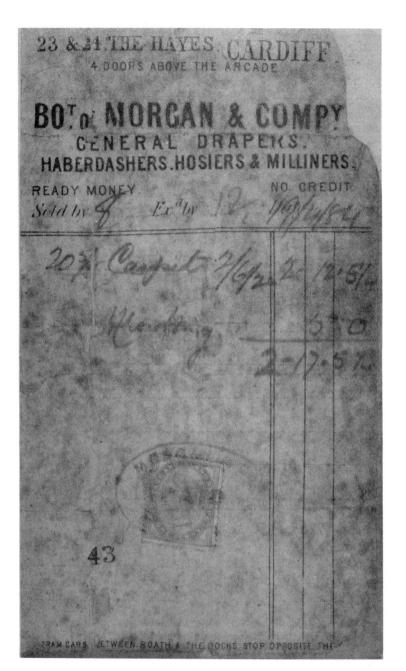

Bill Heading 1884, made out by Mr. Watkeys Morgan who served with the
Company 1880-1954.

MORGAN & CO., Drapers, The Hayes, CARDIFF.

Date _Feb 19th 1895_

Name _John Nicholas_ _left Mar 4. 1896 for B. Evans & Co Swansea_

Age _24_

Name of Parents _Job Nicholas_

Residence _Norchard, Boulston, Haverfordwest_

Last Situation _Greenish & Dawkins_

How long there _3 Years_

Previous Situation _Abram Thomas   Warwick House Brecon_

How long there _12 months_

Cause of leaving _for change_

Salary agreed to _£40_

I hereby agree to give Messrs. Morgan & Company _Fourteen_ days notice before leaving their service or forfeit _Fourteen_ days of my then salary, and will accept from Messrs. Morgan & Company _Fourteen_ days notice to leave their employ or _Fourteen_ days salary in lieu of notice, but should I violate any of the Rules of the House, I hereby agree to leave without notice or salary in lieu of notice.

Signed this _19th_ day of _Feb. 1895_

John Nicholas   _Morgan & Co_

Witness _Richd Howells_

Service Contract 1895.

Bryn Taff, Llandaff: home of David Morgan.

Brynderwen, Llandaff: home of John Llewellyn Morgan.

L. Morgan, son of Mr. David Morgan of Cardiff and Llanbrynean, has successfully passed the Intermediate examination for the degree of B.A. of the University of London. He is now a student of the University College, London."

3 The records relating to this period were all destroyed as a result of bombing during World War II.

4 This episode told me by May Brummitt.

5 Tom Jones, *Rhymney Memories.*

6 According to members of the Hall family it had been understood that Jack was not intended for the business.

17.   Life at Bryn Taff[1]

For thirty-five years, except possibly for the short time he lived in Edgecumbe House, David Morgan lived over his shops. His home life was part and parcel of his business. He was the proprietor in residence, responsible for the housing, feeding and discipline of his staff. His rectitude and self-discipline were conscious efforts to set an example which he expected his staff to follow. Surrounded by the problems of his business, he sought no diversion, friendship or activity which might conflict with his set purpose of developing, expanding and building. As a widower he led a lonely and austere life. Living in a business which employed many women, he maintained a reputation for respectability strong enough to withstand the slightest gossip.

The move in 1893 from The Hayes to a home of his own was a great change. One of the reasons David Morgan made this change in his way of life may well have been his desire to have a home for his son. Over the shop would not be much of a place for a youth to grow into manhood. David's brother James undoubtedly felt that his brother should maintain a home worthy of his position, so it was very much with James' approval that he carried out David's instructions and bought Bryn Taff, a sizeable house in Llandaff Place on the Cardiff Road, in an excellent position facing Howell's School at the front and overlooking the parklike open space of Llandaff Fields at the back.

David complained that James had bought him a castle and asked what was he going to do with so big a house[1a]. Circumstance created the opportunity to enlarge his household. David had promised his brother William that he would pay for the education of William's children. In 1893 when it came the turn of May, the youngest, David proposed sending her to Howell's School as a day girl and having her live at Bryn Taff, rather than sending her as a boarder. He had always shown great affection for May. At Llanbrynean he would insist that she bring his breakfast tray to his room and stay and talk with him while he had breakfast. She had curly hair and he used to spend time brushing it because he did not like curls and hoped thereby to remove them. May knew that he greatly admired her and, in later years, used to say that he fell a victim to flattery very easily.

Before she entered Howell's School he showed his fatherly concern for her by taking her to watch the girls arrive at the school in the morning so that she would get accustomed to the idea of going to school. He bought her clothes at The Hayes. Her mother complained that when May came home she was too expensively dressed for her age. David Morgan replied: " She is only dressed in the manner and fashion of girls of her station ". He sent her to dancing school, doubtless with the customary belief that not only would it add to her social graces, but also to her carriage and posture.

The next year, 1894, when James Hall, the son of David's sister Jane, returned to the firm of solicitors of James Morgan & Co. after a seven-year illness due to a disease of the hip bone, his Uncle David asked him if he also would like to come to live at Bryn Taff. As the result of James' long illness his hip joint was so affected that his left leg was shorter than his right and he had to wear a lift in his left boot; he walked with a pronounced limp and always carried a walking stick.

David Morgan now had some of the family life that might have been his if his wife had lived. Because of her early death and being by nature a lonely man, he was not easily given to friendship; but the presence of the three young people, Jack, James and May, gave him that feeling of family around him which he had previously lacked. James and Jack had their twenty-fifth birthdays in 1894, the year James came to live at Bryn Taff; May was twelve and David sixty-one.

It was good for Jack to have two cousins in the household to make up for the fact that he was an only child, but in some ways the cousins were competitors with him for the affection of his father. James Hall's mind was nourished by a very wide knowledge of English literature due to his reading during the seven years he was an invalid at home. He also had a good bass voice. He sang in the Eisteddfod Choir when the National Eisteddfod was held in Cardiff. James carefully corrected any Welsh idioms that May might use and supported their Uncle David in his efforts to ensure that she spoke grammatical English, without any trace of that Welsh accent that would mark her the moment she spoke.

Reminiscing of the time she spent in Bryn Taff, May said "Uncle David held James Hall's trained legal mind in some respect. Jim could stand up to him in discussion and Uncle knew it. Not so Jack; he could not stand up for himself". It was to James Hall that David Morgan turned for help with his private correspondence when he exchanged letters with his brother William at Llanbrynean about matters dealing with the Breconshire Estate. From the correspondence of James Hall and the comments of May and of her sister Kate, who was responsible for the letters that went from her father, William, to Bryn Taff, it appears that James Hall played much more the role of a son than Jack, who left Bryn Taff after his marriage.

May felt that Jack resented her presence at Bryn Taff. James and Jack played tennis with her on the lawn, and James greatly encouraged her as a tennis player, teaching her to volley, an unusual stroke for a woman at that time. May became a very good tennis player; she recalled that when she came up on Prize-giving Day to receive the tennis prize at Howell's School, the face of her Uncle David who was seated amongst the Governors of the School lit up with a proud smile.

Visitors to Bryn Taff were few and rare. Hospitality was of a very sparse nature. The main meal of the day was lunch, taken at The Hayes, with breakfast and supper being served at Bryn Taff. James Hall and Jack lunched at The Hayes with David Morgan in his private dining room. When May was on a school holiday she would join them for lunch. She noticed that her uncle could not resist the temptation of pork; when the waitress came in with the menu and David Morgan found that pork was on it, he invariably ordered it. The results were always the same: the pork would immediately give him an attack of indigestion which caused him to go red in the face, and he would undo his waistcoat and rub his stomach, indicating that it was a painful experience. This was always followed by a severe attack of asthma, but these painful experiences never cured him of his insatiable desire for pork. Jack was nearly always late for lunch, and when he came in he would say: "Has anybody rang for the waitress?" James Hall would correct him each time, saying "The word is rung, not rang". But Jack never seemed to learn the lesson.

They would all return to Bryn Taff for supper, which consisted of bread and butter, jam, egg and some cheese. James Hall would have a bottle of beer, which would not appear in the household accounts because he had to pay for it out of his own money. Menus had little variety. When Mr. Duncan, the well-to-do shipowner who lived next door at Oaklands, came in to see David Morgan on some matter he would often come at suppertime. May felt his sidelong glances at the table indicated his astonishment at the poverty of the fare. Occasionally a goose would come from Llanbrynean, and this David Morgan relished. It was as much a favourite with him as pork.

There was at Bryn Taff a regular weekly survey of household accounts and expenditure, which kept the housekeeper in line. At times the housekeeper gave them bread and butter pudding. One day David Morgan expressed to her his pleasure at such an economical dish which used up the stale bread and any milk that was left over. She protested, saying: "You have never had stale bread for your bread and butter pudding; I use only the best bread and butter for the ingredients!" He never again ordered bread and butter pudding. However, when he entertained the family from Brynderwen he made a very special effort to see that they were well and properly entertained, and even his grandsons with their schoolboy appetites did not leave his table hungry. But the economy and restricted menus were such that there was no leeway for unexpected guests.

One day Mr. and Mrs. Sankey[2], the previous owners of the house, came to call in the late afternoon. James Hall was instructed to show them round the house so they could see the changes. When Mrs. Sankey asked James where she could put her hat, he realised that they expected to stay for dinner. He slipped away from the guests and went downstairs to inform his uncle of the position. An unfortunate mishap had occurred; Jack had asked the Sankeys to come that evening to play billiards, and had forgotten to tell his father of the invitation. Jack had also forgotten the invitation and had not yet returned from business. May was doing some homework in the morning room when the news was broken to her uncle. He was so annoyed he jumped up and stamped his feet saying: "John this and John that"; May said it was always "John" when something went wrong. Such was his display of temper that she picked up her books of homework and slipped away from the

116

scene. " Poor Jack " did not hear the end of it for some days. (The guests had to be given tinned sardines.)

On special occasions such as David Morgan's birthday a really good spread was put upon the table, and to show that it was a feast day and a holiday, wine was served to the adults at dinner. It was nearly always red wine. David Morgan used to add hot water to his glass of wine, which he believed helped his digestion.

While he lived over the shop on The Hayes he attended Chapel, but when he moved to Bryn Taff he began to attend service at Llandaff Cathedral. Some of the formalities and affectations of the Church of England did not appeal to David Morgan. He took a particular dislike to the manner and voice of Archdeacon Bruce, to whom he used to refer as " Hee-ah Beginneth ", and he made a point of not attending the Cathedral service when the Archdeacon was expected to preach.

In a letter, Kate Morgan described an unusual occurrence on one Sunday when they went with their uncle to attend the Cathedral.

> On a Sunday afternoon, Uncle David, Jack Morgan and Jim Hall, on their way to service in Llandaff Cathedral, passed a man who did not speak to them[3]. A short distance away he met Annie Hall, Nan Hall and May Morgan, then a scholar of Howell's School. He asked Annie if Mr. Morgan lived there and said he had been asked to call. Annie knew Uncle had not asked him to call at Bryn Taff and directed him to Mr. Morgan, the Mount, the last house in the row. The party all went to the Cathedral. On their return Mrs. Parry, the housekeeper, met Uncle as usual to take his overcoat and hat. She said to him, ' I gave the man dinner, sir.' ' What man?' ' The man you told to call here, sir.' To which he said he had not told any man to call. Uncle was furious while everybody else were in fits of laughter, to think the religious old dame had been done. She said he gave thanks before and after his meal and Mrs. Parry was so sure that he was sincere, she gave him a 1/- as he left. As the old fellow rose from the table he said to Mrs. Parry and the maid, ' Thank Mr. Morgan & tell him I have had a good repast.' While the Church party was at tea, they were in fits of laughter, much to Uncle's annoyance.

According to Kate, when Edith heard this story years later she said it was worth recording.

When the time came for May to leave Howell's School, she decided that she would become a teacher; but because of the lack of further training she did not have the qualifications for the better positions. She found in 1899 an opening to teach in the lonely hill village of Upper Chapel in Breconshire. She did not tell her head mistress, Miss Kendall, because she knew that Miss Kendall would disapprove, feeling the appointment not worthy of a girl of Howell's School education. Neither did she dare tell her Uncle David, because she knew he would disapprove of her going away from Bryn Taff to live in this remote village. David Morgan learned of her plans from his brother, William, who met him in the trap at Talybont Station and on the journey to

Llanbrynean told him of May's plans. David never said another word to his brother until after they had reached Llanbrynean.

May saw little chance of promotion or better appointments and began to think of a career in nursing. She applied and was accepted for training at the Cardiff Infirmary in 1908. After she became a nurse she was summoned home to help take care of her brother, William, who was ill with typhoid fever, and she was isolated with him in one portion of the farmhouse. The doctor took it very calmly and said to the Morgan family: " Don't tell anybody about this or you will not be able to sell your milk and cream ". He was of the old school of medicine; when he came to examine his patient and May produced a bowl of water, soap and a towel so he could wash his hands, he was surprised and said " I suppose this is the latest thing from the Infirmary?"

After nursing William, May returned to the Cardiff Infirmary[4]. While working there she saw a great deal of her Uncle David and made a practice of having lunch with him at The Hayes when she had time off or was going to do some shopping for herself. She particularly remembered going to see him in his office at a time when she was wearing a new red skirt and short coat which she had just bought. He turned and looked at her and said: " I see you are wearing the latest fashion ". He always took an interest in the clothes she wore, and it seemed to her that he was fully aware of what was fashionable; which he should have been as a draper and clothier catering for the women's trade, though he did occasionally say that he made his money out of women's folly.

King Edward VII came to Cardiff in 1907 to open the Alexandra Dock and the Free Library; he was accompanied by Queen Alexandra and Princess Marie Louise. David Morgan, having received two tickets for ladies to accompany him to the ceremony, announced, " I am going to take my two favourite nieces " (Annie Hall and May Morgan).

May, with her lively charm and admiration of her uncle, had become an essential ingredient to his happiness. His very strong feelings of disappointment when she left Bryn Taff showed how much her presence meant to him. Mrs. William Morgan discussed May's future with her brother-in-law because he had paid for May's education, but David Morgan would not commit himself to any proposal. Mrs. Morgan got the impression that what he wanted was to have May be his housekeeper and therefore live permanently at Bryn Taff. However May's future plans were completely altered. A young Australian doctor, Bob Brummitt, came to study at the Cardiff Infirmary where he became assistant to Dr. Patterson. May became engaged to Bob Brummitt and they planned to go to Australia and make their home in Adelaide. David Morgan showed his displeasure on several occasions.

While waiting to be married and to leave for Australia, Dr. Brummitt stayed at Brynderwen with Jack and Edith. It was a custom of Edith Morgan's when she was going to Cardiff to walk to Glasses' mews on the Green in Llandaff and ride in the cab that was going to Bryn Taff to take David Morgan into Cardiff. One morning, taking Dr. Brummitt with her, Edith went to Glasses' to take the cab going to Bryn Taff and on to The Hayes. When David Morgan got into the cab and found Dr. Brummitt in it he turned on Edith and rebuked her severely for using his cab without his permission. Edith was completely surprised by his annoyance, because he usually welcomed her presence and appeared to enjoy being driven with her either in or out of Cardiff; but all she did was to look out of the window while her father-in-law voiced his displeasure.

Before leaving for Australia, May and Bob Brummitt went to Bryn Taff to say goodbye to her uncle of whom she was so fond. They were received very coldly at the front door and were not asked inside the house; the farewells were most formal. May was deeply distressed and longed to kiss her uncle on his cheek and say how grateful she was for all he had done for her. But so stern was his appearance that she was unable to say " thank you ". When May left for Australia in 1912, some of the life and gaiety that she had brought to Bryn Taff left with her.

David Morgan was very proud of the success of his niece Agnes in her training as a nurse and, when she graduated first of her class at the Bristol Hospital, he sent her an endearing and revealing letter :

The Hayes   Nov. 12th, 1912

My dear Agnes

I was very pleased to read in the Bristol paper which you kindly sent me, the proud position you stood in the prize list of your Hospital, particularly that a Welsh girl, whom I know the proud people of your city look down on we folks this side of the channel, should head the list. Many years ago I heard a Scotsman say that with the advance of education the Welsh people were the nation they would compete with. I hope that you sent a paper to May in Adelaide she will be quite interested—I was very sorry that I was not at home when you were here. When you are coming next I shall be pleased if you will select one or two evening dresses, possibly they may be useful when you go nursing some family where they dress for dinner. I shall be glad if you can run over soon. I will pay your train fare—trusting to see you soon, drop a P-card a day or two before.

Yours sincerely   David Morgan.

His feeling about the attitude of the English people towards the Welsh may have had something to do with his effort to see that May spoke English as he did, without a Welsh accent.

At the end of her career as a nurse Agnes became Matron   of Mountain Ash Hospital, a hospital financed and administered by the Miners' Welfare. Agnes' success gained her considerable fame and admiration not only among her patients but also the trades union officials who sat on the hospital board.

When David Morgan took a holiday he tended to go to one of the spas: Droitwitch, Leamington, Matlock, Church Stretton, Harrogate, or Tunbridge Wells. He generally took a companion with him; fre-

119

quently James Hall, sometimes James' sister, Rie Hall; included in the holiday would be outings to nearby historic places—castles, abbeys and old parish churches. As the grandchildren got older he went to seaside resorts, Weston-Super-Mare, Cromer and Margate, probably because he was giving the holiday to his son and daughter-in-law and their family.

There is the famous family story of the occasion when, on a visit to Tunbridge Wells, David Morgan and a friend, Mr. Williams of Cilgwyn, who was going with him, missed connections at Cardiff. The story appeared in full in the *Western Mail* much to the annoyance of David Morgan, and could only have been the result of his son telling the story to somebody on the *Western Mail*.

> An excellent holiday story concerning a well known Cardiff tradesman and a friend has just reached us. The two arranged to go to Tunbridge Wells by the 9:58 train on Saturday morning. The cab was longer on the way than was expected, and at the station it was a scramble. The tradesman secured his ticket and got into the train, but the friend lost the latter by just two seconds. Feeling certain his friend would follow by the 10:10 train, the tradesman got out at Newport to wait for him. When the train arrived a hurried examination failed to discover the friend, but the tradesman, little doubting that he was somewhere in the train, got in and reached Paddington at 2:40 and looked round. In the meantime the friend who was left at Cardiff had been informed that the boat train which was about leaving would take him to Paddington by two o'clock, so he travelled by that train, which does not stop at Newport. Disappointed not to find the tradesman on Paddington platform, and concluding he had gone to lunch and then on to Tunbridge Wells, the friend did likewise. Had he waited a few minutes longer the 2:40 train and the tradesman would have appeared on the scene. That poor gentleman, however, arriving later, hung about Paddington till six o'clock, and then, in much natural irritation, he went on to Tunbridge Wells. On Monday a son of the tradesman received two letters from Tunbridge Wells. One was from the tradesman and the other from the friend, each inquiring the whereabouts of the other. Telegrams were despatched, and the tradesman went down to his friend's hotel and asked for him. 'He has just gone out', was the reply; 'will you take a seat until he returns?' Exactly the same thing happened at the other hotel, whither the friend had gone to inquire for the tradesman. Each waited in the wrong hotel for a long time, and then, getting tired, went out and met at last at one o'clock on Monday. The curious thing is that the two hotels are close together, so that the two friends were only a few dozen yards apart from Saturday night till Monday noon. Sunday they spent roaming round the town in the hope of meeting each other. This is a true story, and was not devoid of anxiety, for the tradesman on Saturday night wired home to ask 'Where is Williams?' a question which remained a mystery till the two letters arrived on Monday morning.

Jack left Bryn Taff when he married in 1898 and made his home at Bryn Teilo, a house also in Llandaff Place on the Cardiff Road, only a short walk from Bryn Taff.

David Morgan had another experience of family life when his son, daughter-in-law and three grandchildren (Bernard, Aubrey and Trevil) came to stay at Bryn Taff after Bryn Teilo had been sold and while alterations at Brynderwen were being carried out. Bernard spent only the holidays at Bryn Taff because he was at this time a boarder at Llandaff Cathedral School. The entry of the grandsons in Llandaff Cathedral School was a continuation of the firm belief in the importance of good education which had been transmitted to Jack. It was also an indication of the change which was coming over the social position of the Morgan family after the move from the shop. Mrs. Davenport, a friend of J. T. Duncan, a neighbour of David Morgan's, made a very Victorian comment[5] when she expressed surprise that the son of a tradesman had been admitted to the Cathedral School, which was mainly recruited from the sons of clergymen and other professional men.

Aubrey and Trevil were bathed by their nurse in their grandfather's bathroom in a copious copper bathtub and dried off with some unforgettably rough towels, which looked and felt as if they were woven out of copper wire. David Morgan believed firmly in the vigorous use of these towels to stimulate the circulation. Also in the bathroom was what was called a Turkish bath—a wooden case with an opening of two half circles at the top in the centre, making a circular hole through which one put one's neck and head. Inside was a method of heating a tub of water so that it steamed. The boys were too small to be allowed to indulge in this exciting adventure.

For the two small boys one of the more interesting events of the day was to go and see their grandfather get dressed in the morning. He would be in his underclothing, woollen vest and long-legged pants of oatmeal colour. He would pull over the long-legged pants a pair of knitted stockings up over his knees and tie red tapes below his knees to hold them up. They were heavy stockings of the type working men up the valleys used to wear. Over his woollen vest he wore a striped Welsh flannel shirt, famous for their long-wearing capacity. Attached to the sleeves were a pair of stiff-starched linen cuffs held on by a pair of cuff links, and at the collar of his shirt he attached a starched dickey, which covered the area of his shirt exposed by the opening at the top of his waistcoat. Then came the high point of the performance—the attaching of the collar which folded round his neck without any visible opening, as shown in the portrait. Because the collar fitted so tightly it was an immense struggle for him to get it to meet over the dickey onto the bone-front stud. So strenuous were his contortions and so frequent the asthmatic gasps and coughs that the little boys would wonder whether success was possible, but eventually the great task was accomplished and he would sink down exhausted into his chair. Before putting on his well-polished and substantial boots, which looked more suitable for walking in the country than in the shop, he would get into a heavy woollen suit. When James Hall was asked by the small boys "Why does Grandfather wear such tight collars?" he replied: "Be-

121

cause he believes they help to keep the draught out ". The many layers of heavy clothing were like walls of a fortress built to keep out that ever-present enemy, draughts.

Except for the cuff links for the attachment of the cuffs, he wore no personal jewellery other than a gold watch and chain[6], which had been presented to him by some of his assistants at Pontlottyn. He disliked the use of jewellery. One day he saw May wearing a silver bangle that her parents had given her. " What is that you are wearing on your wrist? You will be wearing a ring in your nose next! " But this attitude toward self-adornment was not maintained in the lifetime of Margaret Llewellyn, who can be seen in her photographs wearing earrings and a gold chain around her neck. Had she lived longer, she would have introduced many more exceptions to the austere rules by which David Morgan governed his life.

James Hall left Bryn Taff shortly after David Morgan's death because the house had been left under the will to the eldest grandson, Bernard. For some years the house was let, but when Bernard married Mary Walker in 1931 they moved into the house, and it was here that their three sons were born. When World War II came with rationing and bombing, Bernard moved his family into Penybont at Pencelli. Bernard, as head of the Fire Watching Organisation for the centre of Cardiff, remained in Cardiff and lived the greater part of the time at Brynderwen. Next door was a Civil Defence Headquarters in the Court, once the home of George Insole.

Under war conditions the Post Office, seeking some accommodation away from the centre of Cardiff, took over Bryn Taff. After the war, Bernard sold Bryn Taff to Howell's School. The headmistress of the school at that time was Margaret Llewellyn Lewis, granddaughter of Mrs. Gething Lewis, the sister of Margaret Morgan, after whom Margaret Lewis had been named. If the family connection was to cease and the purposes of the will of David Morgan were to be altered, it was appropriate that Bryn Taff should become the property of Howell's School, of which David Morgan had been proud to be a Governor.

1   Many of the details in this chapter were given me by May Brummitt, who retained a very clear and vivid memory of her youth, which she spent mainly at Bryn Taff. She was almost as much brought up by her Uncle David as she was by her own parents. On the day of her ninetieth birthday she spoke to me of her deep affection for her Uncle David, and his kindness and generosity to her.

1a Bryn Taff was a three-storey house. On the ground floor were a hall, drawing room, morning room, dining room, kitchens and pantries; on the mezzanine floor an entrance to a billiards room and bathroom etc.; on the first floor five bedrooms; on the top floor three rooms for servants, who included a housekeeper-cook and a maid. This description was given by Mary Morgan, Bernard's wife, who lived in Bryn Taff at the start of her married life.

2   Father and mother of the first Labour Party Lord Chancellor.

3   As told by Kate Morgan.

4 This is May's record:

1899-1901   Taught at Upper Chapel

1901-1907   Taught at Pontfaen.

1908-1911   Royal Infirmary, Cardiff
Went to London to be Senior Surgical Sister at Sir Victor Horseley's Hospital, which was a surgical nursing home. Sir Victor was the outstanding neurosurgeon (or brain specialist as it was then called) of that time.

1912   Married and left for Australia.

5 Source of this story, May Brummitt.

6 This watch is now the property of his great-great-grandson, David George Oxford Morgan, and has inscribed on it:

MR. DAVID MORGAN
from a few late employ'es
as a slight memento of their
RESPECT AND GRATITUDE
1875

18. The Shop

In reply to your enquiry I am not disposed to sell this
business as within the last ten years I have entirely rebuilt
these premises and the trade is a ready money one and
gives me more pleasure than trouble.

David Morgan
July 16th, 1895

The shop was David Morgan. Created out of the bedrock of his
character and the formative experiences of his youth, it was the visible
projection of his personality.

If the weft of his character was honesty, frugality was its warp. To
be thrifty, to be prudent, to save, were a constellation of high virtues
in the eyes of the Victorians. Brought up on an impoverished hill farm
where all commodities were scarce and money was the scarcest, and
descended from generations of poverty, David Morgan had bred
into him and in his early youth driven into him by his mother a sense
of the utmost necessity of frugality for survival, let alone progress in
the world. His background and boyhood made David Morgan aware not
only that every penny counted, but also how difficult it was to acquire
a penny. Soon after he was apprenticed to a Newport draper at the age
of fourteen, he must have realised that if he was going to free himself
of poverty and satisfy any ambition of setting up shop for himself he
must with vigorous self-discipline save every penny he could. It was
said of him that when he was a shop assistant he starved himself to
save money[1]; for he refused to supplement the inadequate meals of
the "living-in" supplied as part of his wage by his employers.

Leonard Woolf in his autobiography wrote that "the road to the Bankruptcy Court is paved with what the accountants call overheads". From
the first day David Morgan set up shop for himself in 1858 in Cwm
Shon Mathew Square Rhymney, he took every possible precaution to
prevent overheads leading him to that court of ignominy and despair.
He made the control of business expenses into a fine art. John Price,
a long-time admirer[2], said of him: "It was not so much what he made
as what he saved". He watched with almost religious fervour for every
possible loophole for waste or unnecessary expense. As with his shop,
so with his personal expenses. Looking back over his life he told his
nephew William Morgan of Llanbrynean: "I have made money because my wants are few".

David Morgan saw to it that his staff practised what he preached.
Every piece of paper, every bit of string, every pin that came into the
shop had to be saved for further use. Any unnecessary use of artificial
light had to be avoided. If the evil of waste was to be successfully
combatted, the assistants would have to be put constantly on their
guard.

His policy for doing business was simple, brief and forthright: " One price, plain figures, no discounts ", to which could be added no bargain sales and no advertisements. Today the first three planks of his policy would seem to be totally unexceptional. During most of David Morgan's lifetime they were so unusual as to gain for him a remarkable and invaluable reputation of honesty and fairdealing. Discounts were given to certain groups of customers who made large cash purchases, such as dressmakers. There was also another form of discount which customers took for themselves by omitting from their cheques the odd pence and in some cases even the odd shillings when settling their bills.

David Morgan set his face sternly against all such practices. In his shop the customer would see the price of the goods marked in plain figures on the attached ticket. The marked price was the only price and it soon became accepted that there could be no bargaining in Morgan & Co., that the marked price was the price for rich or poor, for large or small customer, without any discount being allowed at the time of purchase or later. This simple, but most unusual policy, was maintained against the current practices of the drapery trade because David Morgan by constant observation assured himself that his policy was understood and obeyed.

He told his niece May that ever since he had started on his own in business he had made it a rule to make as little profit as possible on every article he sold. To carry out such a policy and still make enough profit to ensure the success of his business needed sound judgement. The corollary of this policy was the need for maintaining a quick turn-over of his stock if the amount of the mark-up was to be kept to a minimum. His zeal for keeping down the costs of doing business became so well known that it reinforced his reputation for good value at low prices. A number of stories of his care of the pence lived on after him.

The deep concern and careful watch for every form of saving was the hallmark of the training he instilled into his apprentices and assistants, many of whom went on to build their own businesses. How well these men remembered the precepts and example of their master was revealed to Aubrey in a chance encounter on the London express when on his way back to school at Charterhouse. At Newport a man got into the compartment. After looking the boy over for a short time he asked him if he was one of "the Morgans The Hayes". After some comments about what a remarkable man David Morgan was and how fortunate he was to have learnt his trade under him, the man gave the following example of David Morgan's training.

One day when David Morgan, as was his frequent custom, was sitting on a counter chair watching what was going on in the piece goods department, where materials were sold by the yard, a customer came up to this man, then a shop assistant, and asked to be shown some material to make a dress. When she had made her choice and stated the yardage required, he unrolled the bolt of cloth and measured out the amount with his yard stick. Finding he had forgotten his scissors, he borrowed his neighbour's with which to cut off the required length;

then pulling out from his drawer under the counter the topmost piece of paper stored there and taking the first length off his ball of saved string which every assistant kept, he wrapped the paper round the parcel several times, tied it with the string and handed the parcel to the customer. At that moment he found David Morgan standing alongside the customer. Excusing himself, David Morgan took the parcel from the lady. He untied and unwrapped the parcel, smoothed out the paper and asked the assistant for his scissors (the act of borrowing had not gone unnoticed); the assistant had to admit he was without them. " No scissors, no draper " said David Morgan, and, producing his own, he cut the sheet of paper in half. He next asked the assistant for his ball of string, unwound some of it, and, after careful inspection, chose a suitable length; he untied the knot at each end of the length, tied the ball of string together again, and with the short length of string he tied up the parcel. Handing it to the customer, he thanked her for waiting. As she left he said to the assistant: " You see, I do business at fifty per cent less than you do ". " It was a lesson I never forgot " the man added.

If, on his way through a department, David Morgan saw a shop hand pick up a piece of string or a pin he would commend him with the words: " That's the way I built my business ". The importance of saving pins and string was very real to David Morgan all his life. He frequently reminded people that "A pin saved is money made " and " You'll never be rich if you cut string ".

His firm refusal to allow discounts was logically based on his practice of selling his merchandise at the lowest possible profit. The marked price was the minimum at which it could be fairly and profitably sold; hence no discounts. He would not tolerate the omission of the odd pence or shillings when bills came to be paid. He insisted that the missing amounts should be transferred to the next month's account. Coming into the Counting House one day he picked up an account, together with the cheque settling it, from which the sum of five pence had been omitted. He recognised the name of the customer, Mr. Walter John of Penarth, whom he knew. He instructed the head of the Counting House, Richard Horwood, not to follow the usual practice of transferring the missing amount to the next month's account. He would settle the matter when next he met Mr. John. When he did, David Morgan went straight to the matter: " I understand Mr. John, that you and my Counting House have been having a difference of opinion. Let us get this quite straight. Have I been overcharging you or do you owe me five pence?"[3]

Whenever Mr. Walter John told this and similar stories to members of the Morgan family, which he frequently did, he would always express his unbounded admiration for the forthright way in which David Morgan did business.

When it came to dealing with his staff, David Morgan always had an outstanding reputation as a good employer. Careful though he was to see that every penny spent should bring in its maximum worth, he fully understood as a result of his own early experiences the importance of having his staff well-fed, well-housed and proud to be members of his establishment. He knew that the loyalty and devotion of his staff was an important factor in the creation of his business.

When he came to write his will he made bequests to nine employees who were remarkable for their devotion and long service. It was his tribute to this small band whom he must have looked upon as the best example of all he had attempted to achieve in training his staff. The first employee to be mentioned was Richard Horwood who, as head of the Counting House, was responsible for the granting of credit when that was introduced into the business. His judgement, based on long experience, must have saved David Morgan from the losses of bad debts. In the overall running of the business he was David Morgan's right-hand man.

As the business grew so did the Counting House, and with it the responsibilities of Mr. Horwood. He was responsible for the " hiring " and " firing " of staff and therefore all matters of discipline. The staff greatly respected him, knowing him to be a just man. He could be a stern man and, with a few perceptive and penetrating questions, reduce an offender to abject silence. Often his rebuke was enough, and the fear of a summons to his office was a healthy deterrent to slackness or breach of the rules.

The ability of Mr. Horwood to maintain good discipline was a great asset to David Morgan. By example and training, David Morgan set high standards for the staff alike in their personal conduct and business methods. But he was willing to use Mr. Horwood's bark, rather than impose his own discipline, for the maintenance of those standards. It would seem that, as long as the staff did their duty, their employer was prepared to turn a blind eye to healthy high spirits. One day David Morgan was coming down a dark stairway used by the shop assistants; the more lively, given to horseplay, would jump onto the backs of those preceding in the dark down this stairway. One assistant made the awful mistake of leaping onto the back of David Morgan. The identity of the victim being discovered, the whole stairway froze into motionless silence, awaiting the summary dismissal of so rash a youth. David Morgan, giving the young man a very stern look, said: " There are many wiser people than you in Abergavenny ". (Abergavenny was the main lunatic asylum for South Wales.) But no further judgement was made or punishment exacted.

The next employee to be mentioned in the will was John Watkeys Morgan, who, like David Morgan, was the son of a Breconshire farmer. When John Watkeys Morgan entered the business in 1880 he retained Watkeys as his shop name, and Mr. Watkeys he remained, inside and outside the shop, for the rest of his life. He served David Morgan in many capacities, from shop assistant to buyer of various departments. As the business grew, he took charge of all matters relating to supplies and services and was responsible for the receiving department, the parcel office and the delivery service. One of his daily duties during the lifetime of David Morgan was to count out the previous day's takings

127

in David Morgan's private office, which overlooked Barry Lane. The money was poured out of the marked bags of the various cashiers onto the top of a high flat-topped cabinet[4]. Here it was counted and checked against the cashiers' returns, and then sorted into the various denominations of coins, stacked into small piles of stipulated amounts, recorded and placed in paper bags with the amounts of the contents written on them; the paper bags were finally put into a large canvas bag. After David Morgan had scrutinised and approved the final tally on a sheet of paper, the canvas bag was taken by a porter, under Watkey's guardian eye, to Lloyds Bank in High Street.

This daily ritual would be performed behind the back of David Morgan, who, seated at his desk, sideways to the coal fire which always burned except in summer, would be doing his office work apparently heedless to the constant sound of money being poured onto the mahogany top, or the sliding noise of coins being counted, or the chink as they were being arranged in piles. But it must have been to his ears the sweetest of music.

Watkeys just failed to live long enough to complete seventy-four years in the business. His name was followed in the will by that of Hopkin Thomas Joseph, whose enthusiasm for Rugby football brought him to The Hayes after he was dismissed by James Howell for watching the famous 1905 match between Wales and New Zealand from the roof of Howell & Company. Howell's loss was David Morgan's gain, for H. T. Joseph's piece goods department brought many customers to David Morgan's shop and contributed very considerably to his profits. Joseph was a most successful buyer of silks and woollens and built the piece goods department into one of the most important departments in the business. He was also a master of the art of window dressing. He gained the reputation of being one of the biggest buyers of silk in the provinces.

Amongst the others mentioned was Thomas Gwynne Walters, a truly old-fashioned draper. He was known throughout the business as " Daddy " Walters. Trained in the complexities of haberdashery, the bread and butter of the drapers' trade in the days when ribbons and laces, buttons and trimmings and cotton thread played such an important part in the clothing women made for themselves, he became for many years David Morgan's haberdashery, glove and hosiery buyer. Staunch believer in the standards and the quality maintained by David Morgan, he was one of his trusted buyers. After his employer's death, great changes came over the world of fashion. Mr. Walters could not accept the new order of things. His attention was called one day to the lack of range in variety and colour in his stock of silk stockings by Jack Morgan, who was then head of the business. Mr. Walters pulled out a fine pair of woollen stockings and, running his hands through them, praised their quality and asked Mr. John to feel them, saying: "A woman would be foolish to buy a pair of silk stockings instead of these ". Unfortunately for Mr. Walters and David Morgan, Limited[5] his failure to understand the total change in fashion lost the firm its stocking trade, which had been such a strong section in the days of wool and lisle stockings.

Frank Rowlands was a source of great pride to David Morgan. He joined the staff in 1886. He left for two years to get experience in London at the great emporium of William Whitely. In 1894 David Morgan asked him to return to become buyer in the linen department, known as the Manchester department. Frank Rowlands was at that time twenty-eight, the youngest buyer to be appointed by David Morgan. He held the position with great success for fifty-four years. Because of the extraordinary length of time he held this position he was widely known throughout the trade. The great respect in which he was held was due not only to his proved ability but also to his honourable nature and innate courtesy.

Four other employees were mentioned in the will. They were not men who had risen to positions of authority, but David Morgan remembered them as men who, by their long and loyal service, had helped him to build his business. He would have spoken of them as reliable men, an expression of high commendation from him.

Jim Rees, a salesman in the furnishing department, had seen " Morgan's The Hayes " grow from almost its beginning. David Griffiths, whose shop name was Norman, had done likewise. When Norman died some years after David Morgan's death and after the store had been greatly modernised, his drawer under the counter was found full of carefully-folded pieces of packing paper and balls of string, no longer needed since the arrival of standard green packing paper, with the firm's insignia on it, and the issue of balls of green twine. Such had been the indoctrination by his master of the virtues of thrift that the habits of Norman's lifetime lasted until his death. George Atfield rose no higher than shopwalker, whose duties were to see that customers were attended to, to sign the sales check (which indicated that he had checked it for correctness) and to help keep the buyer informed about the movement of stock. Charles Davies spent his long service with David Morgan in the basement where he was the parcel office.

The appearance of the names of these four in David Morgan's will was his final tribute and act of gratitude for what their long service had done for him. The length of years they spent working for David Morgan was also a tribute to him. They were a few examples of his good judgement of men and his ability to find young men to fill posts of responsibility who never disappointed his belief in their ability. They were splendid examples of a large proportion of the staff who spent so many years working at " Morgan's The Hayes ". Miss Glasson, recalling her early experiences in the business, said that the really old employees were all so single-minded in their devotion to David Morgan's that they served as an example for the younger and newer employees to follow. His shop assistants had lived in close association with one another, proud to be his employees. They were treated by him as members of a big family.

Thirty-eight years after David Morgan's death a letter was published in the *South Wales Echo* on 23 October, 1957 from Mr. S. J. Goodman, who was employed at The Hayes from 1904 to 1913. Referring to an article in the *Echo* about David Morgan, Mr. Goodman said:

> I can endorse what Mr. Watkins says of David Morgan's Victorian self-discipline, prudence, forthrightness and uncompromising belief in honest and fair dealing.
>
> From the time he engaged me I never doubted his integrity when dealing either with his assistants or customers. Almost daily he passed through the shop at about 10 a.m. Sometimes he stopped to pick up a pin and bits of string which he handed to the nearest assistant remarking, 'Put those aside, you will need them. I made my business this way'. Sometimes he brought young Bernard with him—a fresh full-faced schoolboy all smiles with grey red-topped hose and school jacket.

As David Morgan walked through his shop his staff would watch him with admiration and awe. (His father-in-law, John Llewellyn, used to say he could always tell from the attitude of the staff when David was about in the shop.) They admired him as the man on whom they would model themselves when they owned their own shop, which was the aspiration of every shop assistant. His reputation for seeing everything, how they made their sales and conducted themselves with the customer, how the stock was handled and shown, gave his staff a deep respect for his all-seeing eyes.

In each section they were organised in a hierarchy based on seniority. When a customer came to the counter, she would always be served by the first hand; if the first hand was still busy, the next customer would be served by the most senior of the juniors; and only when all the juniors were attending customers was it possible for the apprentices to make sales. This order of precedence was jealously guarded because commissions were paid to the shop hands based on their total sales. Further encouragement to sell remnants, slow-moving or old stock was given by putting a small ticket with a marking which would indicate to the saleshand the special premium or " pref " to be given to the person who sold that particular item. The premium earned would be included in the commission paid with the monthly salary.

Miss Harnaman recalls that in the fabric department the senior women assistants used to have new suits made by the French tailor, Monsieur Mangeant. A favourite material for the suits was silk shantung. On an agreed date, they would all come out in their new suits. The ladies in the print and flannel room would have new blouses made by Monsieur Mangeant. There was great competition to have the smartest model.

A well-trained staff knew thoroughly the stock of the section or department and therefore would be able to offer a substitute if the customer's exact requirement was not in stock. It was a matter of pride that a customer should not leave the counter without a sale being made.

Behind the shop assistants, against the interior walls, were high fixtures for display and storage. Where there was no wall, the high fixtures

130

would take its place with wooden drawers for stock or open sections for bolts of cloth which were stacked up as high as an assistant could reach. After the death of David Morgan, his son Jack undertook the first great fundamental change of the interior of the shop by removing the thick interior walls.

Old hands recall the dressing out of the departments the first thing every morning. The goods were removed from display every night and carefully covered with wrappers. Also, long dust sheets were hung to cover the fixtures. The chairs were put on top of the counters so that the floor space would be clear for the cleaners in the morning[6].

When a customer came into the shop it was the duty of the shop assistant to discover what sort of merchandise interested the customer. Then the shop assistant would bring out a choice of merchandise from drawers, or in the case of piece goods the bolts of cloth from high fixtures, or coats and dresses from the cabinets in which they hung, and help the customer make her choice. Because of remoteness of the stock from the customer, this tended to be quite a lengthy operation and often the relationship between customer and shop assistant developed over a period of time into one of friendship and reliance. While this relationship still remains, the nature of the transaction has changed, because in the past so much of the merchandise was kept from the reach of the customers and often out of their sight. There were inevitably exceptions; for instance, carpet squares, rugs, oil cloth, linoleum and other forms of floor covering, and furniture. Although there was dressing-out on the lower fixtures and displays on stands in the aisles, the basic principle remained that the customer handled the merchandise in the presence of a shop assistant.

After the 1914-1918 war more and more goods were being brought forward into the departments, and not kept in distant stockrooms. The fixtures were reduced in height, glass was introduced into counters and the fixtures, the drawers were given glass fronts and spaces were made in the fixtures for display behind sliding glass doors. More and more merchandise was not only exposed to the view of the customers, but put within their reach to handle and inspect. The trend toward self-service had begun. The whole policy of how merchandise was to be presented to the customer was completely changed.

During most of David Morgan's life-time the shop windows were arranged to attract the customer by price and variety of stock. This resulted in the windows being cluttered with a wide range of stock, each with its price ticket, and in many cases resulted in the hideous practice of sticking small articles all over the inside of the windowpane. Gradually the art of window dressing evolved as a general design for a whole window, so that the first impact on the customers was the attractive nature of the display to arrest their attention by its novelty or beauty; when they had stopped to look at it they could notice the price tickets.

David Morgan was an excellent trainer of shop hands, judging by the success of his own business and by the number of his shop hands who went on to make a success of their own businesses. When the day came, as they hoped, for them to walk down their own shop between the counters they would remember the " Govnor " walking through his shop wearing a round-topped Homburg hat with no " bulges " in it, in his right hand a walking stick with an ebony handle and his left arm bent behind him across the small of his back.

He would often sit in a chair watching the transaction of business and sensing the pulse of the shop, which varied according to the days. Besides the regular bustle of a busy day, when the whole shop seemed to throb with activity, there would be the rich sounds of Welsh voices on a Thursday afternoon, which up the valleys was a half-day known as " shut shop day "; the slow calm of a Wednesday morning before the shop closed for Cardiff's half-day; the diminuendo of Friday with a sudden last hour's increase in the evening when wives came in with some of the money which had come home from the weekly pay packet, which was the preliminary to the all-important crescendo of Saturday, which ought to be the busiest day of the week. When he returned to his office he knew what sort of a day it had been, slow, busy or rushed, long before the cash of the day's takings was counted.

" Morgan's The Hayes " became recognised throughout South Wales as a store that had established its own individuality. It grew and expanded as departments logically developed the need for ancillary departments: linens into soft furnishing, soft furnishing into carpets, and carpets into furniture; but during David Morgan's control of the business it was basically a draper's and clothier's shop. He was a draper and resisted the concept of the shop being modernised into a retail department store.

From his account book it appears that he started on 31 October 1879 at Number 23 The Hayes single-handed, except for possibly one or two apprentices, who would receive no wages other than bed and board. The first salaried shop assistant, T. J. Thomas, is entered as arriving on 15 November, 1879, sixteen days after the shop was officially opened. He was followed by Miss Pritchard on 25 November, with a salary of £2-1-8 a month. At Christmastime these two were joined by Miss Williams. So by the end of the first two months the business consisted of David Morgan, three assistants and some apprentices. These people would all be engaged to " live-in ", but where they and their employer lived at that time is not known. Possibly, while the numbers were so small, the floor above the shop at Number 23 was used for the purpose.

From the very beginning provisions were entered into the accounts:

Oct. 28th, 1879	pd	provisions at Restaurant yesterday	6-0
	pd	George Hopkins this morning	3-11½
	pd	Ham & Eggs	8-9

and from that date on there were almost daily entries for provisions. From this evidence it can be seen that David Morgan was providing food for his staff. Because of the detailed purchases of butter, eggs, a quarter of mutton, beef, pork and suet, and so forth, the cooking must have been done on the premises. In May 1880 Edgecumbe House entered the accounts:

> 19th May, 1880 pd for gas fittings Window Rollers and Blinds in Edgecumbe House Wellington Terrace £6-12-6

> 4th June, 1880 pd H. Cohen for Painting and Papering Edgecumbe House £13-13-0.

Edgecumbe House was in Wellington Terrace at the far end of Bridge Street[7] from The Hayes. David Morgan took a lease to house his staff, and probably himself, in May of 1880 seven months after he had opened his shop on The Hayes. The bill for china for Edgecumbe House for £5-19-11 was paid on 21 July. Considering the level of prices in 1880, this must have represented a considerable amount of china, even though it most probably included china for the bedrooms as well as for breakfast and the supper table. The midday meal and tea would be provided at the shop.

Because his name was entered in the Roll of Burgesses of Cardiff in 1881 'and 1882 as having his abode in Wellington Terrace, the address of Edgecumbe House, it can be assumed that when the refurnishing of Edgecumbe House was completed David Morgan moved there until he included living quarters for himself in his first new building between Barry Lane and the Royal Arcade, which was completed in 1884. He continued to use the Wellington Terrace as his address until he moved to Bryn Taff in 1892. But his nieces Kate and May Morgan of Llanbrynean had very clear memories that, when visiting their Uncle in 1888 and later, they stayed with him over the shop[8]. The probable explanation is that having once entered his address in Wellington Terrace on the Rolls of Burgesses he did not trouble to change the entry until he sold Edgecumbe House at the time Bryn Taff was purchased[9].

By Christmas 1882 the names of eighteen people appeared on the salary list. Some of the names on it were to have a long connection with David Morgan. John Arnott Lewis and Thomas Samuel were relatives of David Morgan who, coming to him first as apprentices at Pontlottyn, became shop assistants there and then followed him to Cardiff. Both became successful drapers on their own account, Lewis at Whitchurch and Samuel at Ferndale. R. T. Jones eventually went on to become the owner of the largest drapery business in Merthyr. R. J. (Jim) Rees served the firm all his life, as did the remarkable Watkeys, who came to David Morgan on 12 January, 1880.

The total wages paid to these eighteen men and women for the month of December 1882 amounted to £35-5-6. The seniors received a monthly salary of approximately £2-10-0, or £30 per annum. As examples of the long period in which wages in the drapery trade remained stable, Miss Tippett of Newport, Monmouthshire, was engaged for a salary of £30 per annum in 1911 and as late as 19 October, 1918 an applicant coming from Streatham, London, for the position of first hand in sales for children's coloured coats was offered a salary of £35 per annum. All these salaries were based on the fact that shop assistants would be "living-in". Diligence was encouraged by a commission on sales.

A considerable proportion of the staff were always women. The opportunities for gainful employment open to women were very restricted in the reign of Queen Victoria. It was not until towards the end of the reign of Edward VII that women began to assert their rights, most conspicuously in the Suffragette Movement, which strove for the vote for women. Compared with the life of hard physical labour of the mill girls in their clogs and shawls, or the grim lot of the maid of all work in domestic service, whose nickname "slavey" was indicative of her status and duties, the drapery trade offered a much more genteel atmosphere, which attracted young women of the working and lower middle class and farmers' daughters. To these young women, not yet prepared to take the ultimate step of marriage, the draper's shop provided an opportunity to escape the drudgery of the home or the isolation of the farm.

It was a rule that all female employees should be spinsters. Not until towards the end of the 1914-1918 war were married women taken on as temporaries until their husbands returned from the war. A letter written on 26 July, 1917 to an applicant from Southsea for the post of milliner revealed the importance in the mind of the employer of spinsterhood.

In view of the information now given we do not think it of any use to have the proposed interview. As in neither of your previous letters was any intimation given to the contrary we presumed you to be a spinster . . . The position we have to offer is not a temporary one but permanent and progressive to a suitable Milliner.

The letter closes with evidence that the staff were usually employed by David Morgan for long periods of service: "Our last Milliner was here for about 5 years and her predecessor for 16 years ".

In the fourth year of the war, when heavy casualties and conscription were taking so many men, the walls of prejudice against the employment of married women were beginning to crumble. The Milliner from Southsea, judging from copies of the correspondence of David Morgan, Limited, was a woman of spirit and a very promising candidate. David Morgan, Limited were reluctant to lose her. Her letter in reply to the cancellation of the interview must have been something of a challenge to David Morgan, Limited, who replied to the applicant in a manner which shows the firm was prepared to back down over the question of employing married women.

July 31st 1917

(We) are quite in sympathy with the views expressed therein. We think you have misinterpreted the spirit in which our letter of the 28th instant was written and may mention that we have at present in our employ *several* married Women who have temporarily taken up situations but whose intention it is to retire from them at the close of the War and upon receipt of your letter we naturally came to the conclusion that it would be your wish to do likewise, hence our stating that the position was not a temporary one. If it is your intention to take up a position permanently *which of course would be somewhat unusual and subject to explanation,* (author's emphasis) we are still open to give consideration to your application.

The war of 1914-1918 finally broke the pattern of the Victorian age. Until that time the drapery trade suffered very much from the common evil of all forms of employment, long hours. It was very exhausting for men and women to have to stand for long periods behind counters with nowhere to sit and little movement to relieve the strain on their feet and legs.

David Morgan was no believer in long hours and gradually the original hours of business were reduced over the years, but he always had to face the problem of competitors who put no limits to the hours they would keep their shops open. Even as late as 1913, sometime after the Shop Hours Act had been passed, the hours of business at Morgan & Company were:

Monday	8:30 a.m. to 7 p.m.
Tuesday	8:30 a.m. to 7 p.m.
Wednesday	8:30 a.m. to 1 p.m.
Thursday	8:30 a.m. to 8 p.m.
Friday	8:30 a.m. to 7 p.m.
Saturday	8:30 a.m. to 9 p.m.

Included in these hours were one hour and a half off for lunch and half an hour off for tea, which were provided by the Shop.

David Morgan expressed very strongly his views on the evil of long hours when he was interviewed by a reporter of the *Evening Express* on whether compulsory early closing was advisable. This interview, which reveals so much of the forthright nature of David Morgan, his sense of responsibility to his staff and a glimpse of his early experiences, was published in Cardiff's *Evening Express* on 28 March, 1901.

In this newspaper interview, the only one he ever gave, David Morgan talks freely and vigorously about what he knows most about, the drapery business. Here is a picture of David Morgan, at the age of sixty-eight, looking back over his long life as a draper.

SHOP LEGISLATION
ARE COMPULSORY EARLY HOURS ADVISABLE?
LOCAL OPINIONS FOCUSED

Yesterday morning I called on Mr. David Morgan the well known and widely respected draper of The Hayes and the Royal Arcade. Having spent a lifetime and a long one at that in business Mr. Morgan had naturally formed decided opinions with regard to business affairs and concerning these opinions he talked animatedly. Mr. Morgan, junior was also present and chatted as amicably as his sire.

Just as I was being ushered into Mr. Morgan's office a tall pale young man was leaving and barely had I made known the object of my visit when Mr. Morgan observed 'You noticed that young man who has just gone out. There is a typical instance of the pernicious influence resulting from unreasonably long hours during which shops—or perhaps I ought so say some shops—remain open. That young man has been employed in an establishment in London where they worked from 8 a.m. to 8 p.m. on ordinary days and from 8 a.m. to 9 p.m. in the summer. On Fridays and Saturdays they probably worked much longer. He is now broken down in health as the consequence of our unjust system. Believe in early closing, I should just think I do.'

'I believe' continued Mr. Morgan Sen. 'that Mr. Howell, Mr. Hall and myself are the only drapers in this town who strictly adhere to the rule of closing at seven o'clock on Mondays, Tuesdays and Thursdays and two o'clock on Wednesdays. There are drapers in the town who will not close until they see their neighbour closing, and that practice is common all over Cardiff.'

(*reporter*) 'What is their object?'

'Object? Petty jealousy and nothing else. They are afraid one of their competitors will sell a reel of cotton more than they will. But mind you' pursued Mr. Morgan 'the public are often to blame for the unjustly long hours which shop assistants are compelled to work. People will rush into a shop a few minutes before closing time and thus the assistants are detained by reason of their thoughtlessness. Now in the West End of London many of the shops close at six p.m. and they rarely have a customer after five o'clock. It is because the shop keepers have educated their customers up to it and I don't altogether see why that couldn't be done in Cardiff'.

'But don't you think compulsory closing would be unjust in a case of this sort?' I asked. 'Supposing a man and his wife were running a business on their own account, wouldn't they, in all fairness, be entitled to utilize their personal energy to its fullest advantage?'

'No, I don't think compulsory legislation would be unjust in such a case as that' replied Mr. Morgan jun. 'You must understand that they would not both be in the shop during the whole day, they would take it in turns and would, therefore, not actually work as long as the assistants in the larger shops. Hence the whole body of assistants should not suffer because of the fear of an injustice being done to the smaller shop keepers. I knew one small shop keeper in Cardiff who opened on Good Friday and Easter Monday. After a while I was not surprised to learn that he had closed in perpetuity'.

Mr. Morgan Sen. named a large establishment in London where some time ago this very question of compulsory early closing was voted on by the assistants and to the surprise of the proprietor they nearly all opposed the suggestion. He, naturally, inquired the reason and was told by his assistants that they all aspired to set up in business for themselves and when that happy period arrived they would like to remain open one hour later than the larger shops. In his younger days Mr. Morgan worked in London himself and he was full of reminiscences concerning the experiences of his youth. 'Why we worked so long and so hard at the place I was employed' he said 'that I have gone for a whole week without having my hat on. Another man whom I know worked so hard that he told me he had not put his hat on for two whole years except on Sundays. But then he was rewarded by rising to be head of the firm'.

'In Cardiff I am sorry to say' continued Mr. Morgan 'there are many people who do their shopping on Saturday nights after the public houses close and accordingly many shop keepers remain open till midnight. Nevertheless in this matter of early closing there has been a big improvement in my time. That is in the provinces. I am told that in the suburban districts of London the evil of long hours is growing worse'.

(*reporter*) 'Do you think that in the course of time a workable solution of voluntary early closing will evolve itself out of the present chaos?'

'Never unless you can eliminate jealousy from human nature. That is the prime cause of long hours'.

I mentioned that under the Shop Hours Act assistants were allowed to be employed 74 hours per week and Mr. Morgan jun. told me in reply that their assistants were not employed on an average more than 66 hours. It was his opinion that the Shop Hours Act under local administration was of very little value. A coach and twenty could easily be driven through it. To be made effective the Act must be under the direction of the Home Office.

I asked Mr. Morgan whether he made any reservation with regard to the employment of members of the Shop Assistants Union in his establishment.

'No none whatever' he replied 'I do not care whether they belong to the union or not so long as they do their duty'.

With regard to the provision of seats for assistants[10] Mr. Morgan told me that they were in vogue at their establishment before the Act was passed into law.

I afterwards saw Mr. James Howell but he declined to be interviewed. He mentioned that he favoured early closing himself.

This interview is noteworthy for what was, at the turn of the century, an attitude of moderation towards shopping hours. Judging by the long hours allowed in the regulations which he supported, the current excessive practices must have been as he asserted a heavy burden on the health and lives of the shop assistants. In some of his replies he gives glimpses of the even more arduous hours of employment, when as an apprentice and shop assistant he was learning his trade.

Unlike many a self-made man, he did not feel that just because he had survived such rigorous conditions of employment so could his staff. He appeared to be constantly influenced by the memories of his early days to improve the conditions under which his staff had worked and " lived-in ". Not until the system of " living-in " came under challenge did he begin to realise how great was the change of the relationship

137

between the proprietor and his staff since the days of his start in business. The challenge by the male staff of the whole system of " living-in " and their assertion of their right to sleep out was the most dramatic event to take place at The Hayes during the lifetime of David Morgan.

1 James Hall.

2 Source, Morgan Price.

3 Quotation from D. B. Morgan's short account of the history of The Hayes.

4 This piece of furniture is now in the board room of David Morgan, Ltd.

5 The business, previously known as Morgan & Company, was formed into a limited liability company in January 1916. The newly incorporated company, David Morgan Limited, had an authorised share capital of £160,000 made up as follows:

90,000 6% Cumulative Preference Shares of £1 each
60,000 Ordinary Shares of £1 each
10,000 Employee Shares of £1 each

David Morgan received all the Preference and Ordinary shares in the new company in exchange for the assets (less liabilities) of the former business. (This note provided by Richard Morgan.)

6 Miss Harnaman.

7 One of the early apprentices was David Hall, the oldest nephew of David Morgan. He told his son, Norman Hall, that when he first came to Cardiff to work for his Uncle he lived in lodgings in Bridge Street where Edgecumbe House was situated.

8 May Brummitt told of how she was put under the charge of her cousin Annie Hall when she came to stay with her Uncle over the shop in 1888. She described how Annie used to turn the shower on to her when she refused to get out of the bath. She emphasized this shower as an example of how her uncle was very up to date on the latest things.

9 The late Gerald Llewellyn Morgan, the youngest grandson of David Morgan, presented a strong case that David Morgan did not live over the shop but in Edgecumbe House from the time he furnished it until he moved to Bryn Taff. This argument was based on the registration of David Morgan's abode as in Wellington Terrace until he moved to Bryn Taff and the selling at that time of Edgecumbe House. His son, John Llewellyn Morgan, ten years of age when he moved to Cardiff from Pontlottyn in 1879, spoke about living over the shop but never mentioned Edgecumbe House.

10 This was an innovation of J. Ll. Morgan. He had seats placed in the joins and ends of the fixtures behind the counter. These seats had a spring which snapped them into a flat upright position along the fixtures when they were not being sat upon.

19. "Living-In"

For a long time before David Morgan set up shop in Cwm Shon Mathew Square, Rhymney, in 1858, it had become an established custom of the drapery trade that the staff should be housed and fed at the shop.

"Living-in" played an essential part in the recruiting of staff. It was also a means of keeping the portion of the wages paid in cash to a minimum. The total wage would be a combination of the monthly salary and the value of the "living-in". The actual value would be a difficult figure to arrive at. Many proprietors abused the system by stinting the food and providing crowded accommodation. It therefore became a method of paying low wages. It is difficult to make comparisons which would give some idea of the value of the wages paid. The fifty years before the outbreak of war in 1914 were a period of Free Trade, "The Cheap Breakfast Table", and money went a long way. Nevertheless, wages were very small. Married men would live out, but with the low scale of wages it was difficult for a young man to afford marriage until he either was able to have his own shop or rose to the position of buyer, or at least that of shop walker or senior hand. Some firms would only engage spinsters and bachelors and therefore only candidates for "living-in".

In spite of the abuses of the system, it could be of real value to many employees and offered some genuine advantages for the staff as a whole. The strict rules and regulations which governed their conduct, especially the hours at which they had to be in their living quarters, would win the approval of parents and help persuade them to let their youngsters go to the city to start to make their way in the world and to gain the experience which would one day fit them to run their own shop. A number of apprentices came to "Morgan's The Hayes" one of whose parents and sometimes both had previously done their training under David Morgan.

The conditions for "living-in" at Morgan and Company were better than those in many shops. The room space was ample and the food adequate. A club room was kept for the staff, which included a library, where newspapers were kept, and a popular billiards room. A letter from an Old Timer recalls with pleasure the evenings of singing songs around the piano. A small kitchen was available where the ladies had the privilege of preparing for themselves suppers of food they had bought and giving small parties among themselves. Those who have written about the "living-in" repeatedly refer to the happiness of the staff[1]. There was a sense of comradeship and of being part of a community that gave pleasure to the people employed at Morgan and Company. For the women the companionship was infinitely preferable to the loneliness of the "bed-sitter", which would be all that they could possibly afford. For the younger men there was the special attraction of being able to organise themselves for team games.

In spite of this friendly atmosphere reminiscent of Mr. Fezzywig's Ball, there were some serious flaws. No matter how well intentioned David Morgan was to provide for the well-being of his staff or how much he wanted to offer them conditions better than those he had experienced at the start of his career in the drapery trade, times were changing. The Victorian respect for, and reliance on, paternalism was coming to an end. The traditional responsibilities of the proprietor to his staff were no longer accepted. Young people were beginning to resent the restraints put upon them by a system which had been evolved long before the youth of their parents.

It must have come as a great shock to David Morgan when he learnt that his male staff wanted to have the system of " living-in " abandoned; that they were prepared to resort to a strike in order to gain their demand; and, when their right to sleep out was established, demanded that their salaries should be increased to compensate for the loss of " living-in ". Such a revolutionary idea, challenging so long established a practice accepted by David Morgan as part of his life, must have appeared to him to strike at the very foundations of the drapery trade. He had spent sixty-four of his seventy-eight years as a draper and had always " lived-in " with his staff until he moved to Bryn Taff in 1893. It was part of his business and his way of life. When the Shop Assistants Union presented him with a demand for the end of " living-in ", his reply shows he could not bring himself to believe that his shop family could demand such a change.

The opening shot of the Union's campaign having been fired on 25 September, 1913 with a letter from The National Amalgamated Union of Shop Assistants of 21 Russell Sq. London, David Morgan replied to Mr. Maxfield Mather, the financial secretary:

Sept. 29th, 1913

Dear Sir

With reference to your letter of 25th inst, we have no knowledge of any desire on the part of our staff to live out and see no reason for the proposed interview.

David Morgan

But Mr. Mather was not to be denied. On 4 October 1913, a letter was written to him by Richard Horwood, head of the Counting House, showing that Morgan & Company had changed its position and would be " pleased to give you the proposed interview on Thursday next at 12 o'clock ". The outcome of Mr. Mather's visit was a meeting with a deputation from the Cardiff Trades and Labour Council. The meeting was arranged in a letter of 30 October, 1913, signed " Morgan & Company " in the handwriting of Jack. On 3 November a letter signed " Morgan & Company " by Richard Horwood was sent to Mr. John Turner, the General Secretary of the National Amalgamated Union of Shop Assistants:

140

We beg to acknowledge receipt today of your letter dated Nov. 1st. We have nothing further to add to what has already been stated.

Judging from some of the correspondence, Morgan & Company were becoming increasingly aware of the danger of a confrontation. Advice as to how best the matter could be handled and information about the attitude of other firms which might soon be faced with the Union's protests against " living-in " were sought from the Drapers Chamber of Trade in London. The Chamber sent a telegram acknowledging the request for an interview.

It would appear that the meeting at the Drapers Chamber of Trade stiffened the position of Morgan & Company, because the day following, 6 November, 1913, a letter was sent to Mr. J. E. Edmonds, the Secretary of the Cardiff Trades and Labour Council:

> In reply to your letter of the 4th instant, we think no useful purpose can be served by re-opening the discussion on the question at issue.
>
> It is our opinion that the question has resolved itself into a personal attack on Morgan & Company and no argument to the contrary can gainsay this.
>
> We are told that such action on the part of our male staff was decided upon several months ago and that the date fixed was the period we are now passing through.
>
> We consider it distinctly unfair that the Union should support an action which is directed against one firm only.
>
> Morgan & Company

The tone of the letter, its complaint about unfairness and the charge of a personal attack on Morgan & Company are much more like the style of Jack than David Morgan. David Morgan signed and, judging by its direct simplicity, dictated the first letter; but it appears from the tone of the subsequent letters and the signatures on behalf of Morgan & Company that either David Morgan washed his hands of the whole affair or was persuaded to let Jack try his hand at solving the problem. The problem was the possibility of a strike by the male staff, who were demanding the end of " living-in " and an increase of pay in place of " living-in ". The amount of increase was one of the bones of contention.

On 7 November, 1913 a letter was written to Mr. Quilter, the Secretary of the Drapers Chamber of Trade, giving the details of Morgan & Company's offer to settle the matter.

> With reference to our conversation per telephone today we are prepared to consider personal applications to live out (Dinner and Tea provided on the premises on days of employment) and to pay as additional salary a sum varying from £10 to £20 according to merit.
>
> A little thought will convince you that a fixed sum cannot be stated. As was explained to you, there are instances where employees are paid in excess of their worth owing to Mr. Morgan's aversion to change of staff, and if a

141

fixed sum were stated those who are overpaid must soon terminate their service here.

We are wishful to continue the present relationship that has existed between us and our staff and it is with this in view we make the above offer and to enable the representative of the Union to get out of what we think has become to them an untenable position.

The copy of this letter is signed for Morgan & Company in Jack's handwriting. The reference to David Morgan's aversion to change of staff and the statement about the relationship " between us and our staff " show the letter must have been written by Jack. This effort at compromise attempted to save the face of the Union, and at the same time save the face of Morgan & Company by avoiding abandoning the principle of " living-in " and substituting instead the device of considering personal applications for sleeping out. This is an excellent example of Jack's flexible and ingenious mind and his good-natured tolerance.

According to May Brummitt, when a government inspector came to examine the conditions of " living-in " at Morgan & Company, David Morgan asked him: " Why do you pick on me?" The inspector answered: " The whole question of ' living-in ' is coming up for examination. Because you have the reputation of being one of the best proprietors for looking after your staff, we decided to begin with you ". That many of the staff agreed with the inspector, especially the female staff, is indicated in a letter to Quilter of the Drapers Chamber of Trade:

We are told on good authority that at the meeting last night 41 of our male staff signed to pass in their notices and at a previous meeting 4 of the young ladies were present and we are confident that no others of the female staff have aquised (sic) in the agitation.

In a letter written many years later, Miss Glasson said: " The female staff were very reluctant to live out when the time came to terminate the [" living-in "] arrangement ".

There are no records available, but a guess would number the staff in 1913 at a minimum of 90 males and about 150 females.

On 8 November the expected blow fell and was reported to Mr. Quilter in a letter of that date signed by Jack for Morgan & Company:

The Local Secretary and Local Organizer of the ' Shop Assistants Union ', this afternoon handed us notices signed by 41 of our male staff to terminate their employment on Saturday the 22nd inst.

At present we think perhaps a visit from you to address the staff would be somewhat premature and it would be well to wait a few days to see what development takes place. We shall keep you posted with all that occurs.

We shall require about 26 assistants for the under mentioned Departments and should be glad to hear what assistance you can render us from members of the Drapers Chamber of Trade in temporarily filling the vacancies.

Gents Mercery and Outfitting	2
Dresses (piece goods)	6
Flannels and Prints	6
Linens	7
Soft Furnishing goods	5
	—
Total	26

With the above assistance we think we can make satisfactory arrangements to fill the remaining vacancies. From what we hear we are of opinion that a number from amongst those who have tendered their notices would not hesitate to secede from the 'Shop Assistants Union' but for the fact they will lose the benefit of their past contributions to the Union, including particularly Sick Pay and Out of Employment Pay and for which in some instances they have been paying for years.

With a view of dealing with this point, now that it has arisen we should feel much obliged if you could procure and send us full particulars of the payments necessary to be made to the 'Linen and Woolen Drapers Institution' to enable assistants to obtain equal benefits to those they can secure from membership in the 'Shop Assistants Union' and with the information in our possession we shall be able to deal with the question should the necessity arise.

A letter of 10 November inquired whether or not the London Members of the Drapers Chamber of Trade could be relied upon to lend Morgan & Company some hands should it become necessary. The letter concluded: "We do not think it would be wise to act upon your suggestion as we think it would be suicidal seeing that the policy of the Union is evidently one to entirely abolish the system of "living-in" not only in Cardiff but elsewhere".

From these two letters it can be seen that Jack realised that he was at the forefront of a struggle which concerned the whole drapery trade; nevertheless he was determined not to surrender his control of Morgan & Company's negotiations to the Drapers Chamber of Trade. The Drapers recognised the importance of the role he was playing and invited him to attend their Council meeting. In accepting the invitation, he took the precaution of asking Mr. Quilter to "interview one or two of your leading members so that I may be sure of their support at the meeting". Judging from Jack's tone in the correspondence, what he was seeking was support at the Council meeting from some moderates when faced with diehards who would rather fight it out with a possible lockout as the final counter. That Jack still had hopes of achieving a successful compromise and containing the disaffection is evidenced by the rest of the letter:

With the exception of the 41 who tendered their notice Saturday last, I have no doubt whatever that the whole of the remaining members of the staff will remain loyal. From what I gather I shall not be surprised to receive a few applications to withdraw. I should be very much obliged if you could let me have a reply to my enquiry in my letter of Saturday last regarding the Linen and Woolen Drapers Institution. You will observe from the newspapers that the Union have now commenced to extend their operations by the resolution passed last night to approach our neighbours Messrs. Howell & Co.

While the struggle was continuing some letters of support from people in South Wales were gratefully acknowledged. In reply to one of these, from a gentleman in Troedyrhiw, Jack wrote on 13 November:

> I beg to thank you for your letter of today which is most admirable and I could not state the case more favourably myself, at the same time I am very desirous of avoiding correspondence in the newspaper, as I feel that the less said the sooner mended.

In spite of his reputation for excitability, Jack was keeping cool and counselling others to do likewise. He was aware that some compromise must eventually be worked out, and that nothing should be done that would in any way impede that compromise or jeopardise the good relations with the staff, which persisted in spite of the strike. In reply to an invitation of the Reverend Alick Henderson, the Vicar of St. John's Church, Cardiff, to attend a meeting at the Y.M.C.A., in an attempt to bring the two parties together on neutral ground to find a solution, Jack said he would have much pleasure in attending.

That his tactics were being effective in cooling the atmosphere and eliminating some of the emotional issues which could be used in such a strike, is shown in a leaflet distributed with the *Shop Assistant*, the Trade Union Newspaper:

> The men are not fighting living-in because of the particular food supplied or even the bedroom and other accommodations but merely as a principle.

This in itself was a recognition of the high standards maintained by David Morgan. Jack realised the need for discretion and to avoid the appearance of building up a counter-offensive. So when Mr. Humphries, a draper with shops in Penarth, Whitchurch and Lower Cathedral Road, asked to come and see him, he arranged a meeting at the Bungalow Cafe, High Street, rather than at The Hayes.

One of the tools Jack was trying to use in arriving at a solution was to find some insurance which would replace that of the Shop Assistants Union so that those who withdrew from the Union or did not want to join in could find a good alternative to the main benefit. On 25 November, 1913 he wrote to The National Deposit Insurance Society in London:

> We should be obliged if you would send us a schedule of the different forms of insurance undertaken by you for persons engaged in the Drapery trade so as to enable male assistants to accumulate the necessary capital to start business for themselves and also for the young ladies to secure an endowment on their marriage.

144

While the purpose of this letter was to fashion a tool wherewith to help break this strike, it also shows a genuine compassionate understanding of the lives and ambitions of the staff of Morgan & Company. It was on 11 December, 1913 that Jack could write to Mr. Quilter at the Drapers Chamber of Trade saying he was sending a copy of the terms of settlement arrived at with the assistants through the officials of the Shop Assistants Union.

The terms of the settlement with the Shop Assistants Union were a triumph for the patient negotiations of Jack Morgan. He persuaded the Union to accept most of the objectives of " living-in " which Morgan & Company held to be the most important elements of the system, both for the assistants and for the firm, and at the same time conceded their most important claim for the right to sleep out. The principal points in the agreement were published in the *Western Mail* on 24 November, 1913:

1. All juniors under twenty-one years to live-in.

2. A limited number of seniors to live-in for locking-up duty and control.

3. All male employees to sleep out after August 1st, 1915.

4. Morgan & Company to have the option of engaging new assistants to sleep out or in until August 1st, 1915.

5. No employee to be dismissed as a result of any action in the dispute.

6. Selection of men to have the right to sleep out not to be confined to those who have given notice to the firm. (Position and length of service to be taken into consideration.)

    is signed.

7. Ten members of the male staff to go out every 3 months, the first lot to go out at the end of January 1914. The number that will go to live out at subsequent quarterly periods will be settled before the agreement

8. The sum to be allowed for sleeping out to be seven shillings and sixpence a week. In consideration for this allowance the assistants sleeping out shall provide themselves with all meals except dinner and tea on Monday, Tuesday, Thursday, Friday and Saturday and dinner on Wednesday. (Dinner is the luncheon meal.)

It can be seen that this agreement does not affect the " living-in " system for the female staff or the male junior staff under the age of 21.

In an interview, Jack Morgan said: " I had to fight individually for an agreement, which will act as a basis for all South Wales establishments but I am pleased to believe the negotiations have been conducted in such a way that no bad feeling will be left ". Jack had every reason to feel satisfied with his efforts. He had assured a gradual transition, without the drastic effects of a sudden change, which would enable both the staff and the business to make the necessary changes. Those who

145

would sleep out could have time to find their new accommodation. Those who did not want to live out could continue "living-in".
Western Mail, Monday, 24 Nov. 1913:

(A 'Leader')

There will be much satisfaction in Cardiff at the fact that a strike of Shop Assistants has been avoided, and at a further fact that a settlement has been arrived at which offers an ingenious and easy solution of the living-in problem. The system has no doubt proved irksome to many of those who have been subject to it, and has at the same time proved advantageous to those who have need for the protection it affords. The drapery trade is not esentially different from other retail trades in regard to its employer but it happens to be a fact that many youths in the drapery trade migrate from the villages to the towns and that the living-in system offers them a very welcome convenience, besides an assurance of moral well-being which must be a comfort to their parents. But the position of the employees who have reached legal manhood is different. They demand greater freedom than the living-in system affords and they claim the opportunity to realize the independence of mind, habit and pursuit which fairly belongs to their estate and for which they are willing to sacrifice the material advantage which the living-in arrangements at the larger and better establishments undoubtedly afford. The settlement arrived at may be described as a rational compromise and will probably serve as a model of future settlements. For the female assistant and for the male assistant under 21 years of age the refuge of the living-in system will continue to be available. For the Assistants who have emerged from the stage of legal infancy there will be full opportunity for the realization of the sense of manhood and citizenship.

It had been just two months since the first letter had been received from Mr. Maxfield Mather, the financial secretary of the Shop Assistants Union, and, except for the first letter from David Morgan saying he saw no reason for an interview, the entire matter appears to have been handled by Jack, greatly to his credit.

Shop Assistants Strike

The public will no doubt feel that much credit is due to Mr. John Ll. Morgan for the discretion and ability he has manifested in the negotiations and will hope that the arrangements to which he has assented will restore in full measure the peace and amity which have existed hitherto between the principles and employees of a much respected firm.

Western Mail editorial,
Monday 24th November 1913

Jack's great achievement was in preserving the most important and valuable element to emerge from "living-in", the good relations which the firm had with its staff, which during this strike Jack had made such an effort to retain. David Morgan's well known 'aversion to changes in staff' was expressed by his often-quoted remark when urged by a buyer to dismiss a saleshand: "What's the use; you only change their faces". Though the remark may seem cynical, the staff were fully aware that, provided they maintained the standards expected, they enjoyed

146

at David Morgan, Limited a degree of security of employment very precious in those days, when irascible employers would sometimes walk through a department and, pointing at under-employed assistants, dismiss them with the order: " Go up and pack your trunk ".

That so fundamental a change as the abandonment of the system of ' living-in ' should have taken place with so little ill effect on the progress of David Morgan, Limited or on the relations between the family and the staff was a sure sign of the soundness of that relationship.

1   The following quotation is from a letter written by H. E. Evans: " I have very pleasant memories of my service at David Morgan Ltd. We were all a happy staff, well fed and comfort everywhere. It was ' living-in ' for male and female staff who were mostly from the counties of Caermarthenshire, Pembroke and Cardiganshire, and the staff living outside Cardiff. It was a very happy atmosphere with comfort in bedrooms and sitting rooms, and a billiards room ".

20. The Day of the Sale

When the sale by Lord Glanusk of the Peterstone and Trebinshun estates was announced in April 1918, it was a matter of prime interest to the tenants of these estates, the adjacent landowners, the farming community of Breconshire and even farther afield. According to a report in *The Brecon County Times*: "Since the selling of a part of the Tredegar Estates no disposal of property has aroused so much public interest".

The acreage of these two estates amounted to 2,323 acres. Messrs. Stephenson and Alexander[1], who were put in charge of the sale, described the Peterstone estate, situated in the Valley of the Usk, as "some of the best-known and most fertile holdings in the County of Brecon". This well-known firm of auctioneers announced that the sale would take place at 1 : 30 p.m. on 5 July, 1918, at the Castle Hotel, Brecon.

Inevitably so important a sale near the end of the war aroused great interest as a major test of what agricultural land would be worth. There would be plenty of potential buyers. The wartime boom had put money into the pockets of farmers and also many others who might consider land as an investment, a possession or status symbol. The printed catalogues of the sale ran out in June and Messrs. Stephenson and Alexander had to write to a number of inquirers: "We regret to say that on account of the unprecedented demand for copies we have quite run out of them and shall not have any further copies until the end of the week when a copy will be sent to you". The list of those who had to wait ranged from far and near; one request came from Suffolk and another late applicant was David Morgan's nephew, Mr. Fred Hall of Tynewydd, Llanfrynach.

The interest of another son of Breconshire was aroused. While staying at Llanbrynean, David Morgan had been heard to say at various times that he would like to own the farms he could see from his bedroom window. Some of these farms were well-known to him; indeed he had already bought Blaenant, Pantllyfrith, Llwyncynydd and Pentwyn some time before the sale. The Hall family, into which his sister Jane had married, had farmed Pencelli Court, and Pencelli Castle, and Tynewydd had been the home of Jane and her husband William Hall. David Morgan's brother William a much-respected figure in the local farming community, would know about the farms up for sale, and also the abilities of their respective tenants.

David Morgan's opportunity came to him very late in life. He was nearly eighty-five years of age, but he still had a lively and strong desire to possess this land he had so long coveted.

En route to Brecon and the sale, David, Jack Morgan and James Hall changed trains at Bargoed to get onto the Brecon and Newport Railway. There they happened to meet John Price and his son, Morgan, on their way to their shop in New Tredegar. John Price, who was a first cousin of David Morgan and had bought The Pontlottyn Shop from him, told Morgan Price that David Morgan and the others were on their way to the Glanusk sale, adding: "He is going to buy a number of farms and spend a lot of money[2]".

At Brecon, William Morgan met his brother, David, with the pony and trap, and together the two old gentlemen drove off to the Castle Hotel. This was going to be a momentous day in their lives, and only they could share the memories that lay behind it. William alone would understand the impelling forces which had brought his brother to this sale room. For David it was going to be the fulfilment of dreams that had been with him ever since his mother's impatience had brought home to him his incompetence as a farm boy at Cae Crwn seventy-three years ago; ever since he outbid De Winton for Llanbrynean forty-four years ago; ever since he had built the new Llanbrynean and looked out from his bedroom window on the fair Usk Valley.

His had been a long and successful life. He had been widely recognised as the most successful of the valley drapers, a number of whom had been his apprentices. He had built his great monument, one of the largest retail businesses in Wales, on The Hayes. By frugality, self-discipline, a sense of property, a far-sighted belief in gas as an investment and a profound knowledge of the drapery trade, he had built for himself a fortune. He had come to this sale prepared to spend some of that fortune to fulfil his dreams.

The ballroom at the Castle Hotel was full, and those who could not get into the room stood in the entrance and the corridor. The two old gentlemen sat at the back of the crowded hall, while Jack Morgan and James Hall sat in front with instructions on the lots for which they were to bid and the limits to which they might go.

Those who remember the occasion recall the great buzz of excitement which preceded the opening of the sale, when Mr. Alexander put up the first lot, Pencelli Court, a farm of 143 acres. It had been the home farm of the Hall family and it was from here that William Hall had courted Jane Morgan. It had been farmed by William Hall's elder brother, James, who had married a first cousin of David Morgan, Mary Frances Morgan of Pantycorred. The bidding was brisk, and when the auctioneer's hammer fell Pencelli Court had been sold to David Morgan for £4,025, which was £1,025 above the reserve price. Lot 2, Pencelli Mill, also went to David Morgan; likewise Lot 3, the Royal Oak Inn in the village of Pencelli for £350, a somewhat surprising acquisition for so abstemious a man. Lot 4, a stable in the village, was bought by Captain Hughes Morgan, who had previously rented it.

Lot 5 was the 130 acres of Tynewydd Farm[3], which had for many years been the home of his sister Jane; the tenant at this time was her son Fred. The farm was a good one and in the past had won prizes for being the best-kept in Breconshire. This proved to be a real test of David Morgan's determination. He would have to go way beyond the reserve price of £3,500 up to £5,500 before he could win possession of this farm. According to James Hall: "The bidding for Tynewydd was very keen. Harry Yorath seemed determined to have it, but Uncle was not going to be shaken off by anybody. He was out to buy Pencelli Court and Tynewydd whatever happened[4]".

He followed up the purchase of Tynewydd by buying the next lot, the 314 acre farm of Dolymaes, for £5,000. When David Morgan had been driven in the trap by his brother to look at some of the farms on the Peterstone Estate before the sale, William had strongly advised David not to buy Dolymaes because it was such a rocky farm[5]. William knew about this farm as it belonged to his father-in-law. But David Morgan had the bit between his teeth and, regardless of his brother's sound advice, went ahead and bought it. Lots 7, 9 and 10, described as "Freehold Accommodation Meadows . . . forming part of Dolymaes Farm" in all amounting to ten acres, were bought by David Morgan for a total of £640. Lot 8, a similar meadow of one acre, was bought by David Powell for £80.

What a start to a sale! Of the first ten lots, David Morgan had bought all except this one-acre field and the stable—ample evidence that he had come to the sale to do business. He had already spent £16,275.

The next four lots of small acreage did not interest David Morgan.

Lot 15 was Millbrook Farm. Before the sale Willie Morgan, the youngest son of Llanbrynean, heard his uncle say he would not bid for Millbrook as he wanted nothing to do with its tenant, W. D. Smith. David Morgan had let it be known that he would not disturb any tenant on any farm that he bought. Smith was far from a desirable tenant. William would most certainly have told his brother that Smith was a troublemaker. In the files of the sale there is a copy of a letter which the estate agent of Lord Glanusk had written in reply to a letter from Mr. Smith. It sharply rebuked Mr. Smith, who had apparently complained in his letter about Lord Glanusk's treatment of his tenants in not affording them an advantageous opportunity for the purchase of their farms outside the sale room. Mr. Smith had gone so far as to say that the feeling of anger was so great that Lord Glanusk would not dare to walk among his tenants. The outcome was no bargain for Mr. Smith. He paid the stiff price of £4,400 for the 99 acres he farmed.

Then came Millbrook Mill and house, followed by Tramroad Cottage, neither of which interested David Morgan. The next four farms to come up comprised 1,076 acres of some of the choicest land in the sale. They formed the centre of the estate, and the kernel of the sale. David Morgan was bound to face heavy competition for them.

Highgrove Farm, in some ways not quite the same quality as the other three, was the first and was sold to David Morgan for £2,800, which in comparison with the other prices was reasonable for its 190 acres.

Then came Greenway and Slade Farm, the quality of its 325 acres being evidenced by the high proportion of arable land and the absence of any rough pasture, according to the description in the sale catalogue. The reserve was £5,500, but the bidding passed that figure and also any limit David Morgan set on it; it was eventually knocked down for

£6,800 to Charles Kenshole, the solicitor; he represented the great colliery firm of Powell Duffryn, who wanted it for the rest and recuperation of pit ponies. Here was a pocket far longer than that of David Morgan.

Now came Manest Court, farmed by Brindley Morris. Its 318 acres carried the highest rent of any farm in the estate. It was undoubtedly the best farm in the sale. Its quality and central position made it most desirable to David Morgan. Again the bidding passed the reserve of £6,000 and past the limit of David Morgan's instructions. Jack and James Hall, knowing how much the old gentleman wanted Manest, continued bidding after his limit had been reached. But such was the determination of the bidding by the opposition that they dropped out. It would seem that David Morgan had been caught unprepared for the strength of the bidding.

When David Morgan discovered he was out of the bidding he could not contain himself. His disappointment was so great that, throwing aside all discretion and control, he said to his brother in a loud voice that could be heard all over the room: " He hasn't the pluck of a louse; why doesn't he bid up! [6]" James Hall, telling the same story some years after the sale, gave a slightly different version: " When your grandfather saw your father had stopped bidding on Manest he called from the back of the room: " Don't be a coward. Bid up! "

Apparently Jack had enough courage to resist his father's sarcastic urging and refused to go any farther on what must have been already in his opinion too high a price for Manest. The tenant, Brindley Morris, was absolutely determined to buy Manest, and it was finally sold to him for £9,000. When the auctioneer's hammer fell at that price, the room burst into applause[7]. It was the high point of the sale, and the strong competition of the bidding had built up a tense atmosphere of excitement in which the bitterly disappointed David Morgan had, most probably for the first and last time in his life, lost his head.

This did not however diminish his appetite when the last of these four farms came up. Lot 22, Brynllicci, a farm of 243 acres, brought him back into the battle, and he made his final purchase for £3,450. In all, he had bought 1,038 acres for £22,525 from Lord Glanusk, who was a descendant of Crawshay Bailey, one of the giants of the iron industry. The purchase by a draper of a landed estate from an heir of an ironmaster marked a significant change in the social order.

David Morgan had lost Manest and had shown in public how much he wanted it. In the other bids he had shown, just as when he paid £5,300 for Llanbrynean in 1874, that price had little limit when it came to pay for land he wanted. He must have been absolutely determined to buy Tynewydd when he paid £5,500 for its 130 acres, a fraction over £42 an acre; this was exceeded only by the possibly punitive price paid by the contumacious Mr. Smith for Millbrook. The price paid for Manest worked out at a few shillings over £28 per acre.

It had been a strange and most unusual day in the life of David Morgan. For once he had allowed his emotions to show in a business transaction. Or was it a business transaction? Ever since the purchase of Llanbrynean and later, when he indulged his propensity for building by erecting there a surprisingly large house and massive farm buildings, he had seen Breconshire through different spectacles from those with which he viewed his business and even his personal way of life. He had indulged himself in Breconshire to a degree which, by comparison with the other spheres of his life, came as near to extravagance as David Morgan could bring himself.

On the return journey, David Morgan and his party again met John Price and his son, Morgan, at Bargoed on their way home to Pengam. John Price reported to his son that the party was most excited about the result of the sale, especially Jack Morgan, and added: " The old man is delighted. He has bought all he wants today[8]". So, already in his excitement, the bitter disappointment over the loss of Manest was beginning to be forgotten.

It must have been a very long day for the 84-year-old man. He had made an early start from Llandaff to catch the first train from Cardiff to Brecon to be in time for the sale; he had gone through one of the most exciting and emotional days of his long life in a crowded sale room; and he had returned to Cardiff by the last train from Brecon and then on by cab to Bryn Taff, all in the same day " without apparently turning a hair[9]".

David Morgan had only ten months left in which to enjoy his triumph. But it was time enough to savour the deep satisfaction of having bought the land he had so long coveted; this land, once owned by a descendant of one of the great ironmasters, now belonged to " one of the little boys of Cae Crwn[10]".

1 For producing the files of this sale for me to study, I am much indebted to Mr. Duncan Alexander, in whose office lies a mine of information going back over a long history of property in South Wales.

2 Source: Morgan Price.

3 When the estate of John Llewellyn Morgan was valued for estate duty in 1941, Pencelli Court was valued at £4,150; Tynewydd at £4,320 and Dolymaes at £5,625. It should be remembered these values were arrived at in 1941, the third year of the war.

4 Letter to May Brummitt, November 1918.

5 Source: Kate Morgan, who drove with them in the trap.

6 Source: William Morgan, Llanbrynean and Three Cocks, who was present at sale.

7 The *Brecon County Times* reported only the facts of the sale except adding " amidst applause " in the case of Manest.

8 Source: Morgan Price.

9 James Hall to May Brummitt, November 12th, 1918.

10 Comment by someone on seeing the new house at Llanbrynean: "And to think one of the little boys of Cae Crwn built it." Source: Kate Morgan.

New Llanbrynean, built by David Morgan 1883.

Three Generations:
David Morgan, John Llewellyn Morgan and David Bernard Morgan.

Jack Morgan at Brecon Show.

David Morgan: portrait by Margaret Lindsay Williams.

DEATH OF MR. DAVID MORGAN.

ROMANCE OF A GREAT CARDIFF BUSINESS

THE LATE MR. MORGAN.

THE MORGAN ARCADE

GROWTH OF A GREAT BUSINESS

DOCTOR IN DOCK.

STORY OF FATAL ... FOR PATIENT.

ABOUT HIS WIFE.

ATTEMPTED SUICIDE AT NEWPORT.

NEW ZEALAND WIN.

35,000 WITNESS MATCH WITH WALES.

STOHR'S GREAT GOAL FOR THE VISITORS.

SHEA OPENS THE SCORING

RUGBY

NORTHERN UNION

ASSOCIATION.

SWANSEA BEATEN BY ? GOALS TO NIL AT CAR...

CARDIFF CITY ...

Obituary: Western Mail, Tuesday, 22nd April 1919.

Funeral Procession.

Grave of David Morgan at Llandaff Cemetery.

Llanfigan Church restored by John Llewellyn Morgan in Memory of David Morgan.

21. The Last Winter

In August 1918 David Morgan, accompanied by James Hall, went to the Abernant Lake Hotel, Llanwrtyd Wells, for a fortnight. The holiday did him good, though he complained that "the air was rather too strong and the atmosphere too humid". He was in good health and he enjoyed the company he found at the hotel. "Several Welsh people who met him there for the first time, having known him previously by repute, were delighted with him. One lady, a Mrs. Llewellyn whose husband is a big colliery proprietor said to me (James Hall) one day, 'Why your Uncle knows more about collieries than my husband!'".

He visited Llanbrynean only twice after the sale. The first time his brother took him to task, expressing his disgust over the purchase of the Royal Oak Inn, Pencelli. William was a pillar, indeed the sole pillar, of the Chapel in that village. He felt strongly, as a result of his upbringing, that the publican's trade was not one with which a member of his family should be associated. He finished his rebuke by asking David: "What would your Mother think?" He received the laconic answer: "It is a legitimate business[2]". When the two brothers came to say goodbye at the end of the second visit, some instinct told them it might be the last time they would see each other. Mrs. William Morgan, who witnessed their farewell, described the parting as pathetic.

David celebrated his eighty-fifth birthday on Sunday, 27 October, 1918, the day before the actual anniversary. "Jack and Edith came as usual; also Bernard and Trevil". Aubrey was away at Charterhouse and Margaret was ill with influenza[3]. The new baby, Gerald, was too young to attend this celebration. David Morgan was particularly pleased that Bernard was able to come home from duty with the Welsh Guards. He had received overseas orders on 26 October and was given the usual six days' leave. The party went off successfully and "Uncle, as usual on the occasion of a celebration, partook of everything and was very pleased with himself[4]".

Soon after the birthday party, influenza struck Bryn Taff; fortunately it was in a mild form. James Hall recovered in a week, but David Morgan was in bed for a fortnight. Dr. Pritchard called each day and was concerned about the pulse of his patient. War time restrictions required the doctor to write out a special permit for the supply of the whiskey which he prescribed. "He wants Irish and Jack is getting it. We have Scotch in the house but Uncle does not care for that. Dr. told me [James Hall] Uncle was to take it three times a day. He took a little on Tuesday and on Wednesday but refused it last night which perhaps accounts for the weak pulse this morning[5]". Once when his housekeeper, Miss Rees, was urging him to take whiskey he chided her: "Go on! you old publican".

153

He recovered from this attack of influenza, but his health was never the same again. For the first time he began to complain about his health, telling people how tired he felt. He told his housekeeper: " You know, Miss Rees, I am getting an old man ". What Miss Rees had known ever since she entered his service had only now occurred to David Morgan.

James Hall wrote to Kate Morgan on 8 November, 1918: " Uncle wishes me to ask whether it will be possible for you to send a fowl every alternate week. Miss Rees finds difficulty in getting suitable food for Uncle[6] while he is in bed and he is becoming reconciled to the fact that he will have to spend a great part of the winter indoors ". His thin body felt the cold. He was always conscious of draughts and as he aged he became even more conscious of them. To fend off the ever-present draughts he used to sit in a high-backed chair, covering his bald head with a grey silk cap; on his shoulders was a dark blue shawl, and a rug was thrown over his legs. He always wore suits of a heavy material. He sat so close to the fire that he had to use a small glass screen, which could be moved up and down on a thin wooden shaft mounted on a tripod, so that the direct heat of the fire could be kept from his face. There he sat and waited.

His thoughts must have given him satisfaction. He had built his greatest monument, the business on The Hayes, one of the largest department stores in Wales; he had bought the farms in Breconshire for which he had waited so long; he had made a fortune. All was in order; and on 18 January, 1918 he signed his will, itself a testamentary monument. While he sat by the fireside he still kept in touch with the business. The monthly cheques would come up for his signature. This was no mere formality. Each cheque would be carefully compared with its accompanying statement and each discount checked. He had done this for himself ever since he had entered business. It was his rough and ready method of stock control. He could tell from the account which accompanied each cheque how much each buyer was spending of his money and with what firms he was doing business and on what terms. This life-long practice continued to the beginning of April.

During this winter there was a continuing correspondence between Bryn Taff and Llanbrynean about matters connected with the Breconshire estate. Whilst the majority were written by James Hall on behalf of his uncle, some were written by David Morgan himself. William was constantly consulted and asked for any comment or suggestion he might have about such things as estimates.

Bryn Taff, Llandaff,
27 Jan. 1919

Dear Kate

   Uncle told me on Saturday that he wanted me to write asking you to discontinue sending him a fowl every other week as Miss Rees had told him that the last one sent was a laying fowl and he thought it was a pity you should sacrifice layers. He now tells me to ask you to send a fowl this week but refrain from doing so afterwards for 4 weeks.

> Uncle wishes me to say that he had Mr. Gunter down to see him last Thursday week and liked him very much. He considers your Father has recommended a thoroughly reliable man who will give every satisfaction to him and the tenants.

Mr. Gunter was appointed Estate Agent by David Morgan. The interview must have taken place at The Hayes, because the letter continues:

> Uncle has not been out since Mr. Gunter's visit. He was not well that day and should have remained indoors. He seems very weary but has nothing else the matter. The slight cold he caught on Tuesday before Mr. Gunter came seems to have passed off. Uncle hopes your Father (his brother William) is not venturing much out of doors these days.

Yours sincerely

James Hall

An unusual note for David Morgan crept into the correspondence: "Uncle wishes me to say he is very vexed you have not sent him the receipt he asked for. He wants it ". This note of irritation, so unlike David's customary calmness, was an indication of the tiredness of the old man. Something of a similar nature must have occurred when, in reply to a letter from her brother James, Maria Hall wrote: " Uncle is apparently in his second childhood ".

Winter was over and, with the arrival of Spring, came the Easter Bank Holiday. In 1919 this holiday occurred on Monday, 21 April. All seemed normal at Bryn Taff when James Hall left for London to spend the weekend of the holiday with his brother David at Stroud Green Road. Alone, except for his housekeeper and maid, David Morgan suddenly gave up and took to his bed. Dr. Pritchard was summoned. Word was sent up to Brynderwen, James Hall was recalled from London and Agnes was summoned from Bristol. On 21 April, 1919, David Morgan died of old age. He was in his eighty-sixth year.

In describing his father's occupation for the death certificate, Jack with perception and understanding found the complete answer in the traditional description: " Master draper ".

1 Quotes from a letter by James Hall to May Brummitt, 12 November, 1918.

2 Kate Morgan.

3 This virulent form of the disease was to sweep through Britain in 1918-1919, causing a great many deaths.

4 James Hall to May Brummitt.

5 James Hall to Kate Morgan, 8 November, 1918.

6 By the end of the 1914-1918 war, rationing was very severe. Compared with the way rationing was handled in the 1939-1945 war, it was most inefficiently managed.

22. The Funeral

Long obituaries in the *Western Mail* and *South Wales News* informed the public of the death of David Morgan and gave the details of his life and the story of the building of his shop on The Hayes. Both gave considerable attention to the building of the Morgan Arcade. The *Western Mail* stated " this improvement caused much satisfaction in the town because of the fact that 25 cottages and a public house which had long been an eyesore were demolished ", while the *South Wales News* account described the pulling down of these buildings as " of great benefit to the town " because " some of the most unpleasant reminders of old Cardiff were removed forever ".

The *Western Mail* on 22 April, 1919 printed this editorial:

A PIONEER DEPARTED

The death at an advanced age of Mr. David Morgan removes from our midst a most worthy citizen. ' Morgan's The Hayes ' is a phrase that has long been familiar in many mouths, for it conjures up the image of a gigantic concern that is one of the leading features of the centre of the Welsh Metropolis. The business was probably better known than its creator, for the late David Morgan was a quiet, unpretentious man who shunned the limelight and was intimately known to a comparatively limited circle. . . . Mr. Morgan was one of those who started in the Principality and stayed there, building up from tiny beginnings a vast and prosperous connection and dying full of years and business honours.

The title of the editorial was appropriate, for David Morgan had started his business career early in the development of South Wales and had proved himself an outstanding representative of that generation of Welsh drapers who, having started in a small way, rose to prominence in the economic growth of the Nineteenth Century. This portion of the editorial was moreover an accurate description of the founder and the status of the business he had created.

The writer, evidently feeling the need to say something more of David Morgan than that he was a reserved and successful man, went on to pay tribute to his generosity.

But if Mr. Morgan was a wealthy man, he was also a generous man. In the sweetest spirit of true Christianity he let not his left hand know what his right hand did; but he will be gratefully remembered by the many who often appealed to him and who never appealed in vain.

The writer evidently knew no more than David Morgan's left hand what his right hand did. David Morgan was frugal, not miserly; acquisitive, not avaricious; and not interested in public or private charities. The existing evidence indicates that such donations as he made were of a minor nature by comparison with the income from his hard-earned capital.

In a letter to May Brummitt dated 12 November, 1918, James Hall referred to the generosity of Sir William James Thomas, who had given another 1000 guineas to the Cardiff Infirmary to endow a bed called "The Peace Bed" in gratitude for the Armistice on 11 November, 1918. James Hall continued, "I often wish Uncle had given 1000 guineas to endow a bed there. Many people have whose means are not what his are. However, he has his own ideas on the subject and it is for him to decide". The character and way of life of David Morgan make the concluding passage of this eulogy in the *Western Mail* difficult to accept.

The funeral took place on Friday, 25 April, 1919. A luncheon was given at Bryn Taff for some of his elderly friends coming from a distance, some of whom arrived during the meal. Will Hall was seated by the then fifteen-year-old Aubrey Morgan and entertained him with amusing comments and anecdotes about those whom he described as the blind, the deaf and the halt gathering at the luncheon. As each guest entered the room on one or two sticks, boss-eyed or hand to ear, the funnier Will Hall became. As is often the case at funerals of elderly people, the luncheon was devoted to anecdotes about the deceased. Except for one of the stories told by Owen Owen, these invaluable glimpses into the life of David Morgan have been forgotten and lost forever. Owen Owen, talking about their visit to America, told how they were warned to be on the lookout for pickpockets in the streets of New York, and to be particularly careful of crowds watching a street fight, which was often a put-up show to attract the pickpocket's victims. On the first morning Owen Owen lost sight of David Morgan. Looking up the street, he saw a crowd. Knowing his man, he immediately went into the crowd and found David Morgan in the front row watching a street fight.

Besides the luncheon conversation, the other object of the greatest interest was the presence of the eldest grandson of David Morgan, Lieutenant David Bernard Morgan of the Welsh Guards. Bernard was wearing the distinctive service dress uniform of a Guards' officer, which gave this corps d'elite a more stylish appearance than other regiments in the army. His cap had a shiny black peak, outlined with a narrow band of gold braid and surmounted by the Welsh leek, the badge of his regiment. The grouping of the highly-polished brass buttons on his tunic into two sets of five indicated that the Welsh Guards were the fifth of His Majesty's Foot Guards. He was also carrying a sword. Bernard was paraded by his father around the guests and repeatedly asked to draw his sword so that the fascinated old gentlemen could admire the handsome engraving on the steel blade which framed the leek and the motto of the regiment. The assembly was greatly impressed and delighted; Bernard was not. His increasing embarrassment was spared only when the luncheon broke up and the mourners entered the carriages which were to take them to Llandaff Cathedral.

157

As Aubrey entered the carriage containing his father and his brothers, Bernard and Trevil, he was still laughing at some last remarks of Will Hall. He was sharply rebuked by his father for his unseemly behaviour. One look at the genuine sorrow on his father's face told him his father was in no mood for levity. The awe in which Jack stood of his father had given way to a sense of loss and an anxious awareness of the responsibilities which would now rest on his shoulders.

The carriages of the mourners put them down at the lych-gate which stands on the Green above the Cathedral. Here they were joined by a large assembly, which followed the coffin in double file down the sloping path to the Cathedral. No women were present. On his return home John Price said: "All the old men were there". That is to say, all that remained: Owen Owen, who went to America with David Morgan; David W. Davies J.P., the first apprentice, who later had the help of David Morgan as a partner in his business in Trealaw and later Tonypandy; Alfred P. Morgan the musician, son of D. P. Morgan, the original partner of David Morgan in Rhymney. The three Pontlottyn apprentices and relatives of David Morgan, John Price, John Arnott Lewis and Thomas Samuel, were there; and those early arrivals at The Hayes, Watkeys, Jim Rees, R. T. Jones, draper of Merthyr, and David Hall. The Reverend Jack Croft, cousin of David Morgan's late wife; Gething Lewis, the brother-in-law of David Morgan; Griff Hughes, husband of Lillie, daughter of Gething Lewis; David Morgan's neighbour, J. T. Duncan and his two sons, Frank and John. Hugh Howell and Samuel Hall, Evan Roberts and Charles Marment represented the four leading competitors of David Morgan. The front of the long procession was drawn up with strict attention to the protocol of primogeniture and blood relationship. In front, immediately behind the coffin, walked David Morgan's only son, Jack, with the eldest grandson, Bernard, on his left; behind them was Aubrey, with Trevil on his left. Then, after a small gap, came the relatives headed by William Morgan of Llanbrynean, brother and sole survivor of the children of Cae Crwn; on his left was David Hall, the eldest nephew and the senior member of the family of David Morgan's sister. Behind William Morgan came his two sons and behind David Hall the members of his family. The only member of James Morgan's family present was Wilfred; his two brothers were yet to be demobilized from the army. Wilfred was given the position of walking behind the Llanbrynean family with Fred, the youngest Hall, on his left. These matters of protocol are rarely without their problems. Wilfred managed to create a small scene by refusing to walk alongside Fred Hall. He held that he should not be called upon to walk alongside a man who had been in jail. (Fred had been lodged overnight in the local police station for refusing to pay the fine for removing and keeping some rabbit traps belonging to a neighbour which he had found in a boundary hedgerow.) A photograph of the procession, as it approached the north door of the Cathedral, shows these two gentlemen walking separately on the flank of the family.

The service in the Cathedral was conducted by Canon Jesse Jones,

158

the Canon in Residence at Llandaff Cathedral and Rector of the parish of Gelligaer, the parish which included Pontlottyn. It was at Gelligaer Church that David Morgan was married. The hymns sung were *Let the Saints in Concert Dwell* and *Jesus Lover of my Soul*. The *Dead March in Saul* was played, according to the *South Wales News* " on the grand organ ". Archdeacon Buckley, the Vicar of Llandaff, performed the burial service at the graveside; with typical forethought the deceased had bought the bricks for the vault of the grave when brick was becoming short during the recent war and in his will he had chosen the Celtic cross which was to mark his grave.

The presence of a large number of Cardiff businessmen, representatives of the various gas companies and people from many parts of South Wales who had been connected with David Morgan, together with a very large attendance of employees (estimated by the *Western Mail* between 300 and 400), filled the Cathedral. The number of personal friends were few, but those who came out of respect were many.

The mourners were attending a funeral which would mark the passage of an age in the history of South Wales. The same edition of the *Western Mail* of 26 April, 1919, which gave an account of David Morgan's funeral, reported that a number of the greatest owners of coal royalties in the land were to be summoned to give evidence before the Coal Commission and to produce " the titles to their land, the extent of their holdings of proved mineral land, and other information including their total income from mining royalties ". (It was said that Lord Durham would require a railway van for the carriage of his title deeds.) Title boxes and treasure chests were to be broken open, and the financial secrets of magnates made public. The commission presaged changes in King Coal's Kingdom which would have astonished the mourners.

23. The Will

The funeral was not followed by the customary ceremony of reading the deceased's will. In the language of the law, " The will speaks from death "; David Morgan's spoke in intricate detail and at great length. He had three main testamentary objectives: first, the division of his fortune, valued for probate in 1919 at £245,112, so as to ensure the future of his grandchildren and therefore his family; secondly, the continuation of the business in the family ownership; and, thirdly, the passing in entail of his Breconshire estate.

David Morgan divided his residuary estate into seven equal parts, of which three parts had been originally left to his son, John Llewellyn, and one part to each of his four grandchildren, Bernard, Aubrey, Trevil and Margaret. The will had been signed on 18 January, 1918, and on 12 June of that year a fifth grandchild, Gerald Llewellyn, was born; but it was not until 25 February, 1919, less than two months before his death, that David Morgan, prompted by Gerald's mother, signed a codicil making provision for the new arrival.

David Morgan did not provide for his fifth grandchild by re-dividing the residuary estate into eight equal parts so as to retain the number of parts bequeathed to each beneficiary. Instead, he preserved the division of his estate into seven parts and provided for his new grand-child by reducing his son's bequest from three to two parts. Although arithmetically a simple solution, it deprived John Llewellyn of about £35,000. Considering that he was the father of the five grandchildren, who were all minors at the time of the death, the codicil seemed to take little account of the responsibilities which would rest on Jack's shoulders after his father's death. Jack keenly resented what he believed to be a slight and a demonstration of his father's lack of confidence in him[1]. It could be that it was indeed a demonstration of David Morgan's confidence that the future continuity of the family business lay with his grandchildren. It has already been described how David Morgan " sometimes brought young Bernard with him into the shop, a fresh full-faced school boy all smiles with grey red-topped hose and school jacket ". This was surely no gesture of mere pride, but an expression of his faith in the future: David Morgan was exposing his grandson to what was to become his future responsibility.

David Morgan specifically bequeathed to his trustees, who were his son Jack, his nephew James Hall and his eldest grandson, Bernard, all his ordinary shares in David Morgan, Limited, in trust for his grand-sons. Each grandson was to have one-third of the income from his share at the age of twenty-one; at the age of twenty-four he was to receive two-thirds of his income, together with the income from the accumu-lations invested in the meanwhile by the trustees on his behalf; and when he reached the age of twenty-seven he would become entitled to his capital. The testator was obviously determined to safeguard against an abundance of money boring holes in his grandsons' pockets and particularly against capital being frivolled on the extravagances of youth.

The bequest of the ordinary shares in David Morgan, Limited was, however, restricted to those grandsons who would, in the words of the will, " become actively engaged in the business of the company and in the opinion of the Trustees shall be devoting and shall continue to devote his whole time (except reasonable holidays) thereto ". The use of the expression " except reasonable holidays " caught the eye of the newspapers, who published details of the will under the heading " WELSH DRAPER'S VIEW OF REASONABLE HOLIDAYS ".

The testator was, however, realist enough to know that he could not ensure that his grandsons would become interested and effective managers of his shop. With his long vision of the future of the business, he therefore empowered his trustees, should the trusts in his grandsons' favour fail, to sell the shares in David Morgan, Limited " to the employees of the company, men or women, who are likely in the opinion of my trustees to work well for the advancement of the business ." No doubt mindful of his own early struggles, he added that no employee " shall be required to give more than par value for any share purchased by him or *her* ". Always aware of the important role played by women in his business, he was quite happy to contemplate the possibility of women becoming owners of his business should his family fail to assume their responsibilities.

This liberal attitude towards women, so surprising in so typical a Victorian as David Morgan, contrasts oddly with the provision made for his granddaughter, Margaret. She was entitled to only the income from her one-seventh part of the residuary estate, with a power of appointment of the capital in favour of the issue of David Morgan. He had seen a neighbour of his in Llandaff Place, a Mr. Linton, succeed to the fortune of an heiress whom he had married and who had died young: in David Morgan's own words " Not one penny of it went to the members of her family ". This was not to happen in his family.

The Breconshire estate, to which he added 1,038 acres at the sale of the Glanusk estates of Peterstone and Trebinshun after he had signed his will, he left in entail to his son. It was his wish that his landed property should pass from eldest son to eldest son.

These were the main bequests. But he also remembered in his will the nine employees, already mentioned, who had given long and devoted service, and certain other members of his family. To Edith, his daughter-in-law, and to his brother, William, he left a legacy of £500 each; to the daughters of his brother, William, and of his sister, Jane, £300 each; and to the sons of his sister £100 each. David Morgan did not reward with any greater legacy his nephew, James Hall, who according to May Brummitt was more of a son to him than was Jack. Perhaps David Morgan thought that James Hall's long residence at Bryn Taff and the

161

holidays on which he had accompanied his uncle were ample recompense for the services he had rendered to his uncle.

The will was, however, silent on one problem which today faces the testator, taxation. At the time of David Morgan's death in 1919 estate duty of 12 per cent and succession duty of one per cent for lineal descendants, five per cent for collaterals and 10 per cent for strangers in blood were hardly considered matters of importance. That David Morgan should have died only a few months before the rate of estate duty was increased by the Finance Act, 1919, to 20 per cent in respect of deaths occurring after 31 July, 1919, was in keeping with his reputation for frugality and farsightedness.

"Shrouds have no pockets": none the less David Morgan was determined, by the provisions made in his will, to control his fortune for as long as legally possible. To what extent have his testamentary wishes been fulfilled?

Jack succeeded his father to the leadership of the business at a time when great changes were to come to Cardiff following the end of the war in 1918. His particular gift lay in a keen sense of figures, but he was by temperament disinclined to impose on his buyers the discipline of stock control, so necessary when the post-war slump was depressing sales.

The founder's eldest grandson, Bernard, quickly saw the need for a complete and exacting control of stock. Using to the full the knowledge and experience he had gained in the United States of America, he imposed ruthlessly and without much regard for the buyers' feelings a most strict discipline of stock control. Indeed it was an awesome moment for the buyer when he received a summons to Mr. Bernard's office. Once at Christmastime, when so much of the store was devoted to the toy bazaar and its side attractions, David Morgan's granddaughter, Margaret, observed a notice on the staircase leading to the directors' offices indicating that: "There is no entrance to Fairyland up this staircase"; many were the buyers, summoned to account for their over-stocking, who would agree that the way up the staircase was indeed "no entrance to Fairyland". No matter how irksome was the completion of countless forms or how restrictive were the "stop" orders on buying, Bernard was absolutely unshaken by the unpopularity of his methods and forced his system through. By his drive and determination he saved the business from descending down a slippery and dangerous slope. Bernard fully justified the faith which his grandfather had placed in him! The eldest grandson turned the business into a modern department store, with controls of stock, purchases and details of sales almost ahead of their time.

The late Trevil and Gerald Morgan also played an active part in the management of the store and each made a major contribution towards handing on an outstandingly successful business to the fourth generation. Of that generation, John and Richard, two of Bernard's sons, have taken over most successfully the active management of the business and are joined on the board by their brother,

David and by Elisabeth Parker-Jervis, the daughter of Trevil, who was until his death chairman of the board. The business is still entirely owned by descendants of David Morgan, who control the whole of the company's shares.

David Morgan's wishes for the inheritance of the Breconshire estate have not, however, been so amply fulfilled. Bernard, the eldest grandson, disentailed the estate and sold it at a time when he was faced with the expense of educating his four children. The cost of maintaining the farms to his father's high standards was moreover found to outstrip the rents. Although Bernard was in many ways the grandchild most like his grandfather, his realistic approach had none of the romantic touch which affected David Morgan's attitude towards his farms in Breconshire. Nothing is more certain than that David Morgan, and his son, would have made every sacrifice before selling the land which was a source of pride to both of them.

Indeed, it was in Breconshire that Jack accepted most readily his inherited responsibilities. Breconshire had a special appeal to him: unlike his father's boyhood, Jack's early days spent at Tynewydd and Llanbrynean were happy ones. He added to the estate some 548 acres, including the historic farm of Pencelli Castle. He also set about restoring and repairing the old farmhouses. He was fastidious of the quality of the materials used and his innate good taste and knowledge of architecture prevented him from repeating the mistake of David Morgan, who had rebuilt Llanbrynean in an urban style completely out of place in the rural landscape of Breconshire.

In 1923 and 1924 Jack served as President of the Breconshire Agricultural Society, the oldest agricultural society in Great Britain. There is a very happy picture of Jack sitting at the ringside of the Brecon Show. He was obviously enjoying the scene and the company. As usual when he enjoyed himself he tended to spread himself to the point where his family would feel he was showing off. Not being in the presence of his wife he was able to introduce his three sons, who had accompanied him to the show, to Lord Davies of Llandinam with a flourish of pride. " This is my eldest son, Bernard, who is doing so well in the business; this is my son, Trevil, the cricketer," and then turning to his less-distinguished son, reaching for some similar note of commendation, he added, " and this is my tall son, Aubrey ". He carried off his Chairmanship with such success that he was asked to do it for a second year. His crowning glory came when he, the son of a man who had started life in Breconshire as an unsuccessful farm boy, was pricked[2] by the King for the office of High Sheriff of the County, which he held in 1927 and 1928.

Soon after his father's death, Jack set about planning his great tribute and memorial to his father. He decided to restore the tower of Llanfigan Church and install a peal of eight bells in memory of David Morgan. This he did in spite of his wife's attempt to persuade him to make the gift of a bed to the Cardiff Infirmary instead of this memorial in Breconshire. The following is a contemporary account of the ceremony which took place on 14 September, 1921:

Llanfigan Church
Reopening after Restoration

An interesting ceremony took place at Llanfigan on Wednesday afternoon when the old parish church was reopened. The ancient tower has been restored, the bells recast and four new ones added to complete the octave at a total cost of approximately £4,000, by Mr. J. Ll. Morgan, Brynderwen, Llandaff who was a native of the parish[3].

The old church which presents a very picturesque appearance from the outside is situated amongst a clump of trees in a dingle from which a last spur of the Beacons rises to echo the sound of the bells. At the reopening service the church was filled literally to overflowing. Members of the Morgan family present were, Mr. and Mrs. J. Ll. Morgan, Messers. Bernard Morgan, Aubrey Morgan and Trevil Morgan (sons), Mr. James Hall, Cardiff, Mr. Wm. Morgan junior, Miss K. Morgan and Miss N. Morgan (all three Llanbrynean), Mr. and Mrs. Fred Hall and the Misses Hall, Tynewydd; Miss M. Hall, Miss S. Hall, Mrs. Couzens, Mr. Sam Couzens, and Miss M. Couzens.

The clergymen present were the Lord Bishop of Swansea, the Rev. D. C. Saunders Jones, Rural Dean, who acted as Bishop's Chaplain; the Rev. J. Ll. Phillips D.D., Headmaster of Christ's College; the Rev. J. Simon, St. Davids, Brecon; Rev. Thos. Griffiths, Llanspyddid; Rev. Idris Ll. Roberts, Llanfihangel Talyllyn; Rev. D. H. Picton, Cathedine; Rev. W. R. Jones, Llangynidr; Rev. Joshua Davies, Aberyskir; Canon Beavan, Llanfrynach; Rev. E. Davies, Brecon; and the Rev. R. H. Chambers of Llandefalle.

After the lesson which was read by the Rev. D. Saunders Jones (rector of Cantref) the bells were formally presented by Mr. Morgan, and received by the Rector—the Rev. T. Aneurin Davies. They were then dedicated by the Bishop of Swansea. A short peal was rung during which the Bishop and clergy proceeded to a tablet in memory of the men of the parish who fell in the late war. The tablet was unveiled by Col. H. R. Jones Williams and dedicated by the Bishop. A tablet commemorating the generosity of Mr. Morgan was also unveiled at the bottom of the tower.

After the ceremony, the Bishop gave a short address illustrating how much the social and religious life of the community owes to the voluntary efforts of its members. In his address the Bishop said

The service that afternoon reminded them of the joy of generous and free giving to God's glory and for the good of His Church. He was quite certain it was in the spirit of willing sacrifice and service that the generous donor who provided them with those beautiful bells and the restoration of the tower, had made his offering.

It was a romantic concept, worthy of Jack's creative imagination, that these memorial bells should ring out over the surrounding farms the possession of which David Morgan had so strongly desired. But the memorial was more appropriate to the donor than the man it was to commemorate.

James Hall, who knew more than anybody else about the relationship between David Morgan and his son, gave some indication in a letter written to May Brummitt on 20 November, 1920, of how his father might have viewed Jack's advancement and acceptance in Breconshire:

> You have probably heard that Jack is restoring the Tower of Llanfigan Church and is having four bells recast. He is going to hang four more bells to make a complete octave. The largest bell is to bear an inscription that it is given in memory of Uncle David. I must say I think Jack is doing a fine thing. It is not a thing Uncle would have done nor would he, if alive, have approved of Jack doing it but if he were alive and Jack did it in spite of him, I am sure that after it had been completed Uncle would have been very proud of the work.

Had he been alive and had he been proud of his son's achievements in Breconshire it is more likely that he would not have admitted it to Jack. Poor Jack! [4]

1 Source, James Hall.

2 The list of nominees for the Sheriffs of the Counties is placed before the Sovereign, who according to a long tradition started in the reign of Queen Elizabeth, marks his choice by pricking a mark alongside the name.

3 John Llewellyn Morgan is incorrectly described as a native of Llanfigan.

4 Both Kate Morgan and May Brummitt used the expression " Poor Jack " several times when telling some story about him as a young man. May would also say to me "Your poor father," leaving me with the impression that in their eyes he was fated to commit errors which were bound to annoy his father.

24.   Epilogue :   The Portrait

At the top of the building over the old Green Gardens Court until 1977 was the Counting House of David Morgan, Limited which is now changed to a sales department. On the other side of the staircase, are the private offices and the board room. These were all built after the death of David Morgan by his son Jack.

In the board room there hangs a portrait of David Morgan painted in 1913 by Margaret Lindsay Williams, a Cardiff girl whose portrait of Lloyd George received much notice. Seated in a high-backed chair, David Morgan dominates the room and, as he did in life, the other two portraits which also hang in the board room: a posthumous portrait of his son Jack by the same artist and a portrait of Watkeys Morgan painted in 1950 by Ivor Williams to mark Watkeys' seventy years' service with the business.

Miss Williams posed David Morgan against a dark background. The combination of the dark background, black suit and high-backed chair makes a sharp contrast with his white hair and beard and red cheeks, making the head very prominent. The young artist appears to have been impressed by his 81 years. His pose was one in which he customarily sat in his office or by his fireside at Bryn Taff when listening to someone. The slight, almost transparent fingers of his right hand rest above his knee. The tips of his fingers have the bluntness associated with the hands of people of a practical nature, but the hands are certainly not those of one who has done hard physical toil. They convey a sense of composure. His left hand is held in much the same pose as that of his mother in the photograph taken of her in 1866.

The portrait is unpretentious and lacks any appearance of self-satisfaction or grandeur often seen in portraits of merchant princes. The alertness of the face is intensified by his thinness. First to catch one's attention are the hooded, deep-set eyes, of which his sister-in-law, Mrs. William Morgan of Llanbrynean, used to say: " Deep-set to see far "; his grey eyes had the reputation of seeing all and missing nothing. The outline of his face is covered by his beard, but the bone structure of his skull is clearly defined. His nose is flat with a broad base. The portrait bears out the description of him given by his niece, May Brummitt: "As a person he was unassuming, immaculate and innately honest ." It is a portrait of the man as he was known in his shop.

It is appropriate that alongside the founder's portrait stands the flat-topped cabinet from his old office, on which the previous day's cash takings were counted out every morning by Mr. Watkeys in the presence of David Morgan. This piece of furniture is a visible link between the old autocratic management of David Morgan and today's system of computerised ledgers.

David Morgan never sat in the board room, for it was built after his death. But his portrait has presided over meetings for three generations. Here, in this picture, each generation could in its turn see the source of that heredity of talent which has produced down to the present day continuing abilities in the field of merchandising and the retail trade. There have been many changes since that October evening in 1879 when David Morgan first opened his business on The Hayes; nevertheless he would be well pleased at what his portrait has witnessed, for the board room's occupants have carried out the wishes and fulfilled the ambitions of the founder of the business.

APPENDIX TO "MARRIAGE"

The following were the four children of the second marriage of John Morgan II of Cwmrhibin and Bwlch Farm:—

JAMES, who married Betsy, sister of Eleanor, 2nd wife of John Morgan III and mother of Mrs. Captain Jones (grandmother of Clifford Diamond). James lived near Talybont.

JEREMIAH (Jerry), who went to Australia.

MARY, who also went to Australia.

MARGARET, who was housekeeper to D. P. Morgan, Twyn Carno, Rhymney.

Copies of Letters written to Mary Davies—sister of Jeremiah Morgan— by her nephew David Morgan

PONTLOTTYN
Via. TREDEGAR
Oct. 18th, 1871

My Dear Aunt,

It is now a very long time since I have heard from you, and much longer since I have written to you, but I assure you that you and Mary Ann are not forgotten although such great distance lies between us.

John Owen told me he had heard from you lately and gave me your address, as I had mislaid the one I received from you. No doubt you would like to hear some news from this your native land, I am sure I don't know where to begin first, unless it is with myself.

Since you left I have seen a great many changes. I live now at Pontlottyn and enclose a copy of sketch of the house and shop which is my own. It cost nearly £900 to build three years ago. Three years ago I was married to a young person from this place but it was my misfortune to lose her 7 months ago nearly. She was a loving and affectionate wife to me and I miss her very much. I enclose a " Carte " of her and our little boy taken about 9 months before she died. My little boy is living and is a strong hearty little fellow. My poor wife died of consumption. (March 27, 1871)

Father and mother are still living at Llanbrynean. William my brother is the only one at home with them. Jane is with her husband at Tynewydd and have 6 nice little children, 4 girls and 2 boys. Tom my brother keeps a draper shop at Maesteg, has been there now nearly two years and doing a large trade—6 or 7 clerks and as much as they can do.

James my youngest brother is in a lawyers office in Brecon and he intends some day being a lawyer.

D. P. Morgan and Alfred are still at Pwllgwillim farming—they both enjoy excellent health. David and Lisah were down here about a fortnight ago. Aunt was quite well at Erwood then, Jane had gone on a voyage to America with her husband, he is a Captain of a Vessel, they have had two children, a girl and a boy, but the little girl died some time ago.

Lloyd is still at Aberaman doing an excellent business. He was married about 6 months before I was, and he buried his wife about as much time before I buried mine. He has no children left although there was a little boy born, but died—he did not live many hours. She also died of consumption.

John Lewis, Grocer, and Mrs. Lewis are living but the last time I saw Mrs. Lewis she looked very poorly, worse than I ever saw her. Mrs. Wm. Powell and her husband, David Lewis and his wife and children are all well—there are a good many changes about Twyncarno but the place is almost strange to me now that David is gone away, I very seldom go up there.

The Methodist Association was there about 3 weeks ago, there were a great number of strangers there and some good preaching, but I have heard better.

Rhymney is going on much the same as usual, if anything it is improving, more buildings, more shops, better roads, and the place getting more fashionable and grand—the Railway Station that was opposite the company shop is extended now up past the Brewery and Newtown to Tredegar, Ebbwvale Brynmawr and Abergavenny, and there are 5 trains each way every day for passengers from Cardiff to Liverpool and Manchester, and north of England, and they are busy making a railway from the Rhymney Inn to Dawlins, so you see we are not asleep here but alive and at work.

I will send you the Hereford Times Newspaper next so that you may see something of the old country.

Well I have nothing particular further to tell you but give my best respects to your husband and Mary Ann of course. She must be a bouncing woman now, no doubt about getting married—if so I hope she will enjoy good health as without this the world will not be of much comfort or pleasure.

Trusting these few lines will find all enjoying good health as I am at present, with my best wishes to you all.

I am,

To Mrs. Davies,	Dear Aunt,
North Muckleford,	Your faithful nephew,
Victoria.	David Morgan

DAVID MORGAN—DRAPER

PONTLOTTYN
15th Feb., 1876

Dear Aunt,

I was glad to receive a letter from you, although we are very far apart and a long time since we saw each other, but somehow I have a very vivid recollection of you as I have the " carte " of yourself and Mary Ann, but no doubt she has so altered that I would not know her now. She tells me in her letter that she has two children.

169

I am glad to hear that you are much better than when I heard from you before, and that your husband also enjoys good health.

Things are very much altered in our family since I wrote you before, Mother as you are aware died in November 1873, and father died in May 1875. He had got very weak and feeble for many years but was out and about to within five days of his death. William, my brother, got married in November last to a Miss Jones, a farmer's daughter in the neighbourhood, and I think he was very fortunate in securing a sensible and industrious wife. My sister Jane is quite well with her large family of 8 children. All the rest of us are quite well and single—my little boy is also quite well and going to school every day. He is 6½ years old.

Since the death of father—Aunt Tymaur (Mrs. Samuel of Tymawr who later married Mr. Bevan of Llanganten) has died sometime last autumn. I saw your brother James at Talybont a few months ago, he was quite well. His two sons are married, one of them keeping a farm near Bedwellty Church, the other one is in a large Public House at the Derri.

D. P. Morgan and his son Alfred are still at Pwllgwillim but I have not seen either of them for quite 18 months, neither have I heard from them for a long time, but they are quite well and have been to London lately to see Mrs. Jane Jones. Her husband the Captain, has gone there to live having given up the sea and acts as agent under the company. And Tvizab are still living at Erwood, but I have not been that way for a long time.

Trade is getting very bad here now, never was worse since I have known the hills. In the past twelve months there have been reductions in wages from 8/- to 12/- in the pound, and what makes things worse there is not sufficient work at that price. Some of the pits only work 3 or 4 days a week and it makes things very bad and gloomy, especially after the very good years that are gone by. Cyfarthfa Works are stopped more than 12 months, Plymouth and Aberdare works more than 6 months and Nantyglo Works stopped more than 12 months and very likely will never go on again for many years.

Well I am come to the end of the paper and must close trusting these few lines will find you and your husband quite well as I am, as it leaves me at present.

I am Dear Aunt,
Yours sincerely,
David Morgan

170

APPENDIX TO "THE CREATION OF CARDIFF"

Samuel Gething Lewis of Nythfa, Cathedral Road, was brother-in-law of David Morgan, having married Jane Llewellyn. He was another example of the people who came down from the valleys and prospered in the growth of Cardiff. He established a very successful business called the Bute Works Supply, and played a part in the building of the new Alexandra Dock which was at that time the largest walled dock in the world.

BUTE WORKS SUPPLY

WESTERN MAIL SOUVENIR EDITION AT TIME OF ROYAL VISIT
JULY 13, 1907

Near the place where the Rhymney Ironworks formerly flourished and adjoining the ruins of its long-disused furnaces, there stands a small flat-topped mountain of slag—the waste products of earlier times. That mountain with its precipitous cliff-like sides represents the cast of accumulation of some sixty-six years of industry in what used to be one of the most prosperous and enterprising iron and steel works in Wales. These works were shut down in 1891 as the result of foreign competition . . . It was only in very recent times that its potential value as a mine of material for railway construction and other even more remunerative purposes was anticipated by the Bute Works Supply who purchased the property some years ago. The investment at the time was regarded with amused amazement by the business world. . . . Since those days however nearly a million tons of that waste has been disposed of for just such filling, ballasting and surfacing purposes as that for which it has been and is being used at the Queen Alexandra Dock, Cardiff.

The slag mountain is only a side issue in a concern which is inter alia one of the biggest metal traders in South Wales and deals extensively in railway and colliery plants of all kinds and purveys such essentials as rails, fish plates, bolts and nuts, sleepers and chairs, as well as all the various accessories for the construction of sidings. In addition to these fundamental necessaries the Bute Works Supply Co. purveys engines, boilers, tanks, pumps, machinery and steelwork of every description; there are also departments for locomotives, cranes and ballast wagons as well as bulk staples such as foundry and furnace coke, coal, cinder, mill-scale, pitch, etc. The principal department however is that which deals in railway wagons— sells them, rents them and repairs them—and in this respect alone the Company is one of the largest private owners in Great Britain. This particular branch of the business, which was originally formed to supply the needs of the South Wales Collieries alone, now also includes in its clientele the majority of the larger railways, collieries and contractors in the Midlands and the North of England . . .

. . . The Bute Works Supply Co., which is a private partnership as distinguished from a limited liability concern, was founded in 1889. Mr. Gething Lewis is the present head of this firm . . . On July 1st this year Mr. Lewis took into partnership his nephew Mr. Henry G. Lewis, who has been closely associated with him for about 15 years, and also his two sons, Messers. John Llewellyn and Percy Gething Lewis, who are now all members of the firm.

APPENDIX TO " THE HAYES "

IN AND AROUND CARDIFF JULY 1905
CARDIFF'S COMMERCIAL CHIEFTAINS AND THEIR WORK

ARTICLE NO. 1   MESSRS. MORGAN & CO.

It is extremely doubtful if among the whole of Cardiff's phenomenal examples of business progress a fairer showing of what is possible in this connection may be found than that supplied by the expansion which has positively crowded around the undertaking of Messrs. Morgan and Co. Drapers and House Furnishers, The Hayes, Cardiff . . . . . since the end of October 1879 has completely transmogrified that portion of the town now known as the Morgan Arcade. At the time referred to, the frontage occupied by the pioneer shop of this, at present, huge establishment amounted to 17 ft. and its floor space went back to the extent of a modest 50 ft. The combined floor space, supplied by two floors, was represented by the figures 1,360 ft. and in view of the fact that no year could have been more (apparently) unfavourable for the starting of a new business —seeing that it was the year in which the price of Welsh coal had reached its lowest mark in the ebb—the present proud position occupied by the firm is indeed and truth phenomenal. In addition to the bad state of trade there were other conditions which to a man of less indomitable pluck than was (and is) the founder of this establishment would have proved altogether too much. As may be gathered from our illustrations (a picture of Union Buildings and the entrance into the new gramophone shop in Morgan Arcade) the locality where now stands the lordly buildings erected by Morgan & Co. was the reverse of reassuring, for squalor, poverty and worse were altogether too much in evidence and the reputation of the immediate neighbourhood was such, that to a weaker man progress would have seemed impossible.

It is somewhat difficult when contemplating the 240 ft. frontage in The Hayes and which belongs to the progressive firm, to realize the true meaning of the 17 ft. front which started this remarkable growth. . . . . . Truly has it been said that in these days of keen competition such progresses may not be created with the help of adventitious happenings. Luck has absolutely nothing to do with it. Sheer hard work; indomitable pluck; far seeing wisdom and a determination to let nothing daunt— these are the factors which tend to such ends. These and the one absolutely essential addition of sterling worth. For it is useless to attempt to build a business of this character on second rate merchandise. The best and the best only must be offered for by this means alone is the public confidence so necessary to a sterling advance attained.

A very big feature in this great commercial success has been achieved without resorting to the " sale " which is so dear to the hearts of some of our lady readers or to the spacious kind of hand-bill advertisement in connection with this feature of modern trading which is alas so common in the present strenuous age. Rightly or wrongly—and in the result, the decision must be admitted as of sterling value—the Morgan firm declines to humiliate its patron by suggesting they may secure something for nothing.

APPENDIX TO "THE SHOP"

A letter from Miss Harnaman :

40 Beech Road,
Weston-super-Mare.
Somerset.

20th July 1973

I joined Morgan & Company on the 24th April 1914. My wages were £25 per year, which took into account the fact that I lived in. Only female staff lived in at that time but I think it must have been that male and female staff lived in up to 1913 when the men organised a strike in favour of living out. When I started at Morgan & Co. I was told about the strike. I lived in for many years, in fact, I was the last one to sleep in. I think this must have been in the year 1935. The sleeping-in quarters were on the top floor of the Store. There was one long room for juniors called The Barracks. A Miss Morgan was in charge of the living-in when I started. The discipline and control was very severe. A bell rang in the morning at 7:30; breakfast was at 8.00 and we were expected to be in at night at 9 p.m. As far as I can remember the food was reasonably good, a bit like the saying "God sends the food but the devil sends the cooks."

The Fabric Department was always staffed by men. When I started I was put in the Fabric Department and was the first woman to serve there. When I think back it is about 60 years ago. The merchandise was very limited. We sold a great deal of Welsh flannel, striped, for men's pants and vests at 1/-d. per yard. The men worked down the mines in the nearby Valleys. Wool stockings were for sale in black and brown at only 1/-d. per pair, also lisle hose in fawn, not fashioned. 3 pairs would last a year. Calico, bleached and unbleached was 4/0¼d. per yard. Plain coloured sateens, used for linings, was also 4/0¼d. per yard.

The following are a few of the items sold.—

Navy Serge.	2/0d. yard
Welsh and Scotch Tweeds.	2/0d. „
Delaine for Blouses.	1/0d. „
Plain Silk Taffeta & Cashmere.	2/6d. „
Plain Crepe de chine, Silk and Cotton Velvet Georgette	4/0d. „
Cotton & Corduroy Velveteen.	1/6d. yard.
Mouselline de Soir.	1/6d. „
Printed and Plain Cotton Fabric Nap.	
Wool Velour Heavy weight for top coats.	4/11d. „

The skirts in those days were long and the bottom edge was bound with brush braid at one penny per yard to keep the dust off the boots.

There was a private code for the cost of goods, and for premiums. Not all goods carried premiums—only the slow selling items and short lengths.

This I think was the code:—

B   R   I   C   K   D   U   S   T.   0

1   2   3   4   5   6   7   8   9

so, if a special item carried a large premium, it would be marked D.6 pence. The bill had to be signed by a shopwalker or buyer. I do not remember a sale through the Store until the end of the 1914-18 war. Yes, Mr. Joseph did a big purchase of parachute silk. I think it was sold at 1/-d. per yard.

The assistants wore black dresses. We bought two dresses per year, one for Spring and 1 for Winter. There was great competition amongst the assistants to have the smartest model. I also think we had a discount off purchases made in the store.

During the time I lived in, a bedroom was converted into a kitchen with gas stove, sink and saucepan and frying pan. In the evenings the assistants were allowed to use this for cooking items of food we purchased, such as eggs and chips or bacon and egg. It was a great treat. The woman who was head of the staff Cooking Department was named Sophorra; she would often give us dripping to cook with. She was quite a good sort. The most miserable day of the week was Sunday. Cold dinner winter or summer, and in those days the only place to go was to Chapel. We also had a sitting room with a piano and we had many good times when some-one would play and sing. I personally liked living-in.

BUSINESS HOURS 1914

9 a.m.—7 p.m.   Monday

9 a.m.—7 p.m.   Tuesday

9 a.m.—1 p.m.   Wednesday early closing

9 a.m.—8 p.m.   Thursday (Thursday was half-day closing in the Valleys so the Railway Company ran cheap fares to Cardiff, hence the later hour for closing.)

9 a.m.—8 p.m.   Friday

9 a.m.—9 p.m.   Saturday

Many of the assistants came from Welsh places such as Cardigan, Port Talbot, Ynysybwl.

E. Harnaman

APPENDIX TO " THE WILL "

At the time of David Morgan's death on the twenty-first of April, 1919, his gas holdings were listed for probate:

Quaker's Yard	Ord. Shares	2,104
	Debentures	250
Ammanford G. Co.	Shares	3,000
Rhymney & Aber G. & W. Co.	O. Shares or Stock	17,624- 5-0
	Pref. Shares	1,666-13-4
	Deb. Stock	1,660
Tawe Valley	10% Shares	1,300
	7% Shares	1,600
Garw & Ogmore	Ordinary Shares	750
	P.	1,600
Blaenavon G. & W.	Shares	925
	"	14
Blaina & Bryn Mawr	Cap Stk	120

APPENDIX TO "THE PORTRAIT"

A letter from Leonard Horwood :

My first recollection of Mr. David Morgan dates back to between the years 1900 and 1905 when I would occasionally have accompanied my Mother while she was shopping at "Morgan's, The Hayes". We would often, on such occasions, see Mr. Morgan walking through the shop and I remember him well as an elderly gentleman in a frock coat and a high crowned Derby bowler with a starched single collar and cravat contributing to his strikingly smart appearance. He was a fairly slight figure of medium height with a trim beard and smiling eyes—eyes which I am sure missed nothing as he passed through the various departments of his store. I recall that this courteous and kindly gentleman would always stop to greet and talk with my Mother—they were old friends for not only was my Father in charge of his "Counting House" but my Mother had, before her marriage, also been one of his staff. Before leaving us he would have a few words for me and probably a pat on my head.

In later years when I was a schoolboy I would sometimes call at the office to see my Father and there seemed to be a standing rule on such occasions I had to be sent into the "Private Office" to see Mr. Morgan. This I always found most enjoyable for he was so kind and friendly as we talked of my school and progress and set-backs and other happenings. One memory of these visits is very vivid—Mr. Morgan suffered from severe attacks of asthma and on the table by the side of his armchair he had an apparatus in which burned some patent medicinal powder producing a strangely scented smoke which eased his respiration. This was as fascinating to a boy as it was relieving to his elderly friend.

Later still when I was an articled clerk with a firm of Chartered Accountants I would sometimes sit-in at board meetings of companies of which Mr. Morgan was a director. This enabled me to observe and appreciate his considerable qualities as a man of business with the natural ability to size up situations quietly and quickly and make sound decisions.

I remember the horse-drawn brougham in which he made the journey to and from business from his house at Llandaff—always punctually at set times each way.

It must have been about the year 1885 that my Father, then a junior in the counting house of a London store (Debenham & Freebody I think it was), successfully applied for the post of clerk in charge of the office of Morgan & Co., The Hayes, Cardiff. He remained with the firm until his death in 1936 before which he had become Company Secretary and a director. He was therefore closely associated with Mr. David Morgan for some 35 of those 50 years and we of his family were well aware of his admiration for and loyalty to his "Guv'nor". We heard much, too, of the exciting progress and expansion of the business under Mr. Morgan's guidance. Other old premises in the vicinity were acquired, demolished and replaced with fine new buildings.

I remember the excitement which prevailed when the building which still accommodates the furniture & carpet departments was completed and opened to the public, completely altering the appearance of the area. Until then it had been an open space occupied for most of the year by John Studt's fair ground. Here were merry-go-rounds of galloping horses etc., driven by steam engines with organ music blaring out loud and late, shooting galleries, coconut shies, boxing booths and various other side shows. They were illuminated by paraffin and naphtha flares and the general noise was quite terrific. The fair ground gave pleasure to many but it was no asset to a developing business district and Mr. Morgan must have been pleased with and proud of the improvement which he had brought about.

Of the many outstanding features of Mr. Morgan's business life these are a sample of those of which we heard:

PUNCTUALITY and hard work was expected of all the staff. Working hours were longer in those days—generally from 8:30 a.m. to 7 or 8 and on Saturdays 9 p.m., with a half day off on Wednesday.

HONESTY was imperative. His advice to all was " never take a pin which does not belong to you ". Pins, mark you, were cheap in those days for if you tendered five shillings for an article priced at four shillings and elevenpence three farthings, you received as a " Farthing change " a folded sheet of about 100 pins!

WASTE was to be avoided. In those far off days stock was often stored on shelves or under the solid mahogany counters and many items such as haberdashery were packed in parcels tied up with string. If Mr. Morgan saw a piece of this string on the floor he would pocket it and, tied together, these bits of string were put to good use. As good as the old saying, " look after the pence and the pounds will look after themselves ".

DISCOUNT was not given. If a customer knocked off the odd shillings and/or pence when paying an account then the balance was carried forward and appeared on the next statement. Of course the terms " no discount " were well known and if necessary a polite reminder of this rule would be sent. This must have been one of my Father's responsibilities.

SALES. These became a common practice with the London and some provincial stores: they were usually yearly or half yearly sales. Mr. Morgan did not approve of sales and I believe I am correct in saying that during his lifetime no sale took place at Morgan's.

STAFF RELATIONS. As a young man I knew personally all the departmental managers (or buyers as they used to be called) and many of the juniors. I know that they all shared the general admiration and affection for the remarkable gentleman who was their employer—and the term gentleman meant something in those days. My Father was responsible for " Hiring and firing " and for general discipline and so we heard much that confirmed that good relations prevailed.

Leonard Horwood

179

BIBLIOGRAPHY

The Early Days of Sirhowy and Tredegar by Oliver Jones (Starling Press Ltd.).

The Canals of South Wales and the Border by Charles Hadfield.

Kilvert's Diary 1870-1879. Selection from the Diary of The Rev. Francis Kilvert, Chosen, Edited and Introduced by William Plomer.

Echoes of Rhymney by E. E. Edwards. (Starling Press Ltd., Risca).

The Story of Gilfach Goch by Kate Olwen Pritchard (Starling Press Ltd., Risca).

About Britain No. 6, South Wales and the Marches, A New Guide Book with a Portrait by W. J. Gruffydd, General Editor Geoffrey Grigson.

The South Wales Coal Industry 1841-1875 by J. H. Morris and L. J. Williams.

Rhymney Memories by Thomas Jones, C.H.

The Dictionary of Welsh Biography Down to 1940, under the auspices of the Honourable Society of Cymmrodorion.

The Romance of Wales by A. G. Bradley.

History of Breconshire by Theophilus Jones.

The Encyclopedia Britannica.

Old South Wales Ironworks, by J. Lloyd.

Industrial Development of South Wales, A. H. John.

Cardiff, A History of the City, William Rees.

The Crawshay Dynasty, John Addis.

The Land of Wales, Peter and Eiluned Lewis.

The History of the Iron, Steel, Tinplate and Other Trades of Wales, by Charles Wilkins, F.G.S.

The Life of the People, by Tom Jones.

Hanes Rhymney A Pontlottyn, Rev. D. S. Jones, Haverfordwest. Transl. by G. M. Harries, BA, Published by Gelligaer Historical Society, Vol 9, 1972.

The Growth and Decline of the Mining Valley Town of Abertillery With Particular Reference to Housing Standards and Conditions, a thesis by John Rawlings.

Syren and Shipping 1940.

The Illustrated Guide to Cardiff, Daniel H. Owen.

Glamorgan Historian, Vols. 1, 5, 6, 8, Stewart Williams.

The Rhymney Railway and the Bute Estate, Dr. John Davies, Gelligaer Historical Society, Vol. VIII, 1971.

The Western Mail.

The Economist.

The Times.

Biography of Marc Isambard Brunel by P. Clements.

Sea Power in the Machine Age by Bernard Brodie.

Growth of Cardiff from 1875 to 1880, by Thomas Glyde 1880.

Growth of a City, by C. F. Saunders.

Cardiff Records.

Ordnance Maps.

In and Around Cardiff, July 1905.

The National Trust Guide to England, Wales and Northern Ireland, Compiled and edited by Robin Fedden and Rosemary Joekes.

Royal Wales, by Cledwyn Hughes.

The Cardiff Book, Vols. 1 and 2, edited by Stewart Williams.

Industrial South Wales 1750-1914, Essays in Welsh Economic History, Edited by W. E. Minchinton.

Anatomy of Wales, edited by R. Brinley Jones.

Cardiff and the Valleys, by John B. Hilling.

From the Valley I Came, by Wil Jon Edwards.

The Industrial Revolution, by Keith Dawson.

Children in the Mines 1840-42, Compiled and written by R. M. Evans.

Scenery, Antiquities and Biography, of South Wales, 1807, B. H. Malkin.

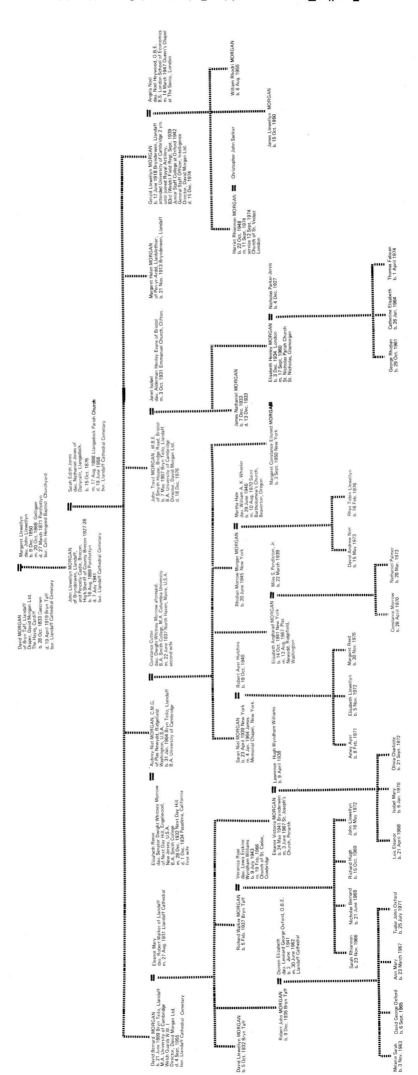

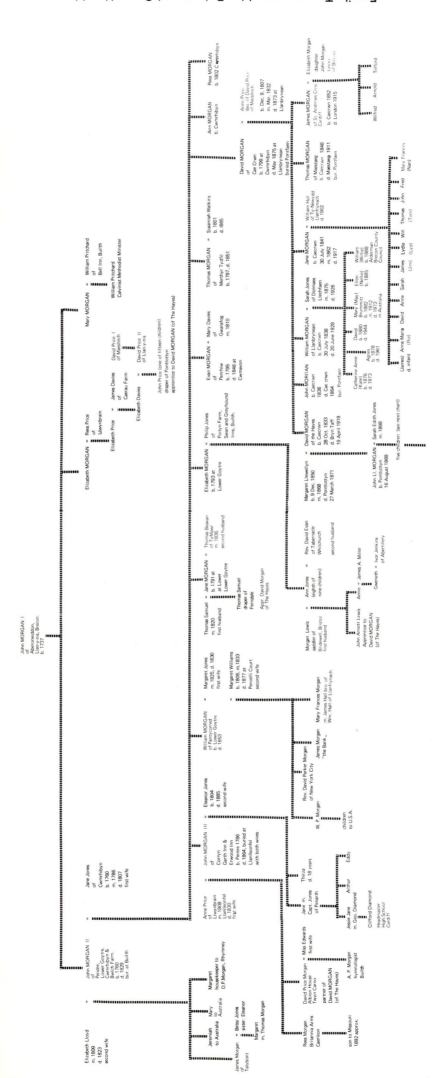